The Belief in a Just World

A Fundamental Delusion

PERSPECTIVES IN SOCIAL PSYCHOLOGY
A Series of Texts and Monographs • Edited by Elliot Aronson

INTRINSIC MOTIVATION
By Edward L. Deci

SCHOOL DESEGREGATION
By Harold B. Gerard and Norman Miller

HUMAN AGGRESSION
By Robert A. Baron

UNIQUENESS: The Human Pursuit of Difference
By C. R. Snyder and Howard L. Fromkin

SCHOOL DESEGREGATION: Past, Present, and Future
Edited by Walter G. Stephan and Joe R. Feagin

THE BELIEF IN A JUST WORLD: A Fundamental Delusion
By Melvin J. Lerner

A Continuation Order Plan is available for this series. A continuation order will bring delivery of each new volume immediately upon publication. Volumes are billed only upon actual shipment. For further information please contact the publisher.

The Belief in a Just World

A Fundamental Delusion

Melvin J. Lerner

University of Waterloo
Waterloo, Ontario, Canada

Plenum Press · New York and London

Library of Congress Cataloging in Publication Data

Lerner, Melvin J   1929-
    The belief in a just world.

    (Perspectives in social psychology)
    Includes index.
    1. Social justice—Psychological aspects. 2. Belief and doubt—Psychological
aspects. I. Title.
HM216.L37   303.3'72   80-16359
ISBN 0-306-40495-8

88·B2434

© 1980 Plenum Press, New York
A Division of Plenum Publishing Corporation
227 West 17th Street, New York, N.Y. 10011

Printed in the United States of America

This book is dedicated to Ma and Pa, Sally,
and especially Mim and Dan

Preface

The "belief in a just world" is an attempt to capture in a phrase one of the ways, if not *the* way, that people come to terms with—make sense out of—find meaning in, their experiences. We do not believe that things just happen in our world; there is a pattern to events which conveys not only a sense of orderliness or predictability, but also the compelling experience of appropriateness expressed in the typically implicit judgment, "Yes, that is the way it should be."

There are probably many reasons why people discover or develop a view of their environment in which events occur for good, understandable reasons. One explanation is simply that this view of reality is a direct reflection of the way both the human mind and the environment are constructed. Constancies, patterns which actually do exist in the environment—out there—are perceived, represented symbolically, and retained in the mind.

This approach certainly has some validity, and would probably suffice, if it were not for that sense of "appropriateness," the pervasive affective component in human experience. People have emotions and feelings, and these are especially apparent in their expectations about their world: their hopes, fears, disappointments, disillusionment, surprise, confidence, trust, despondency, anticipation—and certainly their sense of right, wrong, good, bad, ought, entitled, fair, deserving, just.

Without resorting to the authority of the anthropological archives, it is a good guess that all human beings experience pain and suffering, and possibly grief, at various times in their lives. And there are probably some good candidates for universal human "tragedies"—expected death and "illness," the unanticipated, "accidental" inflicting of crippling pain, the loss of a loved one, the sudden appearance of the dangerous enemy that threatens destruction and suffering. Others might include the consequences of change, aging and the deterioration or loss of abilities, opportunities, privileges, pleasures. One might decide to include the disappointing mystery of the process of satiation—the effect of quite naturally repeating that which was gratifying, to discover that for no apparent reason the expected feeling is gone.

We can see all this in our own lives. At one time or another most people have noted and felt the quite disturbing juxtaposition of the greatly discrepant fates which have been dealt people in our world. One infant dies, others thrive and bring joy to their grandparents. Some people are born to comfort and wealth, and others are born to and live in poverty. Someone is crippled by an accident or disease, some go crazy, some lead wonderfully contented lives, some are raped, robbed, murdered in the streets or in their beds. Some are killed in war, others become revered heroes, and yet others just come home. Some people are ugly, stupid, or suffer greatly because they are black or female; others are beautiful, lovable, healthy, brilliant.

Most people have answers for the implicit question of "why," why is it this way, often before it is asked. They have been taught "satisfactory," if not satisfying or comforting, explanations. "They weren't careful." "They like living that way." "They are just naturally lazy, no good. There is nothing you can do for them." "They come from bad (good) stock—bad genes, bad blood." "They are sinners." "Actually it may be mysterious to us now, but there is a plan, in the universe—everything happens for the best, as it should, as He willed it—it will be made right in the end—in heaven." "Actually it is a tough world out there—those are the breaks, but mostly if you keep your nose clean, keep your eyes open, use your head and are willing to do what is necessary—you will be all right."

At one level of explanation, it is almost certainly true that people will develop ways of coping with disturbing or threatening events, and, if these events are common experiences, then it is quite natural for people to develop a consensus, or shared solutions which are given the status of "reality" within the social unit. It follows also that if these social devices are at all functional, if they do the job of reducing or preventing the threat, then they will probably be retained and transmitted to succeeding generations.

That may be all there is to the story of how people come to terms with, or explain away, the uncontrollable, frightening, painful experiences in life. But, for a social psychologist, at least this social psychologist, living in this society, at this time, that level of explanation provides at most the bare bones of a rough outline. Actually it leaves so much unexplained that it may create a misleading, if not essentially false, image of contemporary social man as the passive recipient of beliefs, truths, and values provided him by his "culture." There is so much more that goes on in people's lives; and the "Belief in a Just World" is essentially a model for the way people make sense out of their environment, and organize their lives, in the realization that there is this "so much more."

The purpose here is not to describe how people achieve order out of the "blooming, buzzing confusion" of their experiences, but rather to concentrate on a clearer understanding of what they do when they discover that they are not living in a "rose garden."

MELVIN J. LERNER

Acknowledgments

Some time ago, as part of a research project, I was asked to list professors who had had a positive impact on me. Since that was a private act, I want to take this occasion to express my deep appreciation and indebtedness to those whom I recognize as having had an enormous influence on my work—not only the way I do social psychology but more importantly the problems I regard as worth pursuing. At the time in my life when I had just decided that I was interested in studying how people affect one another, I had the extreme good fortune to have three warm and generous teachers: John Bennett, an anthropologist; Kurt Wolff, a sociologist; and Mef Seeman, a social psychologist. I then went on to NYU to do my Ph.D. at the Research Center for Human Relations. The director of the program, Marie Jahoda, conveyed vividly, mostly by example, the importance and excitement of doing research that would have an impact on the serious issues of our times. Later on there were many other people who made a difference. Among these, the relatively brief but impressive contacts with Leon Festinger and his students convinced me that social psychological experiments were worth doing. And I am no less convinced of that now.

I am grateful to a number of people who read and commented upon the earlier versions of this monograph. Elliot Aronson, Dale T. Miller, and Camille Wortman were especially helpful in their reviews of the "penultimate" draft. The graduate students and research assistants with whom I had the good fortune to work made the initial just-world research both enjoyable and exciting. Among these were Elaine Agar, Linda Elkinton, Rosemary Lichtman, Gayle Matthews, David Novak, and Carolyn Simmons. I am particularly indebted to Shelagh Towson who not only offered substantive comments on the entire manuscript but functioned as a superb editorial critic and helped greatly in seeing to it that the final draft met at least some of the requirements of acceptable prose. And finally, I am not certain how one can measure, much less describe, the value of the continued support and encouragement I received from Sally Lerner. It mattered greatly to me that she thought the work I did was important.

Much of the research reported in this manuscript was facilitated by the generous support of the National Science Foundation (Grant GS-057) and the Social Sciences and Humanities Research Council, formerly the Canada Council (Grants S70-1251 and S73-0194).

Contents

Introduction   1

There Are No Suffering Children, Only Kids to Make Well!. 2
If I Experience It, It Must Be "Real". 3
Rejection of Victims and Rejection of Counterevidence. 4
The Answers to "How" and "Why" Must Be Protected. 5

Chapter 1. The Belief in a Just World   9

People Develop a "Belief in a Just World". 11
People Construe Events to Fit This Belief. 12
    Generalization from Past Experience. 12
    That Is the Way Our Minds Work. 14
    It Is Functional—If Not Essential. 14
Judgments of What Is Deserved in the "Just World" Reflect
the Norms of the Culture. 15
    Status Role. 16
    Deviant Statuses. 16
    The Generic Norm. 16
    General Cultural Themes—Politicoreligious Ideologies. 17
The Belief in a "Just World" Is Modified by Experiences
with the "Real World". 17
People Employ "Tactics" to Eliminate Threats to the
Belief in a Just World. 19
    Rational Strategies for Dealing with Injustices. 19
    Nonrational Tactics—Psychological Defenses. 20

Eventually, People Develop "Strategies" Designed to
Protect the Belief in a Just World from Any Contradictory Evidence 21
    Extended Time Frame—"Ultimate Justice" 22
    There Are Various "Worlds"—Ours Is a Just One 23
Nevertheless, There Are Continuing Threats to the
Belief in a Just World 26
    Some Basic Myths 26
    Contradicting Experiences—"Realities" 27
    We Need and Create the Belief in a Just World:
    Some Thoughts as to "Why" 30

Chapter 2. The First Experiment: The Effect of Fortuitous Reward   31

The Setting 31
The Findings 34
The Implications for the Method and Theory 36

Chapter 3. The Second Experiment: Observers' Reactions to the
"Innocent Victim"   39

The Questions 39
The Innocent Victim Situation 41
The Experimental Conditions—Creating Degrees of Injustice 43
The Measures—What Do You Think of the Victim? 45
The Findings—How Did the Degree of Injustice
Affect the Observers' Reactions? 47
What Did We Learn? 50

Chapter 4. The Third Experiment: The Martyred and Innocent Victims   55

The Importance of Their Fate, Their Role in Creating
That Outcome, and the Consequences for the Observers 55
    The Importance of Witnessing the Suffering 56
    The Effects of the Victim's Reaction versus Her Fate 57
    The Relationship between the Victim and the Observers 57
The Procedure 58
The Findings 60

Chapter 5. Three Experiments That Assess the Effects
of Sex and Educational Background of Observers, Experimenter
and Observer Influence on One Another, and the Reactions
of "Informed" and Nonimplicated Observers   63

The First Study 64
The Second Study 66

The Third Study... 68
Implications 70

**Chapter 6. Reactions to the Belief in a Just World Theory and Findings:
The "Nay-Sayers"** 73

Under Normal Circumstances, We Don't Act That Way!
"Normally" We All Care about Victims in our World.............. 74
Everyone Knows We Admire Admirable Victims and Condemn
Only Despicable Victims!...................................... 80
We May Reject Some Victims, but We Already Knew about That!...... 83
Some Concluding Thoughts..................................... 87

Chapter 7. Condemning the Victimized 89

The Meanings of Identification................................ 89
  Expecting to "Walk in Their Shoes"......................... 90
  You and I Are Partners: You Could Not Be Bad!.............. 91
  "Disidentifying" by the Powerless...........................92
The Role of One's Fate in the Identification Process................. 94
  The Norm of Social Responsibility........................... 94
  The Effect of Prior Negative or Positive Experience
  on Willingness to Meet Normative Demands................... 95
  The Importance of "Deservingness" in the Norm of
  Social Responsibility.. 97
Some Obvious and Not So Obvious Conclusions................... 101

Chapter 8. The Assignment of Blame 105

The Effects of Outcome on Attribution of Responsibility............ 106
  Fortuitous Reward and Self-Blame........................... 106
  Detached versus Involved Participation...................... 107
The Appearance of "Primitive" Attribution Processes.............. 111
  Who Is to Blame in a Chain of Causation?...................... 112
  The Psychology of "Last Reasonable Chance".................. 115
  Other Examples of Primitive Attributions
  in Experimental Social Psychology........................... 117
Motivation and Information Processing: Some Anecdotal Examples..... 118

**Chapter 9. The Response to Victimization:
Extreme Tests of the Belief in a Just World** 123

The Self as "Victim": Some Puzzling Reactions.................... 123
The Dangers in Identification with Victims...................... 126
  What Can We Learn from a Horrible Example?................. 126

Two Experimental Tests of How We React to "Similar Victims"......128
Identification with Victims—Some Concluding Thoughts.........136

Chapter 10. Who Believes in a Just World: Dimension or Style   **137**

The Rubin and Peplau BJW Scale..............................138
    A Description of the Scale.................................138
    BJW Scale—Reactions to the Victims of the Draft Lottery..........140
    BJW Scale and Reactions to Injustices in Society.................141
    A Test of the "Defensive" Component in BJW...................143
    The "Functional" Use of BJW-Related Acts:
    Appeasing the Gods......................................146
    BJW as a Correlate of Social Attitudes........................147
    Another Look at Reactions to the "Innocent Victim":
    BJW in the Lerner and Simmons Paradigm.....................148
    Construct Validity of BJW-Related Personal Dimensions:
    "I-E," "F," "PEC," and Social Attitudes.....................149
The Belief in a Just World: Styles of "Defense"...................155
    The Effect of Experience on BJW: Abandonment
    or Transformation?......................................155
    Transformation of BJW: Some Earlier Evidence
    of Normative Reactions...................................157
    The Role of Emotional Involvement in the
    Appearance of Just World Beliefs............................158
    Victim's Belief in a Just World: A Strong Test of
    the Importance of the Just World Belief.......................160
    An Even Stronger Test: Victim Crippled for Life................161
    The Religious Perspective as a Form of Belief in a Just World.......163
    The Religious Perspective and Society's Victims: Social Class
    and the Perception of Justice...............................165
    Some Concluding Thoughts................................171
The Penultimate Defense of the Belief in a Just World:
Or the "No-Nonsense-Cut-the-Crap-It's-A-Tough-World-
Out-There" Charade..171
    The Contemporary Model of Man: What Is It, and
    How Pervasive in Our Lives?...............................173
    Is This Model of Man "Mythical"?..........................174
    In What Ways Does the "Myth" Create a
    Functional "Defense"?...................................176
    It Is a Charade—We Only Pretend to Ourselves and
    Others That We Believe in the "Myth"......................180

Chapter 11. Deserving versus Justice   **183**

A Demonstration..183

Deserving versus/and Justice.....................................187
The "Charade" as a Social Device.............................190
A Last Thought..193

References   195

Index   203

Introduction

At the same time and place that Ken Kesey became introduced to hallucinogenic drugs, I did a postdoctoral in clinical psychology. It seemed a good institution, as large mental hospitals go, and there is no doubt that most of the staff were very good; and some were—are—outstanding psychologists. For the first few months, I was assigned to work on an "open ward," where, for the most part, the patients were considered to be in fairly good remission—not acting crazy. My training consisted mainly of acting as co-therapist with an experienced psychologist in small groups which were designed to prepare patients for the move from the hospital to an acceptable arrangement in the outside world.

These "therapy" sessions with the small group of patients, most of whom had a long history of moving in and out of various hospitals, were often stressful, if not emotionally devastating. The therapist in charge of the group would question, and often cross-examine, the patients about their efforts to find jobs in the community. In particular, he would focus on how they had used their "passes"—what they did in town, whom they spoke with, what happened. Of course, we all knew that the patients were frightened by the prospect of leaving the hospital and having to live in that marginal community of crumby rooming houses—working as dishwashers or parking-lot attendants—with no sources of emotional support, and virtually no skills in finding ways to break through their loneliness and isolation. To counter that fear, the therapist—inquisitor intimidated, probed, and badgered them. In what appeared to be ruthless and relentless cross-examination, he would trap them into confessing finally that "yes," they had not actually gone for the interview—"yes," they had lied—"yes," they would not do it again. What a hell of a way to live, in or out of the hospital—how degrading and seemingly hopeless their lives appeared to be. But there were no signs of pity or compassion from the therapist. At weekly staff meetings, we spent considerable time in planning how to get these "manipulators" out of the hospital.

Later assignments on other wards provided essentially similar experiences,

1

adding up to the plaguing question—how could these trained professionals treat sick, vulnerable human beings in such an unfeeling, cruel way? How could they call them names—"manipulator," "burnt-out schiz," "old crock,"—usually, but not always, behind their backs, which degraded them and treated them as bad jokes?

One could stop at this point, and accept the easy answers to this question offered by such eminent critics of mental institutions as Goffman (1963), Kesey (1962), or Rosenhan (1973). But I am convinced that that would be a gross error. I knew and worked long enough with the staff, including the "big nurse," to know that there were no "big nurses." For the most part, they were very bright, sensitive, concerned, warm people who had developed ways of adapting to and functioning within the demands of the system which took into account their own emotional needs. However dysfunctional or cruel their procedures seemed at times, it became clear that they arose out of the desire to help the patients. The name-calling, the sick humor, was a well-understood charade, designed, at least in part, as a way of handling their own strong feelings of compassion, feelings that I was experiencing anew.

I came to realize that this defense was needed for anyone to be able to function for so long with so many people who were suffering, hurt, and would stay that way for a long time—probably as long as they lived (Maslach, 1976). It was obviously a self-protective device, broken through and at times voluntarily set aside when there was a real possibility for trying something new—a drug, a therapeutic program—that offered some hope of help for the manipulators, the crocks, the burnt-out schizes. Nevertheless, I can still recall those scenes—"Didn't you just walk around or sit in the park instead of going to see about that dish-washing job—didn't you?"—and the degrading confession: "Yes".

There Are No Suffering Children, Only Kids to Make Well!

Something quite similar to my hospital experiences happened later when I was teaching in a medical school. A very close friend of ours, Dr. "Annie," who was on the faculty of a department of community medicine, decided to get further training in order to complete her residency requirements in pediatrics. One of Annie's outstanding characteristics was her inability to tolerate sad stories, real or imaginary. She would refuse to see a movie or watch a TV program if there was any chance that it might have a sad ending. Nonetheless, she decided to work on the pediatric ward in order to complete her residency requirements. One visit to a pediatric ward in a university hospital is enough to reduce most people to tears—lumberjacks, old soldiers, and morticians included. The sight of a really sick child can be truly heartbreaking. How then could Dr. Annie spend five minutes, much less hours at a time, in that kind of environment?

After considerable probing and talking with her, the answer became clear. When she walked onto that ward, she literally did not see sick, suffering children. All she "saw" were kids she could help, kids she could make well. The next question, obviously, is what happened when it turned out that one of the children would not get well—would die—and there was nothing anyone would do about it. Dr. Annie did what many physicians do, much to the dismay of the ward nurses. They find every imaginable way to avoid the patient—not to see, talk to, have contact with the patient. What remains is simple denial and avoidance as a way of not "seeing" sick suffering children.

If I Experience It, It Must Be "Real"

My early experiences in the medical school led to at least two other important events. Within months of my arrival, I was assigned to be the psychologist on a university-wide committee whose function was to prepare for disasters—in particular, a nuclear attack. It seems incredible now, thinking back, that we actually went through that mad exercise. But at the time it all seemed so reasonable. I cannot remember all the details, but I do recall that the first meeting was devoted to making preparations for people to live in the shelter for a given period of time after a nuclear attack. We talked not only about food and water, but also about the kinds of recreational activities we should provide—games, crafts, the wonderful things people could do with papier-mâché. Eventually the issue arose of how to arrange admission and exclusion from the university shelters in the event of an attack. If an attack happened during the work day, what should we at the medical center do about our families at home? Should they be allowed in? Should we go get them and bring them to this shelter, or let them go to the nearest to home or the school? Does this seem mad now? It didn't then. And the discussions were thoughtful, free, give and take, light at times. Apparently just like any other committee meeting.

I have no idea what was going on inside the other members' heads, but I do know that the meeting scared the hell out of me. The planning, the discussion, had forced me to "live in" the world of nuclear holocaust. The more we talked and thought about what to do in the event of this or that, the more real it all became in my mind. I was able to create, imagine vicariously, living in one of those shelters, and dealing with the various crises that might arise.

In order to do any effective planning, I had to do that; but the "fallout" of that exercise included a considerably increased level of fear, based, at least in part, on an increased level of certainty that a nuclear war would in fact occur.

Mind you, nothing in the discussion dealt explicitly with the question of how imminent or likely it was that there would be a need for such shelters. Actually, it is unlikely that any direct statement of cold statistics and calculated estimates would have had any real influence on the vivid reality created by the content of the discussion.

Rejection of Victims and Rejection of Counterevidence

As part of my teaching with first-year medical students, I had the task of introducing them to various social factors involved in issues of health and illness. Among the most important are those associated with poverty, and the correlates of poor housing, hygiene and nutrition, infant mortality, decreased life expectancy, poor health care, minimal education, distrust and fear of professionals, etc. This was a particularly salient issue to these students, because there were well-publicized and large pockets of poverty in the mining regions of that state. The vast majority of the students had no interest in hearing that bleeding-heart liberal crap. Typically, very early in that kind of presentation, one of the students would let me know that he grew up with "those people," and I didn't know what the hell I was talking about. Those people were happy living like that. They were just the kind of folks who would cheat and connive and let their kids go hungry rather than go out and get a decent job. There was plenty of work for everyone if they just wanted it—if they'd just go out and look for it. No one had to go hungry. They were lazy, irresponsible. Just look at what they did with their welfare checks. They bought liquor, made payments on a TV while their kids went without meat and vegetables, shoes, decent clothing, etc. What kind of a parent, human being, would live like that?

My initial response to this insensitive assault on these poor people was to assemble an impressive and compelling array of information which would demonstrate beyond any reasonable doubt that they were clearly innocent victims of social, economic, and technological change. During the years surrounding the Second World War the mineworkers' unions were strong under John L. Lewis; the miners made good wages, and had excellent union-sponsored hospitals and health care. After the war, when the demand for coal dropped and automation became economically feasible, the strength of the union was eventually broken, wages went down, unemployment soared, the hospitals closed—and miserable poverty became a way of life for people who had worked hard all their lives and had become accustomed to a sense of well-being and security for themselves and their families. One day a man had a good job, a secure job, with a strong union to back him up, and hospitals to take care of him and his family. The next day, through absolutely no fault of his own—no work, a different union, no hospitals, no hope. Of course, he could leave his home and family, go up north, live in one of the "hillbilly ghettos," and try to find work in one of the factories. It would have to be an unskilled, low-paying job, since he had been trained to do nothing but mine coal—and he would be the last hired and the first fired. And it was lonely. Appalachian immigrants were the "white niggers" in those northern cities—so many went back home. It is a very sad story, but at the end, when I expected the tears to flow and the signs of new awareness to appear on their faces, one of the students would raise his hand and confirm what a casual glance over the class indicated was the general consensus of opinion. "Dr. Lerner, I don't care what you say. I know those people, and they are just lazy, and they just don't want to work. They don't have to live that way—that's what they are like." So much for evidence. The data had no effect whatsoever.

The dramatically "irrational," or was it "nonrational," way they twisted and denied the evidence which portrayed the Appalachian poor as innocent victims resembled most closely the way extreme bigots neutralize any information which might threaten their vicious stereotypes about the "niggers." However, that comparison did not seem to fit either. I had collected considerable data from these students at the beginning of the year, including their responses to Rokeach's dogmatism and opinionation scales (1960), and the "F" scale from the Authoritarian Personality research (Adorno, Frenkel-Brunswick, Levinson, & Sanford, 1950). An analysis of those scores showed virtually no group trends or individual differences which related to this "symptom" of insistence on the contemptible character of the Appalachian victims in the face of any and all forms of evidence.

Actually, whatever the results of the test scores, it would have been clear to anyone who spent time with these students that they were bright, well-integrated emotionally, quite mature by any reasonable standard, with a lively sense of humor, a great sense of purpose in life, and a strong commitment to making a contribution to the welfare of the society. But they simply had "no use for" people who were poor and on welfare, and they refused to believe any evidence in their favor.

There was simply no way that I could attribute this "sick" reaction to an obvious form of pathology. If these truly fine youngsters could react in this way, then anyone could. Any explanation, then, had to fall within the range of normal processes. But how could this reaction be normal? How could rational healthy people maintain such cruel attitudes toward other people who were suffering, and exhibit the most irrational processes in defense of these vicious beliefs?

The Answers to "How" and "Why" Must Be Protected

The answer that emerged from these experiences began with the hunch that these students, no less than the staff at the mental hospital, or Dr. Annie, or any of us, at times create or select ways of seeing our world in the service of an important need. "Need" is used here in the sense that there are strong emotional consequences at stake. In these cases, the need has something to do with the fate of other people in our world—people who are suffering, deprived, crippled, miserable.

Let us look a little more closely at this need. It is reasonable to assume that the students, no less than I, have fairly strong emotional reactions when they are confronted with another person who is a victim. Although this reaction can vary a great deal in terms of experiential content, it is typically a mixture of empathic pain, concern, pity, and maybe at times revulsion, fear, panic. On a simple hedonic scale, the reaction ranges from mild displeasure to excruciating pain, and as a result we are impelled to do something to eliminate the suffering—ours, if not the victim's.

One way to do this is to alter one's view of the event. Dr. Annie arranged her cognitions so that she did not "see" suffering children; she saw children she could help. Some of the staff and medical students at the hospital did not see miserable, crippled victims of forces that no one understood or could control. Instead, they saw objects of derision. And that was not hard to do. All it required was a highly selective perception of attributes and events. Many of the patients did act in ways that were "manipulative" of the staff. The fact that they did this out of desperation and the lack of any other resources to affect their fate could be ignored or forgotten. "Burnt-out schiz" is not an attractive term, but if you are compelled repeatedly to see the same passive, ineffectual, slightly strange behavior which appears impervious to change by any procedure known to man, then that phrase seems to capture some of the sense of futility and hopelessness. And who could deny that people living in those miserable poverty-stricken conditions are lazy? Who isn't lazy from time to time? Who isn't conniving, untrustworthy, from time to time? If we ignore everything else they do and feel, as well as the conditions under which they have been forced to live, then it all becomes clear. They do get in fights, they do drink, they are no damn good, and they brought their suffering on themselves.

If we assume then that the awareness of another person's suffering typically elicits suffering in the observer, we can see the mechanisms that people use to cope with this experience. In some cases we try to help the victim and eliminate the suffering, but even while doing that we may change our view of the victim, either to eliminate our awareness of his suffering, or to persuade ourselves that he really is not suffering at all, or that he is the kind of person who brings suffering upon himself, or that he is somewhat less than human.

For most people, though, these cognitive constructions seem to be relatively tentative or vulnerable defenses which are often breached and at times abandoned when they are no longer functional. The awareness of a terminal prognosis is sufficient to remove the patient from "someone whom I can make well," and so the suffering returns. The "manipulating crock" is treated with enthusiastic concern and warmth as soon as there is some sign, some hope, that he will respond to the new procedure.

But what happened with the medical students? Is it possible that I had been forcing them to go through a process quite similar to my experience as a member of the committee engaged in the quite rational procedure of designing survival procedures in the event of a nuclear war? The more compelling, the more vivid, the more dramatic the portrayal of the misery, and particularly the innocence, of those people, their neighbors living in such hopeless poverty, the more I was forcing them to recognize the reality of a tragedy in their world. But could they acknowledge that reality? If those people living in such miserable and degrading circumstances were truly "innocent" victims of forces over which neither they nor anyone else had any control, what did that mean? How did it make the students feel? Even the hint of it? Could they allow themselves to believe that there could be such undeserved suffering inflicted on so many people in their world?

How do you feel when you see a hungry, sick child? Or have you ever driven through one of our slum ghettoes, and seen the people on the streets and the way they live? What thoughts or feelings do you have? Have you ever known someone who seemed to be doing fine, leading a reasonably decent, productive life, and for no apparent reason—out of the blue—was hit with a disaster—crippled emotionally or physically? Or one of his children died from an accident or sudden illness? What thoughts did you have? What feelings? What did you do then?

How can we make sense, then, of the way we and others try to make sense out of our lives? As social psychologists, by temperament and inclination if not training, we try to build a model, a general theory, and then we do experiments so that we can examine both the phenomenon and the explanation a little more closely. The Just World Theory is one such effort.

In the next section I hope to accomplish two things as a way of setting the stage for the rest of the volume. One of these is to present my understanding of the way the belief in a just world appears in people's lives. Although I may allude to some studies by myself and others, my main purpose is to describe the ideas in a reasonably systematic and plausible form. Later on we will discuss the relevant research in considerable detail, but for now I want to review for you what I think are the personal and interpersonal dynamics associated with our belief in a just world. Where does it come from? How and why do people maintain it? How does it appear in our behavior?

Second, I want to alert the reader to some of the conceptual underpinnings of the Just World Theory and the theoretical issues associated with these assumptions. Many of these will be taken up again in later chapters, and examined more critically. For the time being, let us simply take a first look at some social-psychological processes that may be involved in people's development and maintenance of the belief that the world they live in is a just one.

CHAPTER 1

The Belief in a Just World

The "belief in a just world" refers to those more or less articulated assumptions which underlie the way people orient themselves to their environment. These assumptions have a functional component which is tied to the image of a manageable and predictable world. These are central to the ability to engage in long-term goal-directed activity. In order to plan, work for, and obtain things they want, and avoid those which are frightening or painful, people must assume that there are manageable procedures which are effective in producing the desired end states (Erikson, 1950; Merton, 1957).

Not only are the assumptions of orderliness and controllability of one's environment functional for concerted activity, but there is a growing body of data which indicates that living in a chaotic environment or being rendered "helpless," impotent to affect one's fate, produces deterioration in the physical and emotional integrity of the organism, human and infrahuman alike (Lefcourt, 1976; Wortman & Brehm, 1975).

But a "Just World" is different from, and more than, a "predictable world," or a "controllable world." Conceivably, there are people who can and do function, at least in vast areas of their lives, solely within these latter perspectives of prediction and control. The "objective" posture associated typically with scientific or problem-solving activities, as well as the manipulative egocentric orientation of the true "Machiavellian" (Christie & Geis, 1970) or "psychopath," may be examples of "nonjust worlds," or simply "controllable or understandable worlds." But most people who fall within the range

9

of "normal" processes generate, along with assumptions of order and control, a sense of appropriateness, standards of evaluation which are considered no less "real," objective, than the tangible physical world in which they move (Heider, 1958; Ross & DiTecco, 1975). Certainly the sense of justice varies greatly among people in both form and content, but there may be important constancies in the origins and functions of this virtually universal human process, "justice," the judgment of appropriateness. At least the possibility is sufficiently intriguing to merit our attention.

Most contemporary attempts to understand social behavior have recognized this important reaction. For example, Homans (1961) sees regularities in human behavior as "operants"; in other words, acts which are emitted in a specific social context as the result of prior reinforcement contingencies. Whenever an operant is not followed by a reinforcement, the organism exhibits a certain amount of "emotional" behavior. In the extreme, it squeaks, bites, defecates, engages in behaviors which may appear to be random. That is the prototype of the sense of injustice—how the "is," the regularities or "operants" in human conduct, become transformed into the "ought," the emotional squeaks.

Others, such as Rokeach (1971), assume that the disconfirmation of a "belief," a cognition, elicits a negative state. The more central and important the prior confirmation associated with the belief, the greater the emotional disturbance. Similarly, Festinger's (1957) theory of cognitive dissonance holds as one of its basic propositions the assumption that a negative-drive state results whenever a person holds two cognitions which are contradictory in their implications. In other words, whenever an expectation about one's self or the environment is disconfirmed, people are upset, and motivated to remove that undesirable state of affairs. The negative state elicited by the dissonant cognitions may be the sense of injustice—the violation of that which is judged to be "appropriate."

In a later section, we will devote considerably more attention to the processes that have been presumed to be involved in the development of this sense of what is just or appropriate. The main point to be made here is that evaluative judgments of what "ought" to be the outcome in any event are a natural and inevitable part of the human response to the environment. Although these judgments probably have some roots in the regularities that have occurred in the person's history, they are affectively and cognitively distinct from assessments of control and predictability. For example, in trying to understand the differences between the need or desire for a controllable and a just world, it is important to remember that one of the most commonly observed characteristics of social existence is that people imbue social regularities with an "ought" quality. The way we live our lives is the "right" way. And we become angry, indignant, outraged, when these "correct" ways are violated. Where does this "ought" quality come from? Why do we act that way? Obviously, these are very interesting and important questions, and in the course of this discussion we will try to offer some possible answers.

We can now turn to the descriptive elements of the Just World Theory.

People Develop a "Belief in a Just World"

A Just World is one in which people "get what they deserve." The judgment of "deserving" is based on the outcome that someone is entitled to receive.

A Person "P" deserves outcome "X" if P has met the appropriate preconditions for obtaining X. What is implied, also, is that P desires X. If P does not get X, or receives something of less value than X, then P has not received all he or she deserves. Of course, the outcomes in question can be negative rather than positive. P has met the appropriate preconditions to avoid the undesirable Y.

Suffice it to say that the determination of appropriate preconditions is, for the most part, socially determined. For example, within any society there are rules about what people should do to avoid Y and to obtain X. What kinds of preconditions should have X or Y as consequences? Where no specific rules are appropriate, more general rules of the culture are applied, such as that P deserves what "others" have who are equivalent to P on some important dimension. P deserves less than those who are more "entitled," superior on a relevant dimension, and more than those who are inferior.

Typically, in our society and some others at least, there are two general bases for entitlement or deserving: one's behavior and one's attributes. Certain acts are seen as appropriate antecedents for a range of negative outcomes. If one fails to prepare, take normal precautions, does not produce sufficient quantity or quality, then one is entitled to a certain amount of failure, suffering, deprivation—negative consequences. Certain attributes, including simple membership in the society, entitle one to certain desired outcomes—respect, affection, security. There are other personal qualities which imply superior standing on social standards. To the extent that someone is judged to be kind, friendly, handsome, energetic, conscientious, generous, intelligent, he is seen as being entitled to certain desirable fates. Conversely, failure to meet these standards, or violation of them, is seen as a sufficient precondition for deprivation, suffering, negative fate. People who have been cruel, unfriendly, ugly, lazy, stingy, inconsiderate, or stupid, deserve some degree of punishment.

In a complex, modern society such as ours, the rules for entitlement become organized in complex and interesting ways, which will be discussed in considerable detail in a later chapter. In all cases, however, they are essentially elaborations of these two general forms of entitlement as they appear in various social contexts.

Of course, this and all the other propositions imply the familiar "other things being equal," or "under normal circumstances." Conceivably, the belief in a just world can vary in intensity or strength; however, a certain degree of this belief is natural and inevitable.

People Construe Events to Fit This Belief

This statement may approximate to a truism in psychology, in the sense that "beliefs" are the expression of the way a person organizes his perceptions and cognitions. Any new bit of information is likely, initially, to be coded and assimilated, given meaning within the existing cognitive templates, which also provide the foundation for the person's system of beliefs. But this proposition is meant to convey considerably more.

There probably is a "reality" out there, and so at one experiential extreme are the subjective, autistic reactions which have little correspondence with that "reality." At the other extreme is the objective interpretation or perspective which accurately corresponds to that reality. That person out there *is suffering,* and that person *does not deserve* to suffer. Objectively, that person is not a "manipulator," or a "lazy welfare bum." However, under certain circumstances, people who become aware of that person's fate will construe events, including the personal attributes of the victim, so that the victim appears to "deserve" his suffering.

One can find at least three plausible candidates as explanatory mechanisms to account for this construction of events.

Generalization from Past Experience

Personal Observation. No one sees everything, can know everything that is relevant to a given event. One learns to detect discriminative stimuli or critical cues which are sufficient to generate at least a tentatively acceptable coding of what is happening or about to happen. If in the past there has been a clear association between acts which we consider careless, inadequate, "naughty," prohibited, socially proscribed, and a set of outcomes we call disappointing, painful, undesirable, then it would be quite natural (if not necessarily valid) to assume that, if someone is hungry, rejected, suffering in some way, then that person probably did—or failed to do—that which typically causes this event to occur. Similarly, people who are nice, friendly, clever, handsome, are generally treated well by others, whereas people who are selfish, cruel, uncooperative, are those who end up unhappy as well.

It is simply a very good bet that if you see someone who is miserable and suffering, they were either stupid or careless, or they are merely getting their just desserts for the way they typically treat other people. According to this theoretical approach, the perception of certain important outcomes or consequences leads the observer to infer the antecedent conditions which, he has learned, typically bring about the fate. Suffering often results from the violation of laws—of man and nature.

Cultural Wisdom and Morality Tales. Whatever the person's direct experiences of contingencies between given antecedent conditions and particular consequences, there are strong forces in our culture which convey the belief that this is a "just world." The Western religions stress the relation between sin, doing harm to others, and suffering. Although the ultimate accounting is expected to take place in the next world and for eternity, there are strong themes running through the Judeo-Christian tradition which link signs of one's fate on earth with virtue and a state of grace—Job, in the Bible, suffered long and grievously, but he was more than compensated, not in heaven but on this earth. The Old Testament contains many examples which illustrate that the "righteous will triumph and the wicked be punished." The Christian Reformation created the basis for a world view, the "Protestant Ethic," which permeates our culture (MacDonald, 1972). From this perspective, success, financial and otherwise, is a sign of salvation, and a direct result of the Christian virtues of diligence and self-sacrifice.

Our folk wisdom provides considerable support for this same message. The morality tales which are taught to our children at home and school are variations on the same theme—virtue may be "its own reward," but it is also portrayed as the path to health, wealth, and wisdom. Most children have no trouble generalizing from the fable of the self-indulgent "grasshopper" who suffers during the winter while the self-denying diligent "ant" is safe, secure, and contented as the result of the preparations he made all summer for the long, cold winter. How do people end up hungry, cold, suffering? Obviously they must have been "grasshoppers," rather than "ants."

The mass media recreate the same morality tales with remarkably little variation. The heroes, heroines, are virtuous, diligent, beautiful. The villains are evil, lazy, and often ugly. Whatever the sequence of who does what to whom, the ending is insured. Good triumphs over Evil. The villain is punished—is caused to suffer. He gets what he deserves. Nighttime television, presumably designed for the adult population of this country, contains an incredible number of simple cops-and-robbers shows. Plots are little more subtle than the old-time melodramas, or the adventures of "Batman" and "Robin." Of course, the good guys, the cops, capture and bring to justice the bad guys, the criminals—who are often humiliated, beaten, and reviled in the process. After all, that is what they deserve, and justice will be done.

That Is the Way Our Minds Work

There is some reason to believe that the processes underlying the organization of our cognitions create "balance," or psychological uniformity, in the way we construe events (Heider, 1958). In other words, our minds try to fit together all positive events, traits, and attributes in the same "object" or unit, and similarly bring together all negative cognitions. As a result, we are inclined to believe that goodness, happiness, beauty, virtue, and success are connected in a causal way, just as are misery, ugliness, sin, inferiority, and suffering. We do this, not necessarily because it fits our experiences or morality, but because our brains attempt to maintain a unifying harmony among cognitive elements. In this way we create a relatively stable world for ourselves, comprised of univalent objects. As Heider (1958) states:

> The relationship between goodness and happiness, between wickedness and punishment is so strong, that given one of these conditions, the other is frequently assumed. Misfortune, sickness, accidents are often taken as signs of badness and guilt. If O (the other) is unfortunate then he has committed a sin. (p. 235)

> Common sense psychology tends to hold that any imbalance represents a temporary state of affairs, that is the wicked may have their field day now, but that they will eventually be punished and the good rewarded. (p. 235)

It Is Functional—If Not Essential

Much of the previous discussion, and particularly the anecdotal examples, portrays the "belief in a just world" as inextricably bound up with the person's motives and goals. People want to and have to believe they live in a just world so that they can go about their daily lives with a sense of trust, hope, and confidence in their future. If it is true that people want or need to believe that they live in a world where people get what they deserve, then it is not surprising that they will find ways, other things being equal, to interpret events to fit this belief.

Tannenbaum and Gaer (1965) were able to illustrate with carefully collected data what anyone could testify to on the basis of personal experience. They showed people sections of the very powerful film "The Ox-bow Incident," starting with the scene in which a mob of drunken, miserable characters threatens, out of the basest of motives, to hang three innocent men for murder and cattle rustling. The experimental data revealed that the people watching the film, especially those who felt a sense of identity with the innocent victims, were measurably upset and bothered at that point. They were worried, frightened, angry. Half of the subjects in this experiment then saw a happy ending, where the sheriff arrived in time to prevent the lynching. The other subjects saw the version where the sheriff arrives too late. As one might expect, the happy ending left the viewers feeling good again. The sad ending caused the viewers to be sad and upset.

What appears to be a most common human experience is that people not only populate their world with good and bad characters, they also become emotionally invested in the scenarios, to the point where they need to see the good prevail and only the bad suffer. This urge to see justice triumph is so pervasive and strong that people typically fail to distinguish between "fantasy" and "reality," and invest fictional events with genuine emotional consequences. Efron (1971) reports that viewers of television daytime dramas often write in to demand that the "heavies" not only be punished, but "they want them killed off right away." And they threaten to stop watching the show if the "good" character is endangered.

It is not simply that people identify with characters in their world, fictional or real, or that, as a function of this identification, they respond empathically to the suffering of others (Lazarus, Speisman, Mordkoff, & Davison, 1962; Stotland, 1969). In addition, there is a definite pattern to this arousal, which fits the theme of justice or deserving. People are not upset, in fact they may feel quite good, if the villain, someone who deserves to suffer, is punished. But if an innocent person suffers, then the "sense of injustice" is aroused (Cahn, 1949):

> sympathetic reaction of outrage, horror, shock, resentment, and anger, those affections of the viscera and abnormal secretions of the adrenals that prepare the human animal to resist attack. Nature has thus equipped all men to regard injustice to another as personal aggression. (p. 24)

Along with the "sense of injustice," the belief in justice is often viewed as a "motivationally induced way of adapting to a world in which one is relatively helpless. The individual seeks stability in his world by attributing absolute virtue to the legal system" (Hess & Torney, 1967, p. 52).

Judgments of What Is Deserved in the "Just World" Reflect the Norms of the Culture

Piaget's concept of "immanent justice" (1948) describes an aspect of the belief in a just world as it appears in very young children, the belief that "a fault will automatically bring about its own punishment" (p. 256). Presumably the children not only expect that their parents will punish misdeeds, but they "attribute spontaneously to nature the power of applying the same punishments" (p. 259). Rubin and Peplau (1975) conclude:

> Our analysis of the origins of the belief in a just world suggests that all children have a version of the belief (Piaget's 'immanent justice') at an early age of development. Whether children outgrow the belief quickly, slowly, or not at all depends in large measure on processes of socialization. (p. 85)

Whatever the origins of the child's belief in a just world, there can be little doubt that later experiences with the social and physical environment play an important role in shaping both the way judgments of deserving are made, and the way people adapt the belief in a just world to common experiences in their day-to-day living.

Status Role

Each ongoing social unit includes commonly accepted rules, norms, which define the expectations appropriate to any occupant of that status or position in the unit. These expectations involve prescriptions, proscriptions, duties, obligations, privileges which outline the relationships among the participants in the society. Who is expected to do what to or for whom? Who can expect what from whom? In some cultures it is clear that children are entitled to nurturance, care, and love from their parents. They are expected to reciprocate with respect, deference, and obedience, and generally comport themselves in a way which brings pride to their family. The failure of either parents or children to meet these expectations elicit the judgment of unjust treatment—receiving less than one deserves.

Some of these status entitlements are unique to a given relationship—parent–child, teacher–pupil, worker–supervisor, doctor–nurse–patient, judge–defendant. Others are common to all members of the society in good standing. Every citizen deserves—every woman deserves—anyone who is sick or hungry has a right to—competitors or litigants are allowed or expected to.

Deviant Statuses

Also institutionalized are special statuses which imply either the reduction or the disqualification of specific entitlements. People who occupy these statuses are in a general sense judged to be "worse and different." Minority statuses fall within this category. Commonly held negative stereotypes of minority-group members as diminished in personal worth, harmdoers, norm violators, qualify them for diminished access to desired resources, and often punishment in the guise of retribution for past or future "crimes" to the society. Blacks, Jews, people on welfare, the ugly, the crippled, the mentally ill, criminals, women, are potentially dangerous, inferior, undesirable in important ways, and therefore deserve less, and, indeed, deserve punishment at times.

The Generic Norm

In-group, out-group, we–they—Tajfel (1970) and others have provided careful, compelling documentation of the general process, at least in Western societies, of coding people along dimensions of similar to me, different from me, belonging to my categories, belonging to the others. A seemingly arbitrary dimension, when it is the only basis on which to differentiate between two other people, eye color or a code name for example, leads to preferential treatment in terms of allocation of desired outcomes to one's own "team member." The consequence of this coding is to generate the rule that similarity implies superiority, greater worth, and thus "we" deserve more than "they."

General Cultural Themes—Politicoreligious Ideologies

Even within the same political unit in western societies there are distinct ideologies which provide often contradictory rules for determining who deserves what from whom. Those associated with the left of the political spectrum tend to emphasize rules of "equality" and "manual labor" as the main entitlements, whereas those of the right adhere to the outcomes of "competitive" encounters, individual industry, and the intelligent use of available resources.

The public dialogue among these various orientations takes place in the political arena, and appears as legislation and judicial decisions which create the status quo in which important disputes are resolved and valuable resources are allocated. The consequences of this juridical solution to issues of justice are often remote from any of the individual perspectives.

A striking example of this discontinuity was provided by Kaplan (1973):

> You are sitting on the edge of a pier eating a sandwich and watching the sunset when the fisherman next to you leans too far forward and falls in. He screams to you 'Help, I can't swim. Throw me a life preserver.' You make no effort to get up to throw the life preserver standing only five feet from you even though you could do this with absolutely no danger to yourself and only the most minimal effort. Indeed you sit chomping away on your sandwich and now, along with the sunset, you watch the fisherman drown.
>
> Under the law of essentially every Anglo-American jurisdiction you are guilty of no tort making you civilly liable to the family of the fisherman you permitted to drown, nor would you be criminally liable in any way for his death. (p. 219)

It is possible to present the rationale for this in terms of legislative and jurisprudential wisdom involving compromise among the many considerations of rights and obligations. What remains, however, in stark juxtaposition to this sophisticated "wisdom" is the immediate powerful awareness that this is not justice. Anyone who would "sit chomping away" on his sandwich in this context has violated our sense of who deserves what from whom.

The Belief in a "Just World" Is Modified by Experiences with the "Real World"

Sooner or later, all children learn that their parents, and adults generally, are neither omnipotent nor omniscient. No matter how much we wanted to believe that the "bad" kids would be punished—"you're *really* in trouble, now!''—they often were not. In fact, they seemed to be as happy and well-loved as the goody-goods or the ''boy scouts'' who always did what they were supposed to do. We all had to live with the ''bullies'' on the playground, and the pathetic jerks, whom no one in class could stand for reasons that remained tacit but were generally accepted. And there was the mixture of anger and envy elicited by the ''snobs'' who acted as if they were better than anyone else just because they happened to be better looking, have nicer clothes, and come from wealthier homes. These and many other experiences of the common injustices in the child's world provide sufficient evidence, along with the lessons of chemistry, automotive mechanics, and arithmetic, that we all live in a world where things happen because of natural ''forces'' for reasons that have nothing to do with who has been good or bad. And, of course, we learn to use these forces, laws, to our own advantage. Certainly by adulthood, although there may be some ''simple souls'' who think that ''people's actions are the object of equitable rewards and punishments'' (Piaget, 1948, p. 261), the belief in a world of ''immanent justice'' has been relinquished.

How can we portray the phenomenology of the tough-minded, no-nonsense adult? We might characterize the adult world as one where people give up believing in ''fairy tales'' and learn to deal with reality. Certainly no adult bright enough to tie his own shoelaces would admit to himself, much less to others, that he has some belief that he lives in a ''just world'' where everyone gets what he deserves—or deserves what he gets. It would take a complete fool or naive idiot not to recognize that deserving or justice have nothing to do with what happens to people.

Most of us realize that things happen in our world as a result of biological, social, and physical processes which follow understandable if not understood natural laws. If we know the rules, have sufficient understanding of how things tick, then we can understand, predict, and at times control our environment—what happens to us and others. We know something about human physiology and medicine, so that we modify our diet and way of life so that we stay ''healthy.'' If we become ill for some reason, then we go to the doctor, who knows how to cure us. We know what to do if our car or TV breaks down. We also know that promotions and success at work require a certain combination of effort, talent, and wise politicking, and that the ''breaks'' decide one's place in the hierarchy.

The ''breaks,'' luck, chance, fate, accidents, are important in everyone's life. They are the unpredictable, uncontrollable, though not necessarily magical or mysterious, component. We know, or at least think we know, a great deal about what causes cancer, earthquakes, Mongolism, mental illness, poverty, intellectual ability, automobile accidents, downturns in the economy, crimes, wars—we could even piece together an explanation as to how it happened that *this person* at *this time* was afflicted with *this fate*. Our adult understanding of the ''way life is'' means that we have learned to stop being ''crybabies'' and complaining or having temper tantrums if things don't happen the way we want or think is right. Accidents do happen—some people suffer and some die—the rich get richer and the poor get babies. If you know what you are doing, have enough "power" and the right "breaks," you will succeed. If not, you will fail. That is the way it works in this world.

And that is the way we face "reality"? It is probably true that at times we operate at this level, or at least think we do. But, for most people, this world view is a temporary and relatively encapsulated special orientation which has the appearance of facilitating problem-solving efforts. For reasons that will be discussed in considerably more detail later, I would argue that the experiences and maturational processes which lead to adulthood neither diminish nor eliminate the psychological commitment to deserving and justice in one's world. In fact, there are sound theoretical reasons and supporting data which lead to the opposite conclusion, that adults are much more oriented to issues of deserving and responsive to evidence of injustice than children. But as Piaget (1948) and Kohlberg (1969) have described, this orientation changes in important ways.

It is obvious from what we can detect in our own reactions to what we see happening in our world that adults are highly responsive to, and react powerfully and automatically to, an "injustice." How, then, does the reasonably aware adult accommodate this desire for justice or "need to believe in a just world" to the "real world" of power, "breaks," cause-and effect?

People Employ "Tactics" to Eliminate Threats to the Belief in a Just World

Rational Strategies for Dealing with Injustices

These strategies begin with the acceptance of the "reality of injustice," both its occurrence and one's reaction to it. They appear to be eminently "sensible" ways of dealing with this "reality."

Prevention and Restitution. Social agencies of all varieties, unemployment compensation, aid to dependent children, the Society for the Prevention of Cruelty to Animals, emergency services, the courts, the police and the prison system, life, income, health-insurance programs, Social Security, are among the many social devices designed to prevent or reduce the devastating effects of unjust suffering and deprivation. Our society devotes a great deal of resources to these institutions, and the individual contributes not only taxes and donations, but at times acts directly to help his "neighbors" when they are in genuine (just) need.

Acceptance of One's Limitations. It is obvious that one's resources are limited and finite. No matter how one may feel, there is only so much that can be accomplished with these resources without doing harm to one's self and family. And so priorities and limits are established which take into account the nature of the relationship to the victims, the effectiveness of one's resources, and the potential risks or costs to be incurred in comparison with the probable benefits to others.

For example, Walster, Berscheid, and Walster (1976) found that, if the resources available would be only partially effective in eliminating the victim's deprivation, then the act of help was avoided entirely. The judged cost or potential risk to a benefactor in terms of physical harm, embarrassment, or aesthetic revulsion reduced the likelihood of intervention on behalf of a victim (Bar-Tal, 1976).

Nonrational Tactics—Psychological Defenses

We all know that the awareness of another person's suffering—especially undeserved suffering or deprivation—is often a painful experience (Bandura & Rosenthal, 1966; Lazarus et al., 1962; Stotland, 1969). And most people are interested in reducing their pain. What are the mechanisms we employ that are at least temporarily effective in reducing the distress associated with witnessing an injustice?

Denial–Withdrawal. This is a primitive device, but it works. All it requires is an intelligent selection of the information to which one is exposed. And it has the added advantage of requiring no direct distortion of reality. If you have any sense, you arrange not to see what is happening in the ghettoes, in the poverty-stricken areas of the country or the world. You don't make a practice of hanging around emergency rooms, mental hospitals, or homes for the mentally "disadvantaged." If you do, by some mischance, see a crime or a terrible accident, or meet someone who is blind or crippled, then get the hell out of there. Leave the scene physically, and hopefully, with the help of other diversions, the event will leave your mind. This mechanism played a central part in a set of experiments that will be discussed later.

Reinterpretation of the Event. There are various ways of reinterpreting the "injustice" so that in fact it disappears, and therefore there is no longer any reason to be upset. Some of these methods are rather familiar.

First, one could *reinterpret the outcome.* There are few examples from the experimental literature, but a great number from common observation, in which the victim's fate is seen as rather desirable, where the suffering had later greater benefit, was good for the soul, made the victim a better person. Lazarus et al. (1962) have shown that the powerful emotional reaction attendant upon a vivid film of the subincision rites of an aboriginal tribe can be remarkably reduced if there is an attendant script which emphasizes the valuable function of this ritual for the tribe, and especially the child. It is virtually a cliché in our culture to consider the poverty-stricken, or even the relatively deprived, as having their own compensating rewards. They are actually happy in their own way—carefree, happy-go-lucky, in touch with and able to enjoy the "simple pleasures of life."

Some systems of religious belief see virtue in suffering, and assure restitution in later life. That may help explain why at least one survey (Lerner & Elkinton, 1970) found that the respondents from the very poorest families economically—the ones that were barely able to meet their basic needs—were the ones most likely to embrace fully a "fundamentalist religion," and were also least likely to see any injustice in their situation.

Sometimes one can *reinterpret the "cause"*—if it is possible to attribute the victim's fate to something he did or failed to do, then the sense of justice is often satisfied. Experiments have shown that presumably when the victims' suffering or states of deprivation can be "blamed" on them, then even those people with easy access to the needed resources are willing to let them suffer—"stew in their own juices" (Horowitz, 1968; Schopler & Matthews, 1965). According to the "sense of justice," as with Rollo in the old Katzenjammer Kids comic strip, they "have it coming"—they brought it on themselves.

Finally, one can *reinterpret the character of the "victim."* At various points in the earlier discussion, we noted that our culture, and probably every other (Nader, 1974), has "statuses," socially defined "kinds" of people, for whom suffering and minimum access to desired resources is an appropriate state of affairs. These are the people who, by virtue of some act they committed or would be likely to commit, or some personal quality, are assigned to an inferior position. They are judged to merit "punishment," or are generally disqualified from consideration as worthwhile members of the society (Kelman, 1973). In some subcultures, Jews, gypsies, blacks, Catholics, hillbillies, are normatively defined as "inferior" human beings, and at times dangerous "criminals" (Allport, 1954; Harding, Proshansky, Kutner, & Chein 1969).

It is also quite natural to judge people, who otherwise qualify for full membership in the society, as "social criminals," in the sense that they are likely to violate the rules of decency and consideration for their fellow men. They are selfish, uncooperative, cruel. Although at any given time they may seem to be acting quite normally, it is a virtual certainty that they have harmed someone in the past, and will do it again in the future. And so, it is almost a pleasure, rather gratifying, to see these people get their "comeuppance" once and for all. The sight of their suffering may elicit twinges of compassion or pity, but all that is needed to feel better is to realize that they certainly "have it coming" (Ryan, 1971).

Eventually, People Develop "Strategies" Designed to Protect the Belief in a Just World from Any Contradictory Evidence

These devices and "tactics" are only partial and temporary solutions. It has certainly not been possible, in our society, to eliminate the widespread pockets of undeserved misery and suffering. At any given moment, the recognition of one's limited ability to intervene may relieve the strongly felt demand to respond to these injustices. But no combination of "realistic" tactics is sufficiently effective to restore the trust in one's environment needed to function adequately (Chein, Gerard, Lee, & Rosenfeld, 1964; Jessor, Graves, Hanson, & Jessor, 1968; Merton, 1957), or relieve totally the sense of outrage and threat.

The "irrational strategies" certainly go right to the heart of the matter, and simply eliminate the injustice by redefining or removing the event—but, obviously, as the German citizens and we in this country have learned, through outbreaks of violence in the ghettoes and riots in our prisons, we pay a price for our distortions, and often the defenses are breached with devastating consequences. And, of course, there are limits to how much most people can or are willing to process information in autistic ways.

If it is true that, in order to function, adults have to be "realistic," and that they also must believe in a just world that does not exist, what happens? To begin with, people employ the devices and tactics described, and at times suffer and feel frightened when they are not adequate to the task. In addition, there seem to be points where the basic cognitive orientations of "reality" and "justice" meet, and form the psychological underpinnings of the adult belief in a just world—the *protective strategies*.

Extended Time Frame—"Ultimate Justice"

The easiest and most effective way to protect the needed confidence in the justness of one's world is never to allow it to be tested or confronted with evidence. One must keep the belief separate from the realistic world of everyday happenings. This is accomplished frequently by accepting a certain number of "casualties" or "temporary setbacks" as simply part of life, combined with the unverbalized assumption that in the long run things will work out, are improving, for everyone. This belief in "ultimate justice" replaces the earlier one of childhood which looked for immediate or "immanent" justice where people are punished or rewarded in the next psychological moment.

For those who are unwilling to adopt one of the formal religious systems, the source of ultimate justice can vary from situation to situation. The sight of poverty at times can elicit the trust that one of the many social agencies will help anyone who is hungry or sick. It is not always so obvious which one will actually do the job, but "I am sure there are groups to handle such problems—that's what they are there for." The publicity that follows the apprehension and prosecution of a "criminal," the remarkable strides which medical science has made in eliminating the dangers of disease, can also help engender the feeling that there is a good chance, that "by and large, it will turn out right in the end." And each of us is provided with a version of the history of man, civilization, our country, that provides the most eloquent and persuasive testimony for the assumption that "every day, in every way, we are getting better and better." Obviously, there are forces in the history of civilization which bring us closer to a life of decency and respect for the individual. Notwithstanding the momentary pangs of nostalgia, we all know that it will be better tomorrow than today, which is certainly better than yesterday (Etzioni, 1968). We probably would not say it aloud, but we believe it, we "know it."

It is not easy to overestimate the functional value of this form of confidence, and the accompanying toleration of temporary "errors" derived from the extended time frame. As the story goes, the highly successful Green Bay Packer professional football team, under Coach Vince Lombardi, never admitted that they had been beaten. On those few occasions when they did lose, according to the official record at least, they all knew that it was only because the game ended too soon! Such optimistic trust will enable one to continue after what seems to be an error or failure. You can't win them all—some people die—she waited too long—we're learning more each year—in a few years we'll be able to handle (prevent, cure) this—we know better now—we would not now drop an atomic bomb on civilian targets—unleash vast amounts of chemicals in our environment—fail to test drugs before putting them on the market.

Are these "fictions"? Are they attempts to delude ourselves? Probably not in any way which is amenable to reality testing, and not in any way which inhibits the individual or social organism from engaging in effective problem-solving activity—dealing with "reality." They do enable us to live in a complex, "iffy" world.

There Are Various "Worlds"—Ours Is a Just One

The metaphor of a "just world" is meant to be a more valid approximation of social psychological realities than expressed by the terms "society" or "environment."

People selectively create and populate their environment with people, places, and things. These are organized around various themes and scenarios, problems and possibilities—certain events occur to certain kinds of people for certain reasons. There are plots and subplots, with greater or lesser anticipation of the unknown, but there are usually beginnings and endings which blend together in meaningful ways. The people who are actors in these scenarios, by implication at least, are tied together by common problems and possibilities. "After all, we all live in the same world."

But do we? Who lives in what world? Whose lives are more or less interconnected by common, or at least interdependent, possibilities, goals, ways of thinking, a common ideology? In this sense the metaphor of "world" appears to be synonymous with "subculture," and in some ways that is probably true, as when we think of so-and-so living her life in the "world of the theater," or Sutherland's (1966) famous description of the patterned way of life in the "underworld," and of course there are often entire "worlds" associated with various socioeconomic strata in a given community, like "the world of the middle class" in small-town U.S.A. (Warner, 1963). And there is probably some validity to thinking of certain identifiable statuses as reliable indicators of a style of life, goals, common ideology—the teenage world, the world of the elderly, the urban black world.

Social analysts are able to describe the various statuses each person can and typically does "occupy," and how some of these, involving highly structured networks of formally defined relationships, and others less institutionalized, are often quite distinct, if not contradictory, in the expectations, rituals, and ways of thinking that are required of the individual. Mother, wife, lover, homemaker, citizen, friend, daughter, writer, Republican, second-generation German American, educated woman in her mid-30s, member of ACLU, concerned human being, environmentalist. All of these social categories are intended to locate statuses or positions in the various networks of relationships. They identify various aspects of the social reality through which people move, usually in fairly organized ways. In other words, there are usually identifiable cues of time, place, and other social factors for when a person lives in one of her various worlds—mother, educated woman, environmentalist, homemaker, consumer. And at times they blend and conflict. These are obvious facts of living in a modern complex society.

However, for our purposes I would like to offer the hypothesis that there are some meta-worlds or statuses that are particularly important in the strategy of surviving in our society. In the technical sense, they approximate what is meant by "caste," rather than social status. The boundaries between castes are relatively impervious, and there are rather dramatic and pervasive differences in life experiences associated with each caste.

This is not the occasion to enter into a serious analysis of the "caste" system of contemporary American or Western societies, but there are some aspects of this construction of social reality that are central to our understanding of the common adult form of the belief in a just world. For example, most people probably recognize the world (caste) of the "beautiful people." The actual cast of characters changes fairly regularly, but the common element is that they are viewed as a privileged elite—the rules that you and I live by are suspended or modified greatly for them. At times we may admire, at times ignore them, but generally they are accepted simply as a part of life—with virtually no expectation or hope, except in some obvious fantasy, of gaining admission to that world.

Also I think that most of us believe that there are at least two other worlds. The world we live in is essentially a just world, where, given the qualifiers "by and large" and "in the long run," people can and do get what they deserve. And the other is the "world of victims," the poverty-stricken, the maimed, the crippled, the disfigured—the "losers" in our society. The inhabitants of that world, given any reasonable assessment of the possibilities available, are doomed to live in a world where they cannot affect their fates in any appreciable way. They appear destined to live in a state of chronic suffering or deprivation in terms of goals that we value and expect.

Our world, on the other hand, is set up so that we and those we care about can get what they deserve. The people may look and act differently, with more or less talent, character, and ingenuity, but all of these variations are played out to their appropriate end. It is assumed that everyone is going to turn out all right. But what they actually get out of life, what they make of themselves, is almost entirely up to them—their talent, character, willingness to work—modified in an acceptable way by "connections," and "the breaks."

It may not be a totally comfortable or "nice" world, but it is pretty much a "just world"—where people plan and set realistic goals for themselves and their children which usually work out. With insurance policies, a decent job, money set aside for vacations, a new car, retirement, the kids' schooling, time spent working on the school board, helping the kids with their homework, seeing to it that they live in a "good" neighborhood with the right kind of friends—given Mary's IQ and her interest in music, children, and camping, she will probably go to State U. and get a degree in special education, get married to a nice boy, and so on. Don is a good athlete, he's very bright, gets top grades, and has his eye on law school. I don't see what could stand in his way.

These resemble "typical" middle class aspirations and dreams, although there may be important regional differences in the style of life in this "just world." But it is a real world, and a "just" one, that includes a large part of the population. That probably includes all those who live in families whose incomes are within half a standard deviation of the mean for that region, from the "upper-lower" socioeconomic class to the "lower-upper."

The important point here is that, in a very real sense, possibly the only one that matters most of the time in our lives, we know we do live in a just world. At times, however, we are confronted with members of the other world, the world of victims. Sometimes we react automatically in response to a cue which elicits a sense of identity, concern, compassion, outrage, the desire to ameliorate the unjust suffering and deprivation of these victims. When we are actually confronted with someone in a wheelchair, a blind person, a hungry child, often something happens within us. There is a powerful urge to help, take away the suffering, and make it all better. But, as a rule, we do nothing—except feel very sad for a moment—until the scene changes. Why?

Why do we go about our business and turn our minds to other thoughts? Part of the answer is based on the recognition that we live in different worlds. At times I know we are the same, or at least I recognize the same feelings, needs, and hopes, but essentially, at a much deeper level, I know we live in different worlds, are of different "castes," and mine is a just one and theirs is not. Theirs is a world of victims.

Later we will devote considerable effort to understanding the ways these "worlds" make contact, when and how they overlap, and the various consequences. We all know that there are times when people of the Just World caste give in to the urge to help "victims," but at other times they appear to go through considerable effort to avoid any involvement, any recognition of the hint of any possible relation—they avoid, ignore, and possibly revile them.

In summary, then, it is proposed that the Belief in a Just World is too central a part in the organization of the human experience to be given up simply because the child learns that there is not an all-seeing, all-powerful adult figure who metes out punishments and rewards in direct response to how "good" or "bad" someone has been. The child's belief in a world of "immanent" justice is not simply abandoned. It is modified by the experiences of a rational mind in a world of natural causes, so that its functional components remain as firmly based as ever, if not more so, while its form is altered—to that of the unassailable assumptions of "ultimate justice."

By and large, in the long run, for people like us, it is a just world. We can, for the most part, with our share of "the breaks," get what we want, what we are willing to work for, what we deserve. Of course, we recognize that the world of victims exists, and that something can and will be done about it, but we can't let that interfere with how we live our own lives and what we can do for our families.

Nevertheless, There Are Continuing Threats to the Belief in a Just World

Some Basic Myths

To be sure, the Belief in a Just World is an invention. Adults, no less and possibly much more than children, must believe that the important events in people's lives follow rules, so that when something of importance happens to you, it is both understandable and "appropriate." That is the way it "should" be. But the just world is probably a "myth," in the sense that it is a way of construing events so that they fit a preestablished scenario which satisfies the person.

Before we look more closely at the implications of this myth for our understanding of how people react to one another and themselves, we should note that there are some other important myths which are prevalent in our society, and often found in conjunction with the Belief in a Just World.

Myth of "Rational Man." Most of us walk around convinced that we are objective appraisers of social and physical reality. And our reaction to our own and other's fate is determined by this appraisal. The components of this myth include the presumably rational processing of information relevant to important events in the environment. This begins with the objective assessment of causes and effects. The person's subsequent reaction to this appraisal follows naturally and inevitably the rules of nature and man—compassionate concern, reestablishment of "justice," and acceptance of that which is unavoidable in nature.

If we see someone suffering or in need we consider the facts in terms of who or what caused the suffering or need. Mainly, we discern whether the person did or did not deserve his fate. If the fate is unmerited, then we, anyone, would be concerned about setting things right—helping the victim, and, when appropriate, apprehending and punishing the inflictor. If, on the other hand, the victim deserved his fate, has been stupid, foolish, or derelict in some important way, then so be it.

Good Citizen Myth. Along with the "Belief in a Just World" and "Rational Man," there is the myth of the "Good Citizen." This myth also has a number of components. One is that we help our fellow human beings when they are in genuine need, and we serve as protectors of the weak and the young when it is required.

Another component of this myth seems to reflect elements of the "rational" man. We offer genuine praise and admiration to those among us who exhibit the "saintly" virtues of selfless devotion to the welfare of their fellow men—the underprivileged and the suffering. Only the most cynical among us would question the motives of a "Schweitzer," or the hero who gives up his life in efforts "above and beyond the call of duty" for the sake of others.

On the other hand, we are only human, and we have to be careful not to act like "fools" or "glory seekers" in our efforts to meet our social responsibilities. As good citizens who are not fools, we recognize that we have rsponsibilities to ourselves and our families. And so we do "our part" to help those in need, to deal with injustice whenever and wherever it appears—but that "part" must take into consideration our other obligations. There are realistic priorities and obligations that must be considered in the decision as to what is the "decent" thing to do, and that which is simply an "irresponsible" or a "foolhardy" gesture.

Contradicting Experiences— "Realities"

Emotional-Cognitive Reactions to "Injustices" in Our World. The achievement of adulthood in our society does not bring with it the ability to turn off emotional vulnerability to the suffering of others. The strength of this response is often a function of the vividness of the cues, the psychological proximity of the event, and the severity of the harm presumably done to the victim (Lazarus, Opton, Nomikos, & Rankin, 1965). The more extreme this response, the greater the likelihood that the child or adult will engage in efforts to reduce this distress (Krebs, 1970). These efforts often take the form of the "irrational" strategies, described earlier, that redefine the "blame," the outcomes, or the "characteristics" of the victim. The desire to reduce the observer's distress and the implicit threat to his security appears as an attempt to blame the victim or anyone who can be punished, so that at least the sense of control, if not the belief in justice, can be reestablished (Ryan, 1971). Thus, because we remain emotionally vulnerable to the suffering of others, we often react in ways which correspond little, if at all, to "objective" problem-solving behavior.

   Decision Making in Response to the Fate of Others—The Profit Motive. What does affect how people react to the fate of others—especially those who are in clear distress, need, suffering? The best assessment of the available evidence does not jibe well with the myth of the "Good Citizen." There is, to be sure, a form of rationality involved, but one which appears to be governed by a rather direct self-oriented attempt to "maximize profits"—incur the most gains with the fewest losses.

   Schwartz (1975) summarizes his own and others' findings as a sequence the person goes through in determining whether "humanitarian norms have their impact on behavior," that is, whether someone helps the victim, or does something else. It begins, as one might expect, with the perception of the event:

I. Perception of need and responsibility
   1. Awareness of a person in a state of need, lacking some desired resource.
   2. Perception that this state of need can be relieved if certain actions are taken.
   3. Recognition of own ability to make one or more of the responses which could alleviate consequences for the needy.
   4. Arousal of some sense of responsibility to respond.
II. Activation of personal norms
   5. Activation of preexisting or newly crystallized norms directing that some one or more of the responses be made.
III. Assessment and evaluation and reassessment of potential responses
   6. Assessment and evaluation of the probable outcomes of normatively directed and other responses in terms of their costs.
(The next two steps may be skipped if a particular response clearly optimizes the balance of costs evaluated in step 6; in other instances, however, there will be one or more iterations through steps 7 and 8.)
   7. Reassessment and redefinition of the situation by denial of the:
      a. state of need (its reality, seriousness).
      b. responsibility to respond.
      c. suitability of norms activated thus far and/or others.

8. Iteration of step 6 in light of the new assessment in step 7, repeated until a
distinctly best option emerges.
IV. Action (inaction) response (Schwartz, 1975, pp. 114–115)

The first five steps in this process describe the way each person becomes
aware of the existence of someone in need. During this assessment phase, the
person is probably functioning fairly much as the "rational" "good citizen."
In step 6, however, we come to the crucial "cost-accounting" event in the decision process. The costs here are described as inevitable in helping others:

> By definition, responses prescribed by humanitarian norms entail costs to the ac-
> tor—costs of foregoing own resources on behalf of the needy other with no expecta-
> tion of equal return. (Schwartz, 1975, p. 127)

Obviously, in the final calculations there are "costs" and "benefits" which are
associated with the various alternatives the person perceives possible in the
situation. The final act or sequence of acts reflects what Hatfield (1980) con-
siders the first principle of human social behavior.*

> Proposition I. Individuals will try to maximize their outcomes (where outcomes
> equal rewards minus costs). (p. 2)

Walster and Piliavin (1972) predict that the most likely resolution of this
process will be difficult to predict when the costs involved are relatively
minimal. However, if the costs for "direct help" are high, then "indirect
help," and "justification for not helping and running away," are to be expected. It is only if the person anticipates great cost in terms of social sanctions,
anticipated feelings of guilt (Rawlings, 1970) for not directly helping, and low
cost in the prospective helping act, that people can be expected to actually intervene in a given situation.

If these analysts are right, then the way people actually function is at odds
with the myth of the "good citizen." People are motivated essentially by the
attempt to "maximize their outcomes." In social situations involving the fate
of other people, this involves the reduction of "social and self distress" at
minimum cost to other desired resources (Walster *et al.,* 1976).

When the costs are high, the "Rational Man" myth is threatened by the
person's use of the "justification" mode of restoring "psychological equity"
(Walster & Piliavin, 1972); or, as Schwartz (1975) describes, the "reassessment
and redefinition of the situation." These reactions are essentially the irrational
defenses based upon "denial of the victim's state of need," "denial of the
suitability of norms" which define the victim as someone truly innocent and in
a state of "genuine need."

---

*Readers may be more familiar with comparable versions of this material that appeared in Walster,
Berscheid and Walster, 1976.

What some of our best known theorists have described is that we do not act as "good citizens." On the contrary, we are always trying to make the best deal for ourselves. And when it is the most profitable way to respond, we are not very "rational" in the way we justify our self-interested acts. If they are correct, then it is quite obvious that we must go to great lengths to maintain the belief that we live in a just world. But do we?

We Need and Create the Belief in a Just World: Some Thoughts as to "Why"

Is it really true that most people walk around with a set of cognitions, assumptions, which can be paraphrased as a "belief in a just world"? If this is even partly valid, in what ways is it true? What actually is the source of the "Belief"? How important is it in people's lives? How do people differ in the way they hold it, and in the way it affects their lives? Are normal people actually capable of condemning innocent victims? While they are still in their "right minds"? Is this reaction linked to others, such as helping victims, or attributing blame, through the same attempt to maintain the "Belief in a Just World"? Conceivably, if this is true, we may be able to understand a great deal more about the ways in which we can show more kindness and less cruelty to one another.

In seeking answers to these questions, we will stay fairly close to what happens in a social psychological experiment. Of course, I may as well confess at the outset what will become immediately apparent to the reader. I have enormous faith in our ability to learn from social psychological experiments. I agree with Aronson's (1976) assertion that our experiments give us the chance to

> draw conclusions based on data far more precise and numerous than those available
> to the amateur social psychologist, who must depend upon observations of events
> that occur randomly and under complex circumstances. (p. 7)

There are many issues which arise frequently whenever one describes or draws inferences from experiments. They range from the more technical questions concerning validity and generality of the inferences one is able to draw, to the issues associated with ethical responsibilities of the experimenter to himself, the people who are directly involved in the research, and the members of his society who become aware of what he did to whom, and what he learned. For the most part, these issues will remain in the background, providing an omnipresent audience whose implicit questions will structure at least part of the discussion. In the meantime, though, there should be no mistake about the underlying concurrence with Aronson's statement of faith.

CHAPTER 2

The First Experiment
The Effect of Fortuitous Reward

The Setting

In the fall of 1962, we invited women students from the University of Kentucky to help us in what they thought was a study designed to develop ways of estimating individual contributions to group tasks. When they arrived, they were seated in groups of about five or so in a small auditorium, facing a large one-way mirror. The view from their seats showed two chairs brought up to a table on which were a number of lettered cards and a microphone. Shortly after their arrival a curtain was drawn over the one-way mirror.

All the subjects were to be exposed to the same "objective" event in which two people worked at an intellectual task—making up words out of letters—in which their performances were distinctly different, but indistinguishable in terms of attributes usually associated with "quality," better or worse. The independent variable in this experiment was the "fate" of these two workers in terms of receiving payment. The assignment of the important outcome—large payment—to one of the workers had to be clearly arbitrary, but also legitimate in the sense of violating no moral standards. If that could be accomplished successfully, it was expected that our subjects would try to persuade themselves that the worker favored "by chance" actually performed better, actually deserved the pay after all. To be sure, in order to learn how the subjects' judgments were affected by the arbitrary outcome, it was necessary to vary the recipient of the "luck," so that while the event remained constant, half of the subjects were informed that it was one worker, "Tom," who would be paid, and half were led to believe that it was the other worker, "Dave." Then their judgments of the relative worth of these two workers could be compared. The experiment was set in the context of a project to develop "some reliable and meaningful scales" which could be used to assess "the contributions of individual members to the solution of problems which face the group." As the subjects were informed at the outset, this had become a serious problem in all sectors of our society, since most of the decision making and productivity, at least at the managerial and professional levels, occurred in "teams," or task forces. With the give-and-take interaction involved in these efforts, it was difficult to assess, as every organization must, the relative talents and contributions of each member. These must be known in order to make decisions about who should be promoted, who should be retained, and who should be let go to do something else for which he is better suited. Presumably there were no techniques presently available to make these assessments, so we were employing a "grass roots" approach, in which a number of people would observe a variety of others working in various intellectual group tasks. The observers during the first phase of our research were merely to

> develop impressions and hunches concerning what they observe, then by a process of pooling these various individual impressions I can begin to develop some categories to be used in more specific judgments.

These instructions were meant to make the subjects' tasks seem a worthwhile and obviously reasonable way to proceed. Also, the emphasis on the early states of the research, and the need to rely on "impressions and hunches," was intended to loosen the "reality constraint" somewhat, so that it would be easier for subjects to allow their own wishes and preferences to influence what they "saw" happening.

The subjects were to observe two male students working together on an anagrams task for approximately 15 minutes. The workers' job was to work as a team, making up as many and as complex words as possible. Supposedly to minimize the influence of extraneous cues on their judgments, the subjects were to listen to the work session, rather than observe it visually. Of course this manipulation was intended to increase the opportunity for the subjects' imaginations to influence what they "observed."

Obviously, the success of the experiment depended entirely on finding a way to operationalize the "independent variable." How would it be possible to create the impression of a "valid" but totally arbitrary assignment of differential pay to two workers whose actual performances were not obviously discrepant on any seemingly relevant dimension? And of course this had to be done within the general context of the study, or it would elicit a certain amount of doubt or suspicion.

The subjects were told that, in order to create an experimental task which resembled the real work situation, it was necessary to pay the workers, and to pay them considerably more money than initially anticipated, in order for them to take the task as seriously as if it were an actual job. We had only enough money to pay a sufficient amount $3.50 to half the total number of workers needed for the study. However, we would have to ask *all* of them to work as if they would be paid. And, in fact, we would let the pay be a matter of chance, depending upon the numbers the workers drew from a hat at the beginning of the session. That seemed fair to us, since the workers were actually volunteers who had not expected to be paid at all. Of course, as it was pointed out to the "workers" and the subjects, we would not be able to tell the workers which of them was to be paid until the end of the work session.

After these orienting sessions, subjects listened as the two workers did their job. In a brief initial interview, the workers identified themselves as "Tom" and "Bill." Then subjects heard Tom and Bill being informed about the pay arrangement, and their agreement that it was a good and fair way to proceed. The workers then picked numbers. Tom picked "number 19" and Bill "number 26," and then proceeded to work at the anagrams task, at which they both did a fairly good job. After all, they were actually first-year graduate students, doing their best at the task. At the end of the fifteen-minute session the sound was turned off, and the subjects responded to some "tentative rating scales," using their "impressions and hunches."

The main experimental variable was controlled by one additional instruction to the subjects before the workers began. The experimenter informed the subjects that, since 40 more workers were needed in the experiment, and there were only sufficient funds for 20, we put 40 numbers in a bowl, and would pay the worker who picked an "even number" (Bill-paid condition) or an "odd number" (Tom-paid condition). Of course, they all listened to the very same event.

After these instructions, the experimenter made no explicit link between the numbers drawn by "Tom" and "Bill," who had drawn odd or even, and who, therefore, would be paid. It was assumed that the subjects would care enough about the relative pay issue to be aware of what was happening, and of who would end up with $3.50, and who with nothing. The group discussion at the end of each session confirmed the fact that the subjects correctly identified the worker supposedly being paid. They listened, they believed, and they cared. What happened then? What did they "observe?"

The first question to which the subjects responded subsequent to hearing the tape was the most important, most direct measure of the "dependent" variable. They were asked:

1. How much of a real contribution did each subject make to the group task of forming words?

They were to respond to this question by placing the letters "T" and "B" for

Tom and Bill respectively on a scale divided into 40 equal units. One end of this scale was defined as "virtually no real contribution," and the other as the "maximum, total contribution."

The subjects responded in a similar fashion to four other questions:

2 .   How much effort did each subject seem to put forth in trying to do his task?

3 .   How creative were the ideas of each subject?

4 .   What is your impression of the expectations of the subjects? How certain or uncertain was each subject that he was one of those who was going to receive $3.50 at the end?

5 .   How do you feel about your participation in this kind of task?

The extremes of this scale were "I like it very much, very comfortable," and "Dislike it very much, very uncomfortable."

Finally, the subjects rated both workers on a number of polar dimensions concerned with personal characteristics, such as likeable–unlikeable, mature–immature. These were combined to yield an index of the general preference for or liking of the two workers. In addition to this index, they were asked which of the two workers they would choose to work with in a similar situation.

The Findings

So what did the analyses of these ratings show? One set of totally unanticipated findings arose from the distinct differences in impressions created by the voices of the two graduate students who portrayed "Tom" and "Bill." Considering all the thought and planning that went into every phase of the experiment, it is rather amazing that we had failed to realize that the person who played "Tom" had been a professional radio announcer, with a deep resonant voice and excellent articulation. By comparison, Bill's voice was rather high-pitched, and much more tentative in style. It was "clear" to these young women that Tom was very masculine, and must be quite handsome—"the hero"—whereas Bill was rather meek, and immature—clearly the "second or third banana."

As a result, the two measures of attraction—the general preference index, and the choice of a work partner—revealed what we should have guessed ahead of time. Regardless of who ended up being paid, the women had a clear preference for Tom. For example, in the Tom-paid condition, 10 of the 11 subjects preferred Tom as a work partner, and so did 9 of the 11 subjects in the Bill-paid condition.

This preference for "handsome" Tom over "meek-mild" Bill had an interesting effect on the subjects' liking for the experiment. As in the soap operas, the subjects who believed that "Tom" was the winner liked the experi-

Table 1
Subjects' Comfort in the Experimental Situation[a]

	N	M	SD
Condition 1: Tom paid (attractive)	7	3.30[b]	1.28
Condition 2: Bill paid (unattractive)	11	5.54	4.12

[a]From Lerner (1965).
[b]The lower the score the greater the comfort.

ment much more than those who thought that "Bill" was going to be the one to get paid (see Table 1).

Along with these unexpected but quite understandable results, we found that the subjects did, in fact, generate their own scenario to fit the workers' differing fates, based upon who had been fortunate enought to pick up a lucky number. As one can see from Table 2, the subjects were inclined to ascribe better performance and greater effort to *either* Tom or Bill, depending upon which of them they believed would end up with the money.

Table 2
A Comparison of the Ratings of the "Workers" by the Observers in Both "Payment" Conditions[a]

	Condition 1: Tom paid (N = 11)		Condition 2: Bill paid (N = 11)		t		
	T rating	B rating	T rating	B rating	Condition 1 versus Condition 2	T vs. B	$(T_1 - B_1) - (T_2 - B_2)$
	M	M	M	M			
Real contribution	7.90[b]	11.45	16.72	12.72	2.4 [d]	.10	1.99[c]
Effort	6.45	7.81	10.27	12.36	1.86[d]	1.00	.20
Creativity	8.72	20.54	17.63	21.81	2.17[d]	4.66[e]	2.22[d]
Expectation of money	14.27	12.45	17.09	8.72	.07	2.15[d]	1.39
Overall preference	37.81	56.09	38.54	58.63	.25	5.53[e]	.21

[a]From Lerner (1965).
[b]The lower the score the more "positive" the rating.
[c]$p < .05$.
[d]$p < .02$.
[e]$p < .001$.

There were some other intriguing, suggestive results, but overall there seemed to be two important conclusions. One, as we stated at the time:

> The observers in this experiment construed a social event to fit rather simple and understandable processes. One of these can be paraphrased as "people deserve what happens to them" or "once I know what has happened to someone I will be more comfortable if I can believe that he has earned it. (Lerner, 1965, p. 360)

The other was a little more complex, and certainly not expected. The outcome or fate of each of the workers was important enough to the observers to affect how they construed the efforts of the two workers, but it did not alter in any measurable way the personal attractiveness of Tom and Bill. The observers cared enough about the correspondence between the desirability of the relative outcomes and the personal desirability of the workers to be measurably less satisfied, and more upset, when the less desirable Bill won the money than when hero Tom was paid.

The Implications for the Method and Theory

It was important to find concrete evidence for two presumed reactions. The findings reveal that people will be upset if someone who is relatively unattractive ends up with a better fate than someone who is seen as more desirable personally. Also, people, once they know the desirability of someone's fate, will be inclined to construe the value of that person's effort to fit that fate. In other words, they are inclined to perceive that people get what they deserve. As part of this, they seem to prefer that good things happen to attractive people, and less good things to less attractive people. They are relatively upset if events contradict this pattern.

It was much more important to discover that we could actually study these processes in the laboratory, that we could create the necessary elements of an entire scenario so that those particular people at the appropriate time would be in the "frame of mind" that would enable them to reveal the particular processes we wanted to study. We seemed to be able to do that in a way which would enable us to record, measure, and count the evidence. We had learned not only that the experimental situation was an incredibly complex and therefore "fragile" invention, but also what a useful instrument it could be for looking at important human reactions.

As for the theory—it became clear for the first time that the "Belief in a Just World" was probably more than an extension of "Cognitive Dissonance." The work that has been generated out of the theory of cognitive dissonance has been very important in helping us understand how people react when their experiences do not seem to conform to their expectations. When a person is confronted with evidence that the world is not just in some sense, then we can reasonably expect that a state of dissonance has been created, and can rely on the body of literature on that subject to help us predict how that person will react subsequently (Aronson, 1969). Dissonance theory cannot, nor was it intended to, enable us to understand why people are strongly committed to cognitions like the belief in a just world. The belief that one lives in a just world, just as the belief that one is a decent, worthwhile person, seems to play a central role in the organization of the person's life. The clear implication here is that what is at stake for the individual when these cognitions are threatened is not only the negative drive state generated out of holding dissonant cognitions, but the very integrity of their conception of themselves and the nature of their world.

This is easier possibly to recognize with reference to the belief that one is a worthy human being. The evidence suggests that, if and when that cognition is altered significantly, then there are widespread and dramatic effects on people's lives. They are not for all intents and purposes the same people with different cognitions about themselves. The range of affect they experience, ways of relating to others, kinds of thought processes thy engage in, ability to mobilize themselves, are radically altered if their sense of self-worth is reduced. If our understanding of the belief in a just world is correct, then we would expect that the effects would be equally dramatic if that belief is shattered, or diminished to any important degree. The emotional consequences associated with the loss of this confidence in one's environment, the attempt to find alternative ways of coping with one's needs, fears, and the threats from the environment, would produce "deviant" behaviors in the pejorative sense (Chein *et al.*, 1964; Jessor *et al.*, 1968; Merton, 1957). Although our research will not attempt to test this hypothesis by creating such an extreme event in people's lives, we do expect to be able to show the kind of motivational committment to this central belief that would fit this degree of importance to the person.

Also, a simple, or possibly naive, construction of a theory of "cognitive balance" seemed lacking. In the first place, it is much too "bloodless" to have the right feel when applied to the problems of how we react to people's lives. The emotional components of compassion, fear, indignation, etc. are such central, if not dominant aspects of our reactions, that any psychological demands derived from the attempts to find "balance" in our cognitions seem relatively trivial. Who cares about "balance" when I learn that one of my daughter's friends had "accidentally" slipped and tumbled to his death while meditating and watching the sunset from the top of Diamond Head? When I heard his parent's worried voice before anyone was certain what had happened, all we knew was that this fine, highly reliable young man had not come home or appeared at work the previous day. Something was very wrong! "Cognitive imbalance"? Is this what was happening? And then they found the broken body.

Certainly any prior inclinations to find "balance" theory inadequate to the phenomenon were supported by the rather selective way the subjects in the initial experiment responded to the event. The observers altered their cognitions of the worker's behavior—his effort and creativity at the task—as a function of the anticipated "outcome." So why did they not then also change their cognitions of the worker's personality to fit the relative merit of his efforts and the value of the outcome? The answer seems to be that the observers did not care that much, were not motivated sufficiently by the form of "balance" among their cognitions which matches the valence of someone's fate, his personal worth, and his efforts. Instead, the observers were a bit more upset when the less desirable person was to be paid the money; but they seemed to deal with the entire event satisfactorily by altering only one set of cognitions—that attached to the worker's efforts at the task—making up words out of letters on cards. There appeared to be no attempt to bring all the cognitions into a univalent system of balance.

And so, there were a few points which established the outline for the next steps in the Just World Theory. First, the person's attempts to find evidence for "justice" in his environment probably involve something more than seeking to reduce dissonance or create "balance" among his cognitions. Second, the awareness of someone's fate can have an effect on the perception of his relevant behaviors, while having no noticeable effect on the perception of his personal attributes.

CHAPTER **3**

The Second Experiment
Observers' Reactions to the 'Innocent Victim'

The Questions

There was no question of what the next study should be. We wanted to look at the plaguing tragedy of the derogation of innocent victims in our society. It so obviously happens, and the problem has so many facets, from learning to make fun of the "class jerk" in school, to stigmatizing the mentally and physically crippled, and perpetuating the vicious stereotypes applied to the victims of our social and economic system. Is it possible that the motivation to find justice in our world could lead to the perpetuation of the very social stereotypes which stand as a major impediment to the creation of actual social justice?

There was a definite set of goals guiding our efforts. We assumed that, if it should be possible to recreate enough of the "right" elements in the laboratory, then we might be able to look at the phenomenon carefully enough to answer this and the related questions of why we reject some of the victims, sometimes, and help others at other times. If the theoretical hunches were valid, then it might be possible through this research to learn how to channel the very same motivation into effective social change, rather than cruel degradation of victims.

To begin answering some of these questions, we needed to create an experimental situation in which people who were merely going about their daily routine would be confronted with another person, also merely going about routine activities, who was suffering undeservedly. Subjects would become aware that this other member of their society was suffering through no apparent fault of his/her own—an innocent victim—having done nothing stupid or careless to merit this suffering.

If the theory is correct, then the observers should be upset for a number of reasons, not the least of which is the implicit threat to their belief that truly innocent people do not suffer, at least not in their world. To eliminate this threat, they would need to restore justice. That could be done in a number of ways. For example, they could simply leave the scene and try to pretend it never happened, or at least try to forget about it. Or they could see to it that justice was done in the situation by rescuing the victim and having the inflicter punished. Or they could engage in various reinterpretations of the event, so that the victim was not seen as so "innocent." If they could persuade themselves that the victim actually brought about the suffering by some misdeed, then their sense of security, if not finely tuned sense of justice, would be restored. Or they could come to view the victim as the kind of person for whom suffering is not a clearly undeserved fate. This last reaction is, of course, the one we wished to examine in this initial effort. Could observers, normal human beings, actually engage in victim derogation? Or show some evidence that they would invent or find negative attributes in a victim clearly innocent by more objective criteria?

The expected answer to these questions was of course yes, but more detailed information was also anticipated. If people are motivated to maintain the belief that they live in a "just world," for the sake of their own security and their ability to pursue goals which require long-range planning and extensive effort, then the following hypotheses also make sense.

Witnesses of an innocent victim's suffering will attempt to reestablish justice in the situation by compensating the victim. If they are unable to provide compensation, they will attempt to reestablish justice by finding the victim blameworthy, as a function of his/her actions or personal characteristics.

What about the relation between these two kinds of cognitive attempt to find justice? Our reasoning was:

> If the person is motivated to believe he lives in a world where he can obtain the things he wants and avoid threatening events, then it seems likely that these two paths to reward (performance versus personal worth) can be ordered in terms of preference for the individuals. It would be preferable for a person to believe that desired goals come as a result of appropriate acts rather than of personal characteristics, since he is more able to change and control his behavior than his intrinsic personal worth. (Lerner & Simmons, 1966, p. 204)

If this is true, then, in order to discover whether innocent observers would condemn victims, we needed to make it difficult for them to assign blame for something the victim did or failed to do. And to determine if this "rejection" arose out of the observer's commitment to justice, we should find a way to vary the extent of the victim's undeserved suffering, while keeping everything else the same. If the theory is correct, the greater the undeserved suffered, the more the derogation of the victim.

In addition, it would be important to allow some observers the opportunity to come to the victim's aid. According to the theory, they would accept the chance to help the victim, and, if successful, would have no need to condemn the victim in order to restore their confidence in the justness of their world. They would see the victim in relatively objective terms.

The Innocent Victim Situation

To examine some of these hypotheses, undergraduate women enrolled in introductory psychology courses were enlisted to participate in a study of "cues of emotional arousal," fulfilling the course requirement that they participate in some psychology experiments.

When they arrived, in groups of 4 to 10, they sat in a small auditorium, facing a large curtain covering a one-way mirror. Carolyn Simmons, a very "professional-looking" young woman dressed in a white lab coat, introduced herself as the Research Associate who was conducting this experiment on cues of emotional arousal. She explained to each group of subjects why it was important to develop a set of "behavioral cues" which would reliably indicate how "upset" or "disturbed" another person was. Since these cues would not depend upon what the person said, they could be most helpful in the early detection of disturbing conditions in situations where people wanted to hide the extent of their distress, or when, as with young children, they did not have the verbal skills to convey their feelings adequately to a teacher or parent. So, if supervisors, parents, or health personnel had this simple behavioral screening device, they could, by observing people, determine whether psychological first aid was necessary. In that way, many serious crises might be prevented. The undergraduate women were participating in the initial stages of the development of this "check list" of stable cues of emotional arousal.

Carolyn informed them that, at this stage in the research, a number of people were being asked to watch someone whom they knew was undergoing a known degree of stress. The observers would attempt to detect what behaviors exhibited by that person led them to infer a given level of stress—something in the movement of the body, arms, facial gestures, sudden rigidity in posture, anything they felt was a cue. Of course, these would be their "hunches"; however, by pooling these impressions across observers and situations, commonly used cues would be revealed, and then the more exacting tests of these cues could be started.

The subjects were then told that their experimenter was taking advantage of the fact that another psychologist, Dr. Stewart, was doing research in human learning that was likely to produce stress in her subjects. She had students come in for a study of human learning, and once they arrived they learned that it involved receiving various kinds of "reinforcements" in a paired-associate learning task. In some conditions (positive reinforcement), they were given 25 cents for each correct answer, and usually earned between two and eight dollars. In another condition, they received no money, but rather strong electric shock (negative reinforcement) for each incorrect answer. In the third condition, they were merely given neutral verbal feedback about their performance. The ostensible purpose of that experiment was to study the effects of strong reinforcement on human learning. This is a "plausible" experiment for psychologists; although the use of electric shock was not typical, it was also not unknown to these students at that time.

The paired-associate learning task was chosen by us because it was virtually impossible for anyone to avoid making errors, and these introductory psychology students knew that. They also knew that there were many studies of human learning going on, and it was quite natural for a student to quite innocently sign up for one of them as part of the normal routine of completing one's course requirements.

After these preliminary instructions, the curtains covering the one-way mirror were opened to show the test room, where a memory drum was seen on a table with two chairs drawn up to it. Dr. Stewart was observed "adjusting" the shock equipment and electrode leading to the memory drum. A technician was also adjusting the television camera. Carolyn then explained to the observers that the curtain would be closed once more, and they would observe the learning experiment over the black and white TV monitor in front of them, because:

> Previous observers had relied most heavily on changes in skin color of the subject as an indication of her emotional state, and that in order to see what other possible cues could be used the observers today would watch the task over a television monitor.

Of course, we really wanted the observers to watch a TV monitor because it was important that all groups see an identical event, and so we had made a videotape which the observers would believe was actually a direct transmission of the events taking place in another room.

By this point in their instructions, almost everything had been done to create the appropriate set for the observers. To add somewhat to the realism of the situation, Carolyn announced that she believed that the student who had signed up for Dr. Stewart's experiment was in the room with the observers. And, sure enough, one of the young ladies raised her hand. At about that time, Carolyn looked at her watch, and commented that Dr. Stewart should appear shortly; she did, asking if her "subject" was here. They then started out the door at the back of the auditorium, and at that point Carolyn asked Dr. Stewart what condition she would be "running" today. It was only at that point that the observers, and presumably the "victim," knew what her fate would be. Dr. Stewart said that she was doing the "negative reinforcement" condition. The "victim" would receive strong electric shocks, rather than money or simply neutral feedback.

The lights were dimmed and, all attention was focused on the TV screen, where the subjects saw Dr. Stewart and the student who had been sitting in the room with them; Dr. Stewart attached electrodes to the subject's wrists, strapped her into the chair, and began the experiment on human learning. The videotape was actually totally staged. The "victim" was a department secretary, who was instructed to do her best at learning the list of paired nonsense syllables. She was not actually shocked, we used a loud rasping buzzer to signal the administration of the shock, and she acted as if she were being shocked through the electrodes attached to her wrists whenever she heard the buzzer. It worked very well, and the first few takes were extremely credible. Quite spontaneously, our confederate lurched and moaned at points. Initially she seemed concerned, and while being strapped in she asked if the shocks would hurt. The rather cool and detached Dr. Stewart informed her that they would be strong but would cause no damage. Later in the tape the victim turned to Dr. Stewart, and wistfully asked, "Will they continue to be this strong?" and she was reassured by Dr. Stewart that she was doing just fine, and should continue to do her best. The entire session lasted about eight minutes. Subsequent observation and research with the tape have confirmed the fact that it is extremely moving and believable.

Hopefully we had created a situation where people were observers of an event going on in their world which involved the undeserved suffering of an innocent victim. The victim's suffering was understandable from the perspective of what happens to students who sign up for the "wrong" experiment. But certainly the gains for the student were rather minimal, and not enough to compensate for her pain. If she had known what was in store for her, she certainly would not have signed up for that experiment. But, once there and subtly led into the next phase of the experiment, she had been tricked successfully, and she faced the "unknown" dangers of defying someone in authority in order to get out of the situation. At that time, it was not considered illegal, and probably not even unethical, for a psychologist to inflict this kind of pain on an undergraduate for the sake of science. Nevertheless, it was clearly an exploitation of that person—she had been victimized.

The Experimental Conditions—
Creating Degrees of Injustice

All the people in this experiment saw the same videotape, and all but one of the experimental conditions was created by the instructions given immediately after the tape ended and the lights were turned on.

In one condition (Reward), subjects were told that Dr. Stewart needed only the first session to be "negative reinforcement" for her experiment. The next session with this same subject could be any of the three possible conditions—positive reinforcement, neutral, or negative reinforcement—and she would leave it up to the people in the "emotional cues" study to decide. Carolyn then announced that the observers could decide, with secret ballot, what condition would help them confirm the impressions they were forming about the cues they employed to detect the level of arousal. In this manner, subjects were given the power to cast their vote so that the victim's suffering would end and she would be compensated by earning between two and eight dollars in the next session. After Carolyn collected the anonymous ballots, she riffled thorugh them, pretending to examine the votes. Regardless of the actual vote, Carolyn announced that they would be observing the victim receive positive reinforcements in the next session.

A slightly different experience was created for some other observers (Reward Decision). They were given the same instructions as those subjects in the Reward condition. The only difference was that, after the ballots had been collected, the observers were told nothing about the outcome of the vote or the victim's fate in the next condition.

The observers in the other conditions were given no opportunity to affect the victim's fate. Some of them (End Point) were led to believe that the observation part of the experiment was over, and the victim's suffering at an end. Others (Past Event) were led to believe they had seen the videotape of a session that had occurred in the past, and that the victim was fine now. To create a condition of increased unjust suffering, some observers were told that after this brief intermission they would watch the victim in her second session of "negative reinforcement" (Midpoint).

Finally, those observers in the Martyr condition were confronted with the most complex and probably most interesting set of experiences. In the course of designing this experiment, we tried to think of the circumstances most likely to make people admire a victim. The answer that came to mind readily was, when the victim has chosen her fate, inspired by altruistic socially responsible motives—in other words, chosen to be a "martyr."

In our society, we admire and respect our martyrs. On the other hand, if we take the Just World Theory seriously, then the suffering of a good, nobly motivated victim should be considerably more threatening to one's belief in a "just world" than that of the comparatively neutral innocent victim. If we were able to create the appropriate experience for the observers, they should be highly motivated to find evidence that the victim is actually a truly undesirable person. If the theory is right, and the experimental situation does its job in creating the appropriate compelling experience for the observers, the martyr victim should elicit the most derogation.

The procedure employed to create the Martyr condition for the observers was based on a little vignette among the two experimenters and the "victim" at the back of the room. It occurred at the point in all the conditions when Carolyn asked Dr. Stewart which of the three conditions she was running that day, and Dr. Stewart responded with "negative reinforcement." In the Martyr variation, the observers then heard a brief dialogue between Dr. Stewart and the victim in the doorway just behind them. It began with the victim asking Dr. Stewart, "Does that mean that I will be getting electric shocks?"

Dr. Stewart responded affirmatively. The victim then stated that she was frightened of shocks, to which Dr. Stewart replied that she understood, but, after all, she (the victim) had signed up for the experiment on human learning, "But of course, it is up to you." The victim restated her anxiety about the shocks, and then Dr. Stewart pointed out that the decision was up to her, but, after all, she had signed up for that experiment, and she was depending upon her participation, as were the observers who would not be able to receive experimental credit for their experimental participation if she did not go through with it. "But of course, it is up to you." The victim then stated something to the effect that, since everyone was depending upon her, and "if it is necessary for them to get credit," then she would go through with it. The observers then saw the same videotape as all the other subjects. This situation was similar to that in the Endpoint condition, in that the victim's suffering was supposed to be over when the session on her videotape ended.

That essentially was how the six experimental conditions were created in this experiment—Reward, Reward Decision, Past Event, Midpoint, Endpoint, and Martyr. When the videotape was over, the observers had been through a very moving experience; they had witnessed someone receive rather strong electric shocks, and they thought and felt it to be very real. It was not at all unusual to see them reacting visibly to the rasping sound of the buzzer and the jerking of the victim's arms and body when she supposedly received her first "strong electric shocks."

The Measures—What Do You Think of the Victim

Immediately after they were given the instructions designed to create the appropriate experimental condition, the subjects were given a set of instruments to complete. The first one was designed to enhance the credibility of the entire situation. It was a brief check list of cues which others supposedly had found useful in detecting emotional arousal. The subjects were to check those they used, and then add others of their own not on the list if they so wished.

The most important task was to find a way of measuring the subjects' impression of the victim—in particular, their evaluation of her personal attributes. This had to be done in a way which fit the experimental context and would not arouse the observers' suspicions. Two measures were included for this purpose; they were introduced with a brief comment to the effect that there was reason to believe that people with different kinds of personalities would exhibit different kinds of cues under stress, and so the "victim's" social personality was being assessed. Social personality was defined as the impression she gave other people of her personality—not what it might be in some more private or basic sense, but the kind of impression she created of herself. The subjects then had a plausible reason for relying on their "hunches and impressions" of the victim's personality in completing the two instruments. One was composed of a set of 15 bipolar descriptive adjectives which were all highly evaluative in connotation (e.g., intelligent–unintelligent, friendly–unfriendly, mature–immature, kind–cruel). Each pair of adjectives was separated by nine dashes, and subjects were to check the dash which indicated the degree to which the victim created the impression of possessing the attributes. The evaluation of the victim on this measure was computed by assigning a score of 1 to 9, based on the proximity of the check mark to the negative adjective. To further refine the measure, subjects completed the same set of scales for themselves, and their own attractiveness score was subtracted from the victim's. The more positive this index, the more attractive they saw the victim. The more negative, the less attractive she was in comparison with their view of themselves.

The second measure of attractiveness, "Social Stimulus Value," was based on five questions concerning the observers' hunches about how people in general would react to the victim after a brief acquaintance. They referred to the extent to which people would be interested in getting to know her better, admire her, like her, and the extent to which she would fit in with the observers' friends. Finally, observers estimated the extent to which she would have to struggle for what she wanted out of life. Each of these quesitons was scored from 1 to 6, with a higher number indicating a more positive impression, and then added together to yield a total "attractiveness" score.

In addition to these instruments, we constructed our own measure of the observers' perceived similarity to the victim. This was intended to be relatively free of the "evaluative" component, and so a forced-choice procedure was used, involving twenty items that provided the subjects with two alternatives roughly equal in social desirability. The subjects were to check which of the two were applicable to the impression created by the victim. For example, "good sense of humor," or "good sense of fairness." Another was "tends to be insecure," or "tends to be selfish." The subjects' choices for the victim were compared with those they assigned to themselves. The degree of similarity could vary from totally different (0), to entirely similar (20).

At the end, the subjects were asked to respond freely to two general questions about their reaction to the experiment. "Were the instructions given clearly?" and "What, in your words, was the experiment about?" Then they were given an opportunity to express any other reactions.

The Findings—How Did the Degree of
Injustice Affect the Observers' Reactions?

The main findings of this experiment can be seen in the data of Table 3.

Data not found in the table are the observers' votes in the two conditions where they were given the opportunity to select the one of three possible conditions—positive reinforcement, negative reinforcement, or neutral, for the victim's next session that would enable them to "clarify their initial impressions and hunches." Apparently 23 of the 25 subjects given this opportunity felt that it would be best for them if they were to see the victim in positive reinforcement, where she would be free from any further shocks and would be paid between two and eight dollars, depending upon her performance. The other two observers elected the Neutral condition for the victim, where she would not be shocked, but merely informed of whether her answer was correct or not.

Referring now to Table 3, subjects' ratings of the victim in the Reward condition were, on the average, at a neutral point. The victim was rated just slightly less attractive than themselves. If we look at Endpoint and Past Event conditions, we find that the victim appears to be somewhat less attractive than in the Reward condition. Although the differences do not yield an acceptable level of significance, given the variability in the responses, they are certainly in the expected direction. The observers who believed the victim would continue to suffer (Midpoint condition) described the victim as even less attractive. This time the evaluations were reliably lower than in the Reward condition, and on one measure (Social Stimulus Value) significantly lower than in the Endpoint condition. And that makes sense—the more undeserved the victim's suffering, the more negative her evaluation by the observers. The Martyr victim elicited the lowest evaluations. Even though the duration of her suffering, her martyrdom, was no longer than in the Endpoint condition, she was seen as having dramatically more negative attributes.

Generally, then, the results were very much in line with our theoretical hunches. When the observers had the opportunity, they elected to rescue and

Table 3
Ratings of the Victim[a]

	Past event $(N = 10)$	Reward $(N = 14)$	Reward decision $(N = 11)$	Midpoint $(N = 14)$	Endpoint $(N = 14)$	Martyr $(N = 9)$
Attractiveness[b] (bipolar scales)	−11.10	−5.07	−25.18	−25.78	−12.85	−34.00
Social stimulus value	18.70	19.21	15.27	14.71	17.00	14.11
Similarity[c]	11.60	9.42	9.36	9.36	9.82	8.78

[a]From Lerner & Simmons (1966).
[b]The more positive (less negative) the rating, the more attractive the victim.
[c]The higher the rating, the greater the perceived similarity.

compensate the victim. And, when successful, they saw the victim in a rather neutral, objective light. When the observers were unable to intervene on behalf of the victim, they showed signs of reevaluating her personal worth. The more unjust her fate in terms of duration of suffering or the motives which made her vulnerable to suffering (Martyr), the greater the tendency to find negative attributes in her personality to denigrate her.

There was even more to the findings than this, however. The two conditions where the observers were given the opportunity to intervene on the victim's behalf were included in order to find out if it were possible to distinguish between a "cognitive dissonance" prediction and one based on the assumption that people will attempt to maintain their "belief in a just world." As we designed the Reward Condition, we realized that, if the subjects did as we expected and elected to help the victim, and then showed no relatively negative evaluations of her, their actions would fit a dissonance theory explanation. After all, if I have chosen to help someone in need, it follows that I should believe that that person is someone who is worthy of being helped. And so I certainly would not want to create "dissonance" for myself by derogating her.

Presumably the observers' "belief in a just world" would be affected, not by their decision and attempt to help the victim, but mainly by the victim's fate. So, according to that theory, even though the observers attempted to help the victim, they would be likely to derogate her unless and until they had evidence that the victim was in fact rescued.

The crucial variable for a "dissonance" prediction of the observers' cognitions of the victim's worth is the observers' cognitions of their decisions to act on the victim's behalf. The important event in determining the observers' evaluation of the victim, according to the Just World Theory, is the observers' cognition of the victim's fate.

In a rather ambitious attempt to discriminate between these two positions, some of the observers were given the chance to help the victim with no assurance that their act had been successful—the Reward Decision condition. Other observers (Reward condition) were told quite explicitly, after an examination of the ballots and before they filled out their evaluations of her, that the victim would be in the positive reinforcement condition. Subjects' reactions in these two conditions were remarkably different. Their ratings of the victim in the Reward Decision condition were clearly lower than in the successful Reward condition, and virtually no different from those in the Midpoint condition where the subjects were not able to intervene.

Does this finding speak directly to the issue of "dissonance" theory versus the "Belief in a Just World?" Not really. It would have been consonant with a dissonance-theory prediction if the evaluations of the victim in the Reward Decision condition had been no less positive than those in the Reward condition. That is, the important cognition in their evaluations would have been the perception of their own willingness to help (Jecker & Landy, 1969). On the other hand, the fact that the data do not bear this hypothesis out is not acutely embarrassing for dissonance theory. One can assume, with some theoretical integrity, that the observers could have resolved any dissonance generated by the circumstances in the Reward Decision condition by persuading themselves that, "Yes, I tried to help that person, but that is because I am a decent, civilized person, who is willing to try to help anyone who is suffering, even the least deserving 'schnook.' "

The fact that it is possible to generate these two discrepant "dissonance theory" predictions of the observers' reactions in this situation does not necessarily indicate a weakness in that theory. If anything, it suggests that the conditions appropriate to test the theory were not created. On the other hand, the initial prediction of no difference between the two conditions in which the observers decided to help the victim, regardless of the apparent success of their efforts, is a more natural, more "mainline" prediction from dissonance theory, as we will see later in the discussion of another similar experiment (Mills & Egger, 1972). The finding, then, that subjects in the two conditions differed radically in their reactions to the victim, seemingly as a function of her fate, regardless of their acts, is a little more awkward for a dissonance explanation than if no differences had been found. Not a critical finding, by any means, just slightly dissonant with the most obvious "dissonance" prediciton.

If one can have confidence in inferences based on the lack of significant differences on a measure which has no established empirical validity, then it may be interesting that the observers' perception of their similarity with the victim remained uniform across all conditions. The observers attributed similar characteristics to the victim on about half of the twenty items they were given, regardless of the victim's fate. Unfortunately, it is probably best not to attempt to interpret the scores on this instrument until we have additional evidence as to what it actually measures.

Analyses of the subjects' responses to the open-ended questions concerning their perceptions of the experiment yielded one of the most encouraging findings. One of the questions asked directly for comments and constructive criticism. As it turned out, most of the subjects (65 out of 72) provided comments that were readily coded as either positive or negative, and the majority of these (40) were clearly positive. Since numbers were too small to do a within-conditions comparison, subjects were simply placed in one of two categories in terms of their reaction to the experiment—positive or negative—and their evaluations of the victim were compared. The results were quite intriguing. Those who condemned the experiment rated the victim, on the average, as -5.16 on the bipolar adjectives, an essentually "neutral" rating on that measure. On the other hand, the ratings of those who evaluated the experiment positively were extremely negative, -24.35, and reliably lower than those of the experiment condemners ($t = 3.73$, $df = 63$, $p < .001$).

This finding fits so well with our theoretical speculations that it is extremely

tempting to accept that interpretation. Confronted with an instance of undeserved suffering, the observers had two alternatives. They could accept the situation
at face value as unjust, and react with indignation, fear, and compassion for the
victim. A minority of the observers—20 out of the codable 65—seemed to take
that course. On the other hand, the majority seemed to elect the alternative of
reestablishing justice in their world by deciding that the victim was a relatively
"inferior" person who happened to be suffering for a good cause—a valuable,
interesting experiment. The latter is certainly the more comfortable reaction; it
eliminates the fear of living in a world where an injustice can, and, in fact, *is* happening. The comfort of this solution to the conflict between condemning the
authority figure who is inflicting suffering, or the innocent victim who is endur-
ing it, can be very expensive and self-defeating in the long run, as many of the
citizens in Nazi Germany discovered.

What Did We Learn?

When fitted all together, the data create a compelling picture. Normal people *will* reject, or at least devalue, an innocent victim, if they are not able to intervene effectively to correct the injustice. In the circumstances we created, our
normal subjects preferred to act on behalf of the victim; it was only when this
alternative was not available that they condemned her. In addition, the victim
was evaluated more negatively as the extent of undeserved suffering increased.
To be sure, there were some people, a distinct minority, who continued to view
the victim in a rather objective light, and chose to condemn Dr. Stewart's experiment as an instrument of injustice.

The key to the observers' evaluation of the victim was clearly the victim's
fate; it was not simply their being confronted with her suffering for a given
period of time. The same "suffering" could elicit their help or their condemnation. The "injustice" attached to the suffering seems to be the defining event,
since the scene of greatest injustice, created in the Martyr condition, elicited the
greatest condemnation from the observers, although the victim's actual suffering
was no different from that in the other conditions. The observers' reactions to the
suffering victim did not seem to be an attempt to reduce cognitive dissonance;
the justness of the fate of the victim seemed to be the important event, regardless
of the observers' power to intervene. And there is some reason to believe that the
observers' final image of the victim was not designed simply to find her a "different" kind of person, but much more specifically directed by the attempt to
portray her in a negative light. It is doubtful also that the observers' condemna-
tions of the victim derived from generalizing their empathically induced discom
fort. Their reactions seemed to be much more selective; they tended to feel
negatively about either the experiment they witnessed or the victim, and did not
react to all the cues available in the environment.

We should remind ourselves at this point that these inferences and conclusions are generated entirely by analyses of check marks made on pieces of paper. These dependent measures were completed after the experiences we created for our subjects, and that observation moves us in two almost opposite directions.

The first can be characterized by an impatience with the reliance on these methodological devices. Those check marks are a barely visible, sterile representation of obviously powerful human events involving the interlockig of important cognitive and affectively tinged motivational processes. Witnessing that victim suffer under those compelling conditions is a very moving experience for the subjects. Their involvement in what is happening to that girl is almost palpable, and it is certainly observable. Typically, at the first shocks almost everyone jerks empathically with the victim's movements and the sound of the rasping buzzer. Some titter or giggle a bit at what is happening. By the second and third shocks the nervous laughter usually ends, and the subjects stare intently at the screen. Some do look away for a moment, some shake their heads, and a few continue to show visible signs of empathic involvement with each event.

What the experimenter cannot observe directly is reported by the subjects as she chats with them at the end of the session. Most of them will describe how they literally felt the first shock with the victim, and how furious they were with Dr. Stewart. Most of them decide that the victim is a fool or a weakling for sitting there and allowing herself to be shocked. They assert most emphatically: "I would never sit there and let anyone do that to me!"

As a way of exploring this reaction, they are then asked to think back to the earlier part of the session, and to recall how they felt. Their answers are some variant of expressions of indignation, fury, outrage, at the injustice they were witnessing. "I was really mad." "I felt like getting up and walking out." "I thought it was disgusting." "She (Dr. Stewart) was certainly 'breaking a law.'" At other times, during other demonstrations of the experiment, some observers directed their anger toward the experimenter who had them watch the scene. "I was really pissed off at you." A number of medical students stated how it was nothing short of a miracle that they didn't "slug" their male experimenter, who was a rather short, physically unimposing man. The chairman of an interdisciplinary department designed to train personal and community change agents, who witnessed the videotape as part of a colloquium, felt that it was extremely arrogant and cruel to inflict people with the experience of watching someone else receive electric shocks, even in that most protected context.

The facts of the matter are truly remarkable in the face of these certainly genuine, strong affirmations of the anger felt during the initial phase of watching. None of the people from all walks of life, who have watched and felt the victim suffer, demonstrated their disapproval in any overt way. Not one of literally a thousand or so students in medicine, dentistry, nursing, psychology, arts and sciences, people with experience in one of the helping professions—medicine, psychology, social work—complained. Actually, one person, a faculty member in the same department as the chairman mentioned earlier, got up and left in the middle of the tape. But that was it! No slugging, no threats, no complaints; she merely got up and left the room.

They all sat there and swallowed their sense of outrage, their empathically felt pain, their anger at the injustice of it all, without so much as a mild protest or query, and yet the commonly expressed reason for condemning the victim is that she did not protest or act to end her pain! Could it be that there are many reasons for wanting to condemn the victim, and some people simply discover that she is a rather unappealing person? Others look for and find a reason for their condemnation which is plausible, and might add a bit to their comfort. "She was a fool to sit there and take that. I certainly wouldn't have. I would have ripped off those electrodes." A very brave reaction from people who sat in silence as they "suffered" from watching someone else suffer.

Two other "distortions" are commonly found in an audience of observers. One is a denial of the event. "I think she was just overreacting with all that jerking and moaning. The shocks were very mild." The other is simply an interesting alteration of the details of how the victim happened to find herself in that situation. "She knew what she was getting into when she signed up for the shocks. I really thought she shouldn't have made so much out of it." The facts are: (1) At two critical points in the experimental situation, the shocks are described as strong electric shocks—"They are strong, they will be painful, but cause no permanent damage." Both Dr. Stewart on the videotape and the experimenter emphasize the strength of the shocks. (2) The observers are told in some detail that the victim is purposely not forewarned that the experiment involves electric shocks when she is asked to participate, since "they probably wouldn't sign up if they were told ahead of time." Both of the observer reactions appear, then, to be an attempt to find a set of cognitions that will eliminate the injustice. Condemn the victim in one case, minimizing the degree of pain and injustice caused by the shocks, and in the other decide that the victim brought her suffering on herself, so that she is to blame and there is no serious injustice involved.

This entire sequence, beginning with watching the victim, the subsequent ratings of her attributes, and the ensuing verbal descriptions of what they saw, felt, and thought has been so predictable that it was successfully used for years to introduce students to social psychology. The students invariably found it a moving experience, and reactions were so dependable that a set of lectures could be planned to follow from the discussion of their observations and reactions. Undoubtedly, the most compelling "data" and confirmation of the theoretical processes occurred in those scores of classrooms as the students who had experienced the Midpoint condition described what they felt and saw, and how their reactions changed over the eight minutes they watched the victim suffer.

There was one time where everything "went wrong." One of the early occasions when this situation was used for teaching was a lecture to a freshman class of medical students. Approximately 75 of them were in the tiered auditorium watching the victim receive her shocks over two large TV monitors. When the victim received her first shock, there was, as usual, some laughter. The experimenter said and did nothing at that point. With the second shock the laughter got much louder, accompanied by some stomping of feet. With each succeeding shock the laughter became increasingly loud, so that by the end of the tape the entire group of 75 students roared with hysterical laughter and thundering foot-stomping with each shock. In spite of the fact that this was taking place in a new medical sciences building designed to have soundproof lecture halls, the class immediately below was disrupted to the point that it had to discontinue. We learned that the hysterical reaction can be short-circuited or prevented rather easily, for example, by an indirect comment from the experimenter to "please concentrate on the monitor," which implies that this is serious business. All the same, it was interesting to find that our "victim" situation could elicit "collec-tive behavior"—mass hysteria, literally. The obvious inference is that these medical students had found another way of reducing the tension and minimiz-ing the threat created by watching the victim suffer.

By contrast with these classroom sessions, the information obtained from statistical analyses of check marks on scales assumes the character of a sterile ritual designed to objectify very moving human experiences. It is time, however, to take a questioning, if not critical posture, and begin asking the required ques-tions of what we can legitimately infer with some degree of confidence. Where are the gaps and problems which require more data? What kind of additional in-formation is needed to evaluate the plausibility of the Just World theoretical in-ferences in comparison with alternative explanations for the reaction patterns ex-hibited by subjects in various conditions? So let us take a more careful look at the check marks, the situation, and the observers of the Innocent Victim.

CHAPTER 4

The Third Experiment
The Martyred and Innocent Victims

The Importance of Their Fate, Their Role in Creating That Outcome, and the Consequences for the Observers

The Just World Theory implies that, in effect, people work backwards in their reactions to victims. They assess what is happening, and then calculate what it would take for someone to deserve that fate. If these preconditions are not met, then the observer is confronted with an "injustice." Response to the injustice can vary as has been described earlier, but typically it begins with a degree of negative affect, "upset," that is roughly proportional to the magnitude of the injustice. This distress is followed by efforts to reduce it, by restoring justice, or "leaving the field." An important derivation from these ideas is that, if observers are virtually prevented from leaving the field psychologically and physically, *and* they are unable to reestablish justice by acting on the victim's behalf, they will be motivated to find or create additional evidence that the victim actually deserved his fate. And if they cannot locate their victim's culpability in some act or lack of action, they may have to resort to finding his character personally deficient, labelling him a relatively undesirable person who is likely to cause other people harm. We can arrive, then, at the prediction that innocent and "helpless" observers who are confronted with prima facie evidence of someone's undeserved suffering will be increasingly likely to reject that victim as a function of the degree of *injustice* associated with the victim's fate.

Although the findings of the previous experiment seem to support these conjectures, no single set of data can be sufficient to counter the view we all hold of ourselves, that we feel compassion for innocent victims and admiration for altruistically motivated martyrs, and only blame victims who have done something reprehensible, who are truly blameworthy. And certainly our reaction to victims is not determined by their fate, but by an objective appraisal of the merit of their intentions and the quality of their acts; good intentions and noble deeds elicit praise regardless of the ultimate outcome. Obviously, we need to generate further and more careful tests of these alternative views of the way we react to victims. It would be particularly valuable to focus on the singular role of the victim's fate in determining the way innocent observers view the victim.

In our next effort, "innocent observers" were again confronted with an "innocent victim" or an altruistically motivated one—a "Martyr." And again the general strategy was to use a videotape of the event, so that all the observers would see essentially the same "victim," the same person acting in the same way, except where the experimental variables were introduced.

The Importance of Witnessing the Suffering

One potentially troublesome aspect of the situation employed in the Lerner and Simmons experiment is that all the observers saw and literally felt the victim's suffering. Is it possible, then, that the condemnation of the victim was a form of retaliation against the person who was the "cause" of their suffering? The victim's suffering via their empathy led to their suffering, and therefore they came to dislike, be angry with, the cause of this grief. This is not a very rational process, but certainly it is no less so than the condemning of an innocent victim as a way of restoring one's confidence in the justness of the world.

One way of reducing the plausibility of this "Frustration Aggression" explanation is to present the situation in a sufficiently vivid way so that the observers are emotionally involved without compelling them to actually witness the victim's suffering. The observers will be informed of what will take place—they will be aware of an injustice—but will not have the opportunity to experience the victim's suffering vicariously.

So, in this second experiment, we altered the procedure so that all observers would view the victim engaged in a relatively neutral initial task. At the end of the task, they would learn of the victim's fate in the next situation. She would suffer—or not. Although in this situation the observers would not actually see the victim suffer, and there would be a different young woman acting the role, we expected the outcome again, as in the previous study, to be a critical event in determining the observers' evaluation of the victim.

The Effects of the Victim's Reaction versus Her Fate

Probably the most startling single finding in that earlier experiment was the severe condemnation of the "Martyr" who agreed to go through with the experiment, even though she was frightened, because "it was necessary for all of them to get credit." In this study, the Martyr sequence was added on to the videotape after the victim learned of her fate in the next situation. Subsequently, some of the observers would be informed that there actually had been an error and the victim would not suffer at all. It was expected that the Martyr victim would elicit the strongest condemnation, but only if the observers expected that the victim would actually suffer. Her willingness to be of help should lead, if anything, to admiration and liking when it turned out that she would not have to be shocked after all.

The Relationship between the Victim and the Observers

An unexpected finding in another study (Lerner & Matthews, 1967) led to the inclusion of a third hypothesis. The particular characteristic of that situation was that either the observer or the victim would have to undergo strong electric shocks. By the chance picking of one of two possible slips of paper out of a bowl, it was determined that the victim would receive the shock, and the observer would be in a relatively desirable condition. It was found that observers who believed they could just as easily have been the victim did not reject the victim, but actually enhanced her attributes. The explanation offered for this finding was that the situation elicited a kind of identification with the victim based on the perception of a possible common fate, as well as an element of gratitude—"There but for the grace of God go I." Since this condition was the only one of a number of conditions studied which elicited an enhancement of the victim, it was important to learn if it was a stable finding, not unique to that particular experimental context. Although there are no compelling theoretical explanations for this serendipitous finding, it was expected that it would generalize to different situations.

The strategy employed in this study was to have the subjects observe a "model" in a neutral learning situation which was to be followed by a second learning task. After observing the model in the first task, the subjects made ratings of the model. The experimental conditions were created in the following ways: (a) Observers were informed that the second task would involve (1) strong electric shocks (negative reinforcement), or (2) no shock for the model;

(b) Immediately after the first task but prior to the ratings, observers in the Martyr condition saw the model engage in an interaction designed to elicit the impression that she would undergo suffering for the sake of the observers; (c) The subjects were led to believe (1) they could just as well have been the "model," or (2) it was clear that the observers' fate was unrelated to the model's misfortune.

The major hypotheses were:

1. When the observers (subjects) believe they will see the model undergo electric shocks, they will describe her as less attractive than when they do not expect her to be shocked.

2. When the observers believe the model will be shocked, the Martyr condition should elicit greater rejection than the Nonmartyr.

3. When the observers believe the model will not be shocked, the model in the Martyr condition should be described as equally, if not more, attractive than in the Nonmartyr condition.

4. When the observers believe the model will be shocked, but also believe that the model is to be shocked instead of them, the model will be described as more attractive than when this perception of possible common fate is not present.

The Procedure

The subjects were 57 female students who volunteered to participate in this experiment as part of the requirements for a course in introductory psychology. They were exposed to the experimental situation in small groups of four to eight, preassigned on a nonsystematic basis to one of the various conditions. No subjects doubted the experimental ruse.

The experimental situation and procedure were very similar to the one employed in the initial innocent victim study (Lerner & Simmons, 1966). The videotape they saw was of course somewhat different.

Martyr and Nonmartyr. The videotape employed in this experiment contained an initial sequence in which the model entered the room, received her instructions, and performed rather well in a digit-span task. At the end of this sequence, Dr. Stewart informed the model that she was running negative reinforcement conditions that day for the second task. Upon receiving this information, the victim explained that she was terrified of being shocked, and exhibited great resistence to going on with the rest of the experiment. Dr. Stewart then urged her to continue for the sake of the observers, who would not be able to obtain lab credits for participation in an experiment if she refused to do her part so they could observe her. After a few moments of persuasion, based on the elicitation of altruistic motives, the victim agreed to go on "if it is necessary for all of them (the observers) to get credit." This scene, except for the use of a different confederate as the model, was virtually identical with the one employed by Lerner and Simmons. The observers in the Martyr condition saw the entire tape, whereas those in the Nonmartyr condition saw only the first sequence, ending with the completion of the digit-span task, before making their ratings.

Fate of the Model. The subjects in this experiment were run under one of two conditions of anticipated outcome for the model: a condition in which they were led to believe that the model would receive electric shock (Shock), and a condition in which they were not told that the subject would receive shock (Nonshock). The Shock outcome under the Martyr condition was created merely by allowing the observers to view the entire videotape. The Shock outcome under the Nonmartyr condition was established by the experimenter's informing the observers after the initial task that the model would be run under negative reinforcement conditions in the second task.

The observers in the Nonshock condition were led to expect, initally, that they would observe the model in two "control" situations. After seeing the model in the first session, they were informed by Dr. Stewart that the model would be run under negative reinforcement in the second task. The experimenter picked up the head phones, and had a brief conversation with Dr. Stewart, in which Dr. Stewart was reminded of the original assignment. Dr. Stewart then agreed that she had made an error. The model would, in fact, be run under a control condition in the second task. The observers then made their ratings.

Independent versus Dependent Fates. To test Hypothesis 4, it was necessary to provide conditions comparable to the Martyr–Shock and Nonmartyr–Shock conditions described above, except that the observers would have to believe they might have been shocked instead of the model. In the Martyr–Shock and Nonmartyr–Shock conditions described, the observers had signed up to participate in a study of emotional cues, and the model had volunteered for a study in human learning. Clearly, from the beginning the observers and the model were on different paths (Fates Independent). To create the impression that the subjects' and Model's fates were interdependent (Fates Dependent), subjects, upon entering the observation room, were asked to pick a slip of paper out of a bowl. Once seated, they were told that it was necessary for one of them to be the "subject in a learning task," in order for the others to observe her under various conditions of arousal. They also learned that one of the slips that had been in the bowl had "learning task" typed on it. The person who had picked that slip would serve as the subject in Dr. Stewart's experiment on human learning. The subjects were then requested to examine the slip they selected from the bowl, to see which of them had the one with "learning task" typed on it. It was arranged so that the experimenter's confederate, the "model," always turned up with the appropriate slip. The subjects then went through the same procedure as those in the Fates Independent conditions.

Following exposure to the videotape and the experimental instructions, the subjects filled out essentially the same scales as in the initial study.

The Findings

By and large, the data in Table 4 confirm the hypotheses. As predicted in Hypothesis 1, the observers described the model as less attractive when they were led to believe she would be shocked than when they were not told she would be shocked (Nonshock $\bar{X}$ = 96.14, Shock $\bar{X}$ = 82.00, t = 3.08, $p <$ .005). The Martyr model did elicit more rejection than the Nonmartyr when the observers expected the model to be shocked (Hypothesis 2) (Martyr–Shock $\bar{X}$ = 75.22, Nonmartyr–Shock $\bar{X}$ = 89.63, t = 2.14, $p <$ .05). However, under Nonshock conditions in the Martyr model is described as being as attractive as the Nonmartyr (Hypothesis 3) (Martyr–Nonshock $\bar{X}$ = 96.70, Nonmartyr–Nonshock $\bar{X}$ = 95.64).

To test Hypothesis 4, the subjects' ratings of the model who was to be shocked were compared under two conditions. In one condition, observers believed the model had been scheduled for a different experiment than they, and therefore their fates and the model's were and had been independent. The mean rating of the model's attractiveness in this condition (Shock-Independent) was 82.00. Under a second condition, observers were led to believe that if they, instead of the model, had picked a certain slip out of the bowl, they would have been the one shocked instead of the model. The model's mean rating under this condition (Shock-Dependent) was 98.00. A comparison of the ratings under these two conditions yields a t of 3.46, $p <$ .001, confirming Hypothesis 4.

The most important findings of this study focus on the Martyr sequence, which had been used in two experiments to create the impression of someone agreeing to suffer from altruistic motives. It is clear that, in two separate studies (Lerner and Simmons and the present one), this Martyr sequence led to in-

Table 4
$\bar{X}$ Ratings of the Model's Attractiveness
(Bipolar Adjectives)[a]

Kind of model	Nonshock (independent)	Shock (independent)	Shock (dependent)
Martyr	96.70	75.22	92.33
	$(N = 10)$	$(N = 9)$	$(N = 9)$
Nonmartyr	95.64	89.63	103.10
	$(N = 11)$	$(N = 8)$	$(N = 10)$

[a]From Lerner & Simmons (1966).

creased rejection of a model if the observers believed that the model had suffered or would suffer in the future. The findings of the present study indicate that this rejection is not the result of something inherently distasteful or pathetic in the Martyr sequence. When the observers believe the martyr will not suffer, they describe her as being as attractive as the model without the Martyr sequence. This evidence should make it quite clear that the Martyr sequence does not, in itself, lead to rejection; however, if observers believe a martyr will actually suffer, they will be compelled to reject her even more than if her suffering were not so nobly based.

It is intriguing to note that in this experiment, as in a previous one (Lerner & Matthews, 1967), the observers did not appear to condemn the victim when she "blindly" drew a slip out of a bowl which sealed her fate. There are at least two plausible reasons for this reaction. One is that an observer who believes that he could just as easily have been the one to suffer, as the victim feels a sense of "identification" with the victim. It is possible that the sympathy and compassion exhibited by some members of one minority group for the suffering of others reflects this same kind of identification with the "underdog."

An alternative explanation is that the observers were not identified with the victim in the sense of feelings of compassion, but rather they felt relieved, with little if any threat to their sense of justice. At the outset, the observers and the victim were in a situation of equal risk, equal jeopardy, and it was the victim who had the "bad luck" to pick the "wrong" slip. This situation appears to meet our norms and expectations about the "fair" and just way to handle this kind of problem. Someone had to be the victim, and it could have been any one of us. In effect, there was no "injustice," and no innocent or martyred person; there was one of us who had to suffer a little because of the "breaks." Conceivably, then, when people in our culture believe that there is a situation of direct or indirect competition for a scarce resource, and if everyone has an equal claim to the desired outcome, then there are fair ways to decide who is to "lose" and who is to "win." And the winners need not feel guilty, or see the losers as "victims." Of course, one of these ways is to leave it to "chance," or the variant we know of each person drawing straws or picking a number.

Unfortunately, there were no additional data available in this experiment which would help us shed light on whether either of these processes were involved in the "neutral" reaction to the victim's fate when the observers believed she drew the slip which decided that she would be shocked rather than earn money. Later efforts will tell us considerably more about the determinants and consequences of "identifying" with victims, and also about the social psychology of "parallel competition," and the norm of "justified self-interest." For the time being, the finding remains as an intriguing description of the circumstance in which victims are not rejected.

CHAPTER 5

Three Experiments That Assess the Effects of Sex and Educational Background of Observers, Experimenter and Observer Influence on One Another, and the Reactions of 'Informed' and Nonimplicated Observers

Although the findings of the initial experiments were nicely compatible with the theoretical hypotheses, other plausible explanations could be entertained.

Observers' attempt to reduce "guilt." Most people have internalized the obligation to defend the innocent and punish the wicked. This moral obligation can require acts that are uncomfortable or costly in terms of other goals. It is reasonable to conjecture, then, that the observers in the Lerner and Simmons (1966) study may have felt guilt for not intervening, especially in the Martyr condition, where the victim agreed to suffer for their sake (so that they could receive needed "lab" credit). To eliminate a feeling of guilt without having to intervene and risk the consequences of intervening, the observers condemned the victim.

The rejection of the victim is based on a veridical perception. Another equally plausible explanation assumes that the observers did not need to alter or distort their perceptions of the victim to condemn her. After all, the victim allowed herself to undergo a rather extended period of severe electric shocks merely for the sake of meeting a requirement that she participate in one experiment or another. Anyone with a normal amount of integrity would have refused to participate after the first severe shock. An observer might infer that the failure effectively to resist indicated an objectionable weakness in the victim's character. The observers merely reflected these unadmirable qualities in their ratings of her.

The effect of subtle influences by the experimenter and other subjects. A third explanation rests on questions of method. There was considerable opportunity for the experimenter to influence, albeit unconsciously, the reactions of the observers—especially since the instructions were administered verbally (Rosenthal, 1966). A variant of this issue points to the fact that the observers participated in small groups. All of the subjects in each group were in the same condition. It is possible, then, that the observers tended to influence one another by nonverbal signals to react in a relatively homogeneous fashion, thus artificially increasing the likelihood of finding differences among experimental conditions.

Characteristics of the observers—"fundamentalist women." There is an entire class of explanations that stems from the characteristics of the observers employed in the initial study. They were all female undergraduates who were similar to the victim in many respects, including the fact that they all were taking introductory psychology courses and participating in an experiment to meet a requirement. These attributes would point to a sense of identification with the victim as a mediating variable. Also, most of the observers were white, Protestant, and from central Kentucky. Possibly more sophisticated, urbane observers would exhibit less judgmental reactions, and be less influenced by "fundamentalist" orientations to reward and punishment.

The three studies reported here provide some evidence concerning one or another of these explanations.

The First Study

The first study in this series compared the reactions of male and female undergraduates to the "innocent victim." In addition, the hypothesis that the victim's behavior in the situation was inherently reprehensible because of her failure to resist her persecutor was tested by having some observers aware that the victim was merely acting. The observers in this condition (Denatured) were to judge the victim and predict how naive observers would react to her. The reaction of observers to the opportunity to intervene by substituting themselves for the victim was also explored.

The observers in this study were 31 male and 30 female undergraduates from various sections of an introductory sociology course. They were recruited as volunteers to participate in a study of the perception of cues of emotional arousal. Their participation was encouraged by their instructor, but in no way was related to their grade in the course. They were exposed to the experimental situation in small groups comprised of both males and females. All subjects in each group were in the same experimental condition.

The procedure was similar to that employed in Lerner and Simmons (1966). There was an introductory statement by the experimenter outlining the value of obtaining information about the way people appear under stress. The subjects then learned that they would observe a student from a class in introductory psychology who was participating in another experiment—concerned with the effect of strong negative reinforcement on paired-associate learning. The observer's task was to look for signs of arousal as the subject performed. They were then given a plausible reason why it was necessary for them to observe the session via closed circuit television. Then subjects watched what was actually a 10-minute videotape, during which the victim received several apparently painful electric "shocks" for incorrect responses, and reacted to them with expressions of pain and suffering.

The various experimental conditions were created in the following manner:

Denatured. The subjects in this condition were told at the outset that they were observing a videotape of someone acting as if she were being shocked. This tape was to be used in other studies of the effect of suffering on impression formation, and their task was to provide baseline data concerning the impression that this subject gave of herself. After viewing the videotape, the observers rated the victim's attributes, and then were asked to predict how she would be rated by observers who believed that she was suffering, and would continue to suffer in a second session.

Midpoint. This condition is directly comparable to the one employed in the earlier study (Lerner & Simmons, 1966). After watching the videotape, the observers were told that they would watch the victim in a second similar session of equal length. They then rated the "personality" of the victim, after being told that one of the purposes of the study was to determine the way people of different personalities reacted under stress.

Opportunity to substitute. This condition was similar to the Midpoint condition, except that the subjects were told that they might find it helpful, in clarifying their hunches about the cues people exhibit under stress, if they could watch someone other than the original subject (victim). They were then given the opportunity to indicate, privately, on a slip of paper whether they would be willing to be the "subject" in the next session. The experimenter

Table 5
Mean Ratings of Victim and Analysis of Variance: Study I[a]

	Condition		
Sex	Midpoint	Denatured	Opportunity
Male	− 15.55	− 3.44	− 10.2
N	12	9	10
Female	− 15.75	+ .72	− 13.6
N	9	11	10

[a]From Lerner (1971a).

would then pick one from among those who volunteered. This rating occurred just prior to the debriefing.

After receiving the experimental instructions, the subjects completed some forms, including a rating of the personality of the victim. This measure consisted of the 15 highly evaluative bipolar scales. The subjects then rated the "average college student" on the same set of scales for purposes of comparison. The main dependent variable was derived by subtracting the average college-student rating from that of the victim.

Analyses of variance (see Table 5) indicate that the only significant effect was attributable to the experimental condition ($D = 4.71, p < .02$). Neither sex of observer nor the interaction between sex of observer and experimental conditions approached significance. Apparently the ratings in both the Opportunity-to-substitute and Midpoint conditions were more negative than those in the Denatured condition (Midpoint condition versus Denatured condition, $t = 2.92, p < .01$; Opportunity condition versus Denatured condition, $t = 2.16, p < .05$), but they did not differ reliably from each other.

In the Denatured condition, the observers' predictions of the ratings of naive subjects resembled very closely their own ratings of the victim. The male ratings yielded a mean of − 3.44, whereas their predicted mean was − .11. Female ratings had a mean of .72, and the mean of the predicted ratings was − .81. It should be noted, also, that none of the observers volunteered to take the victim's place.

The Second Study

This study took place in the context of a regular class meeting. Its main purpose was to determine whether these students—both male and female of various ages, all of whom had some commitment to a helping profession— would react to the victim's suffering in the same way as had the younger groups of undergraduates in the previous studies. In addition, all of the subjects were exposed to the same experimental situation at the same time. This procedure was employed to eliminate the possible effect of the experimenter's communicating his expectations to the subjects, and also the possibility of subjects' influencing one another to achieve relatively homogeneous responses.

The subjects were 29 students from one advanced undergraduate–graduate class in sociology of health-related behavior. Approximately half the students were male, and half female. The ages, academic status, and majors of the students varied greatly, from undergraduates expecting to enter medical school or majoring in sociology, to mature adults returning to obtain advanced degrees in pastoral counseling, vocational rehabilitation, and health education. The single common denominator among them was a concern with one of the helping professions.

The experiment took place in the context of a guest lecture. The experimenter announced initially that in preparation for his lecture on stress he wanted the class to observe someone undergoing a stressful event. He then related to them a rationale for the importance of their learning the cues indicating that someone was under stress. An assistant then distributed envelopes containing instructions and scales for the observers to complete. The packets were identical, except for slightly different instructions designed to create the differing experimental conditions. Of course, the packets were distributed on a more or less random-chance basis, so that the subjects in the varying conditions were mixed throughout the audience, and the experimenter had no idea of the condition for any given subject.

All of the instructions led the observers to believe they would see the victim in two sessions. The ratings occurred after the first. After reading the preliminary instructions, the students saw the same videotape employed in the earlier studies. They believed they were observing an actual event over closed circuit television.

Two of the conditions employed in this study were virtually identical with those of the previous study—a Midpoint condition, in which the observers were naive, and a Denatured condition, in which they were informed that the victim was acting. The third condition, Reward, was similar to the Midpoint, with the additional statement that, unknown to the victim, she would receive ten dollars at the end of the experiment. The measures were identical with those employed in the earlier studies.

Table 6
Mean Ratings of Victim and Analysis of Variance: Study II[a]

	Condition	
Midpoint	Denatured	Reward
−7.88	7.00	9.55
(N = 9)	(N = 11)	(N = 9)

[a]From Lerner (1971a).

The ratings were similar in the Denatured and Reward conditions (see Table 6). The victim, however, was described more negatively in the Midpoint condition (Reward condition versus Midpoint condition, $t = 2.16$, $p < .05$; Denatured condition versus Midpoint condition, $t = 1.83$, $p < .10$).

The Third Study

Probably the most provacative finding in the Lerner and Simmons (1966) study was the comparatively extreme rejection of the victim who agreed to undergo shocks so that the observers would receive credit for participating in an experiment. The intent in creating this condition was that the victim be perceived as altruistically motivated. The severity of condemnation supposedly reflected the extent to which the observers were motivated to perceive that this apparently martyred victim deserved her suffering after all.

One alternative possibility is that the subject's status of "innocent observers" was altered by the Martyr condition. Although the subjects were not consulted about their wishes in the matter, the victim was pressured into and agreed to accept her suffering, for the sake of the subjects. They may have then come to feel guilty over their complicity in the injustice, or angry over their enforced indebtedness to the victim.

Another possibility is that the martyr scene, rather than creating the impression of someone acting generously from altruistic motives, portrayed the victim as someone who conforms easily to unreasonable demands of authority figures, or is willing to suffer unnecessary humiliation and suffering for others' approval—a "sap" or "sucker."

The strategy employed in this study was based upon two assumptions. If it is true that the Martyr condition actually portrayed the victim in a negative light, then observers who did not believe that the victim was suffering, or who believed that the suffering victim would be appropriately compensated, would still describe her negatively. In other words, the victim would be perceived in a uniformly negative manner, regardless of her fate.

The second assumption was that subjects who were not observing the victim in order to meet the requirements of a course in introductory psychology would exhibit fewer, if any, feelings of guilt or obligation toward the altruistic victim. Therefore, to the extent that guilt or resentment are the effective determinants of the rejection of this victim, subjects from a class that has no such requirement should not devalue the victim. Other observers may be implicated, but these subjects are not, and therefore should exhibit no rejection.

The subjects were 46 women students recruited as volunteers from various sections of an introductory psychology class. When the subjects appeared for the experiment, they were given the standard rationale for observing someone under stress. They were also led to believe that some of the observers in the room were from introductory sociology, while others were there meeting the introductory psychology requirement. The experimenter explained that they would observe a student from introductory psychology participate in her experiment over closed circuit television. The tape and the measures employed in this experiment were identical to the ones used in the Martyr condition of the earlier experiments.

Each group of observers was assigned to one of four experimental conditions. In three of them, they were led to believe that the altruistic victim would suffer severe electric shocks. In one of these conditions, they were told that, unknown to the victim, she would be paid $30 at the end of the session, in another, only $10, and in the third, that there would be no compensation. The subjects in a fourth condition (Denatured) were informed that the subjects were merely portraying a victim, and would not suffer shocks.

The alternative hypothesis can be stated quite simply. If there is something inherently repugnant in the martyr's behavior, then she will be condemned uniformly across all conditions. On the other hand, if the rejection of the martyr is a function of the observers' being implicated, then there should be no rejection from these sociology students in any of the conditions. However, if the evaluation of the martyr is a function of the degree of the undeserved suffering, then we should find the most rejection in the condition where the martyr receives no compensation, less in the condition where she will receive $10, and even less in the condition where she will not suffer at all, or be paid $30.

Apparently the observers in this study were affected by the various experimental conditions. Those who believed that the victim would suffer without compensation described her as considerably less attractive than did the subjects who believed that she would receive $30 at the end of the session (see Table 7) (No-reward condition versus $30 condition, $t = 3.72$, $p < .001$), or who believed that she was not actually going to suffer (No-reward condition versus Denatured condition, $t = 4.76$, $p < .001$). The reactions of the observers in the $10 condition resembled those exhibited by the subjects who believed that the victim would receive no compensation. Although the mean rating in this $10 situation was slightly less than in the No-reward condition, it was not significantly so. The $10 condition did yield significantly lower ratings of the victim than either the Denatured or $30 conditions ($10 condition versus $30 condition, $t = 2.71$, $p < .01$; $10 condition versus Denatured condition, $t = 3.75$, $p < .001$).

It is also worth noting that observers in the Denatured condition were relatively unsuccessful in predicting the reactions that naive observers would have to the victim under conditions of no compensation. The mean predicted rating for naive subjects (-2.09) was lower than their own rating of 5.81, but decidedly higher than that actually found in the No-compensation condition (-26.58).

Table 7
Mean Ratings of Martyr Victim and Analysis of Variance: Study III[a]

Condition			
Denatured	No reward	$10	$30
5.81	−26.58	−19.75	−1.27
(N = 11)	(N = 12)	(N = 12)	(N = 11)

[a]From Lerner (1971a).

Taken together, these findings appear to offer clear support for the hypothesis that the observers' reaction to the altruistically motivated victim is affected by the extent of her undeserved suffering. The alternative hypotheses—that the condemnation of this victim is the result of something inherently repugnant in her behavior, or is the result of the observers' guilt and resentment—do not seem to fit the reactions of the observers in this study.

Implications

These studies confirm the earlier finding that the victim of undeserved suffering runs the clear risk of being condemned by those who witness his or her fate. In general, the observers in these studies thought considerably less of the person portrayed on the videotape if they believed her fate to be one of undeserved suffering than when they understood that she would receive considerable compensation for her pain, or knew she was acting and not really suffering at all. This tendency to condemn the victim held true whether she was altruistically motivated or merely "innocently" pursuing her normal routine.

Of more importance than the general finding, which is probably part of our common wisdom, is the attempt to understand its psychological origins. Why do people tend to condemn victims of undeserved suffering? The evidence from the studies reported here seems inconsistent with two alternative explanations. All three studies contained a condition in which the observers were informed that the person portrayed on the videotape was not actually suffering, and were asked to react to her. These observers consistently viewed that person as considerably more attractive than similar observers who believed that she was a victim. Also, those informed subjects were unable to predict the more negative evaluations of naive observers. These findings offer good evidence that *the victim's fate, rather than her behavior in the situation,* elicits the observer's condemnation.

Study III dealt mainly with a "guilt" explanation. The volunteer subjects in this study were not the implicit beneficiaries of the martyr's largess, and yet they condemned her when they believed that she would not be sufficiently compensated.

The results of Studies I and II bear most directly on the methodological questions raised in the introduction. A comparison of the ratings given the victim by the subjects in Study II with those in Study I suggests some interesting similarities and differences. Although the differences between the ratings given the victim by the subject in the Midpoint condition versus the Denatured condition are virtually identical for the two studies—approximately 15 points—the victim is seen as somewhat more attractive by the subjects in Study II. This result was not predicted, but would be consistent with the notion that people who are oriented to helping others (Study II) would tend to see victims in a more positive light.

The results of Study II also tend to disconfirm the hypothesis that subtle cues from the experimenter or other subjects can account for the observed condemnation of the victim. The experimenter in this study had virtually no contact with the subjects, and did not know which subject in the classroom was in a given condition. It is extremely unlikely, then, that he could have induced the subjects to respond as he hoped they would.

The hypothesis concerning the observers' influence on one another, and the resultant tendency to give a common response, can be tested by comparing the within-condition variance in Study II with those studies where the subjects were run in experimentally homogeneous groupings. The within-condition variance in Study II, 321.96, is comparable to that found in the initial Lerner and Simmons study, 344.9. This is especially noteworthy, given the relative heterogeneity of the subjects in Study II. The within-condition variance of these two studies, though, is somewhat larger than in Study I, 247.72, and in a similar study using this same measure, 262.9 (Simons & Piliavin, 1972). Apparently, whatever subtle communication occurs among the subjects and the experimenter in this situation does not account for the main findings of the series of studies, nor does it appear to introduce an increased homogeneity of responses when subjects are given the same experimental instructions.

In summary, it seems safe to assert at this point that the devaluing of the victims employed in these studies was probably *not* the result of (1) something inherently repugnant in the behavior of the innocent or altruistically motivated victim, or (2) the experimenter's silent signals to the observers or theirs to each other, or (3) something unique to female undergraduates from ''fundamentalist'' Kentucky. It also appears that (4) one does not have to be the beneficiary of a martyr's largess to end up condemning her.

The most consistently reliable determinant of the reactions of these observers—powerless as they were to help the victim—was the degree of injustice in her fate: the less deserved or compensated her suffering, the greater the likelihood that the victim would be devalued.

CHAPTER **6**

Reactions to the Belief in a Just World Theory and Findings
The 'Nay-Sayers'

The central theme of the "Belief in a Just World" theory creates a rather chilling image of humanity. It begins by describing how we live in a society that tolerates the widespread suffering and deprivation of innocent victims. Then the evidence is added that, for the sake of our own security, we either avoid these injustices, or we add to them by finding reasons to condemn the victims. We do this for quite understandable reasons. We want to—have to—believe that our world is so constructed that terrible things happen to people who deserve them because they were "terrible" to others.

When our behavior is described in this bald, dramatic fashion, it becomes clear how disturbing such knowledge must be to our self-image and to our sense of security. To the extent that the findings and the metaphorical description of the relevant processes are persuasive, then we must feel degraded. Not only is there the implication that we may be directly responsible for adding to people's misery by our rejection, but the reasons for our actions seem not only selfish, but rather petty and simpleminded.

That is a very difficult pill to swallow, and an immediate reaction is that I am a much better and sensible person than that. I am not that selfish or callous,

73

and certainly not so naive as to try to maintain a fairy-tale image of my society. Only a fool would try to pretend that it is a just world, and it would take a sick fool to condemn innocent victims in order to protect such a foolish belief.

It was with thoughts such as these that the exploration began. At its best, it took the forms of fascinating experiments, which served to clarify and elaborate the processes underlying this belief in a just world, and our reactions to victims. And if the analysis of these efforts is correct, they produced a completely unintended bonus as case studies of the motivations underlying the "Belief in a Just World"—as this belief appears in all of us, even social psychologists.

Under Normal Circumstances, We Don't Act That Way! "Normally" We All Care about Victims in Our World

One of the most natural reactions to the assertion that we reject innocent victims is to recall the considerable evidence that we, in fact, do just the opposite. Much of the time we feel great compassion and concern for victims, even those we are not in a position to help. Most civilized societies, including our own, devote considerable resources to institutions as objective expressions of this compassion for those who are deprived and suffering.

Aderman, Brehm, and Katz (1974) realized that there was considerable experimental evidence that people normally react with "empathic" distress when they see someone else suffering (e.g., Bandura & Rosenthal, 1966; Lazarus *et al.*, 1962). Of most importance in their thinking were Stotland's (1969) findings. When he gave his observers instructions to just "watch" a victim suffering, rather than to imagine how he felt, or how they would feel if they were suffering, then the psychological indices of this normally elicited empathic arousal were remarkably reduced.

The situation employed in the "Just World" experiments which resulted in rejection of the innocent victim contained instructions to the observers to "look for cues of emotional arousal." Aderman *et al.* noticed that those instructions were remarkably similar to the "watch him" instructions Stotland used. It appeared eminently reasonable, then, to conjecture that:

> Lerner and Simmons (1966) gave their observers empathy-inhibiting instructions. These instructions, rather than just world considerations, would appear to lie at the root of the strong derogation effects of the Lerner and Simmons study. (p. 346)

The strategy they employed to test these ideas was quite straightforward. They modeled their experimental situation after Lerner and Simmons, and presented their observers with one of three sets of instructions prior to their watching the "victim" receive electric shocks in the "learning experiment" situation.

To appreciate the meaning of their data, it is important to be aware of the actual instructions the subjects were given. In one condition, Imagine Self, they read:

> In a few moments you will be watching the learning experiment. While you are do-ing so please imagine how you yourself would feel if you were subjected to the same experience. While you are watching the learner, picture to yourself just how you would feel. (You are to keep clearly in mind that you are to react as if it were you who were the learner. You are to react as if it were you having the experience.) While you are watching the learner, you are to concentrate on yourself in that experience. You are to concentrate on the way you would feel while receiving the treatment. Your job will be to think about what your reactions would be to the sensations you would receive. In your mind's eye, you are to visualize how it would feel for you to be the learner in this learning task. (p. 344)

In the Watch Her condition designed to be "empathy-inhibiting" they read:

> In a few moments you will be watching the learning experiment. While you are doing so, please watch exactly what the learner does. You are to watch all of her body movements that you can see. Your job will be to watch her bearing and pos-ture. You are to notice everything she does, whatever it is. (While you are watching her, don't try to imagine how you would feel in her place or how she is feeling. Don't think about how she feels or how you would feel. Just watch her closely). (p. 344)

The observers in the third condition were given instructions designed to re-semble those employed by Lerner and Simmons:

> In a few moments you will be watching the learning experiment. While you are doing so, please watch exactly what the learner does. Your job will be to observe closely the emotional state of the learner and to watch for cues which indicate her state of arousal. (p. 344)

After watching the victim situation, all subjects completed scales similar to those used in Lerner and Simmons, and a check list designed to assess their mood. The effect of the various instructional sets on the observers' view of the victim can be seen in the following table, taken from Aderman *et al.*

Table 8
Mean Relative Derogation Scores for Subjects in Each Condition[a]

| Audience size | Observational set | | |
	Imagine self	Watch her	Lerner & Simmons
Alone	5.67[b]	− 2.33[c]	− 2.33
Group	− 0.56	− 7.44	− 8.50
Combined	2.56	− 4.89	− 5.42

[a]From Aderman *et al.* (1974).
[b]cell $N = 18$.
[c]Minus scores indicate that the subjects rated themselves more favorably than they did the innocent victim.

If one looks at the "combined" means, they appear to be in line with the hypotheses. Given the positive ratings of the victim in the Imagine Self condition, and the significantly lower and equally negative ratings in both the empathy-inhibiting Watch Her condition and the Lerner and Simmons replication, the authors conclude that:

> The present results suggest that the Lerner and Simmons findings are generalizable only to those observational situations in which empathy does not occur to an appreciable extent. Although the evidence from laboratory studies indicates that such situations are rare, there may be certain real world settings which actively inhibit empathic responses. (p. 346)

This experiment is important because it not only presents an alternative explanation for the findings in the initial Just World victim-rejection experiments, but also reaffirms the view that people normally, naturally, are empathic to victims, and therefore do not condemn them. But does it? What can one safely conclude from these findings?

It is probably true that most people, under most circumstances, experience something like empathically or vicariously induced suffering when they are confronted with vivid cues of someone else in pain. So far, so good. But, is there any evidence that the observers in the Lerner and Simmons situation did not experience this empathic arousal with the victim?

The measures of the observers' mood in the Aderman, et al. experiment produced essentially uninterpretable data. The only difference they found among the conditions was in terms of self-ascribed aggression. On the other hand, anecdotal evidence based on observations and self-reports of the way subjects reacted to the victim in the Lerner and Simmons replication condition indicates that they were extremely aroused, empathically. And that is what the theory would suggest.

There are some data which support the observers' verbal testimony that the victim situation is an extremely powerful empathy-arousing situation. Probably the only reliable and understandable findings resulting from our attempts to examine the physiological correlates of response to the victim (Lerner, 1973) is that subjects do respond consistently and strongly, as measured by changes in skin conductance. This "arousal" is considerably lower when the subject is aware that it is only a videotape of someone who is acting as if she were being shocked. Also, as might be predicted, the observers see the victim in a more positive light when they are *less aroused,* and aware that the victim is not actually suffering. (See Table 9).

In other words, according to these findings, rejection of the victim will *not occur* unless the subjects are aroused empathically. Obviously, without the sense of personal threat, i.e., empathic arousal, there is no need for the observer to arrange his view of the event to construe the victim's suffering as deserved.

As we will see in more detail later, the issues surrounding the processes called "empathy" or "identification" are much more interesting and complex

Table 9
Mean GSR Responses and Derogation Scores Per Condition[a]

	Disabused ($N = 10$)	Naive ($N = 11$)
Mean GSR responses	13.4	46.0
Mean evaluation of victim	− 5.4	− 15.6

[a]From Lerner (1973).

than we need to deal with at this time. Nevertheless, it is probably safe to assert that (a) the subjects in the Lerner and Simmons experiment were highly empathically aroused, at least initially, and therefore (b) simply inducing empathy in an observer does not prevent derogation of a victim. In fact, the evidence tends to suggest that (c) other things being equal, the greater the empathic arousal, the greater the likelihood of rejection of the victim. If this is true, how can we explain the ratings of the victim produced in the Aderman *et al.* experiment?

The most plausible explanation begins with a reading of the instructions used to create the Imagine Self and Watch Her conditions. It appears that Aderman *et al.* confused two rather different orientations—"empathic" and "sympathetic." Sympathy is quite different from empathy—that automatic arousal one experiences in response to powerful cues of another person's suffering. It seems that we respond sympathetically, with compassion and a sense of concern, when we feel a sense of identity with the victim. In effect, we are reacting to the thought of ourselves in that situation. And, of course, we are filled with the "milk of human kindness" for our sweet, innocent selves.

The instructions for the Imagine Self condition certainly are most explicit in telling the subjects that the experimenter wants them to be sympathetic, in the sense of identifying with the victim and feeling sorry for her. Whether the subjects' responses were a result of being "good" subjects in the sense of trying to see the victim in a positive light for the experimenter, or their ability to role-play the reactions of a sympathetic observer, the net effect would be the same. They certainly would not show any signs of derogating the victim.

The relatively positive evaluation of the victim elicited by the explicit and repeated instructions to imagine that the shock is happening to you, "You are the victim," has been found in other experiments which used more indirect means of establishing this sense of identification with the victim. Sorrentino and Boutilier (1974) reported that observers of the innocent victim who thought they might be selected to be the victim in the next "learning" session gave the victim positive ratings. Of course, no one had to tell them explicitly to imagine that the victim was one's self.

It appears, then, that Aderman *et al.* provided us with a demonstration of how the awareness of a common identity with the victim can not only prevent condemnation, but may elicit rather positive sympathetic reactions. What they have not done, however, is to demonstrate that the vicarious arousal elicited by cues of another person's suffering—empathy—will prevent rejection of that victim, and certainly not that the condemnation of the victim found in the Lerner and Simmons situation is a result of the *inhibition* of this arousal. "Empathy" can and does elicit rejection of the victim—the desire to avoid a sympathetic attachment, a sense of "identity" with the victim.

Before going on to the next experiment, we may note that both in the real world we share with Aderman *et al.* and in the laboratory, there is good evidence that "empathy" is quite different from "sympathy." If that is true, then how is it that Aderman *et al.* came to believe that the rather automatic natural reaction of vicarious arousal was artificially inhibited in the Lerner and Simmons experiment to produce the derogation? Would that mean, then, that people do not reject victims in the real world, and that they are generally, typically, automatically sympathetic? That would be a very comforting thought. However, have you ever talked to, seen the look on the faces of people who stop and crowd around the scene of an accident? Are they aroused? Are they sympathetic?

For example, imagine being the subject in the Lerner and Simmons situation when this happens: You are led to believe that the learner you will be observing will be given an "easy list" of nonsense syllables to learn, with considerably less chance of making errors and receiving shocks than in the "difficult list" condition (which most closely resembles the Lerner and Simmons conditions). Very shortly after beginning, the following scene takes place as the victim begins to receive the shocks:

> At that moment an experimenter who was seated in the back of the room rushed forward excitedly. He exclaimed loudly to the other experimenter that the girl was being given the difficult list using the procedure that was supposed to be used for the easy list. He noted that it would be next to impossible for the girl to avoid being shocked under these circumstances.
>
> The second experimenter, who had given the subjects the initial instructions, went to an intercom and ostensibly tried to correct the situation. He was informed by a voice from the TV monitor room, loudly enough so that all could hear, that nothing could be done about the situation because no one could reach Dr. Stewart in the experimental room. Perplexed and agitated, this experimenter then turned to the subjects and said, "Well, it seems that the machine has fouled up and there's nothing we can do about it." (Piliavin, Hardyck, & Vadum, 1967, p. 6)

After watching the remainder of the tape, the subjects evaluated the victim. Obviously, the histrionic reactions of the two experimenters made it clear that it was all quite unfair and unjust, and something of which they certainly did not approve, especially given their "perplexed and agitated" state. It is no surprise, then, that the observers who witnessed this introduction to the Midpoint condition did not lower their ratings of the victim to whom the experimenters were so obviously sympathetic (see Table 10).

Table 10
Mean Attractiveness Ratings of Lerner & Simmons Victim
(Bipolar Adjectives)[a]

	Endpoint	Midpoint
Nonjust	− 6.6	− 3.3
	(N = 10)	(N = 13)
Just[b]	− 3.2	− 14.1
	(N = 10)	(N = 10)

[a]From Piliavin, Hardyck, & Vadum (1967).
[b]The "Just" conditions were essentially replications of the Lerner & Simmons instructions. Mean Square Error = 131.1.

In the second study using the "innocent victim" shock situation, the experimenters altered the introduction in another interesting manner. They had the subjects read the following instructions just prior to watching the "victim":

> This experiment studies the way people react to other people who, through no fault of their own, fall victim to some uncontrollable outside force or action. Victims of a hurricane or earthquake are examples, another would be a person attacked by a stranger on a city street. To study reactions to these people, we are showing students "victims of misfortune." Each group of students sees only one; we can then compare their reactions. (Simons, 1968, App., p. 2)

The subjects saw the videotape, and the instructional set was repeated. The subjects who received these instructions did not show signs of devaluing or rejecting the victim (see Table 11).

Table 11
Means and Standard Deviations of
Index of Attraction of Victim by Condition[a]

	Deception[b]	Partial truth[c]
Past event		
$\bar{X}$ =	1.58[b]	3.40[c]
SD	10.8	14.3
N	(19)	(20)
Midpoint		
$\bar{X}$ =	− 8.27[b]	2.89
SD	15.5	14.0
N	(21)	(19)

[a]From Simons & Piliavin (1972).
[b]These conditions were replications of Lerner & Simmons.
[c]These conditions were created by the additional instructions quoted in the text.

Simons and Piliavin (1972) point out that the findings of these two studies bear a "striking resemblance" to one another, and that when you "suggest to them (subjects) that they are observing a victim of misfortune, they do not devalue her at all." On the basis of this reassuring conclusion, the next step becomes obvious. All we need to prevent good citizens from publicly derogating suffering victims is to have people with the authority and fate control equivalent to a psychologist experimenter define in a compelling way that the victims are truly innocent and worthy of compassion. Also, as in these experiments, they must continue to remind us before we react on each occasion.

That message may not be particularly surprising theoretically, or have much possibility of realization in the real world, but it shows that people are capable of acting, at least neutrally and sometimes sympathetically, to clearly innocent victims.

Everyone Knows We Admire Admirable Victims and Condemn Only Despicable Victims!

One of the most natural reactions to the just world research is to recall the overwhelming evidence in support of the common wisdom that we all feel sorry for the innocent victims of undeserved suffering, and the only victims we condemn are those who deserve it. A fascinating experiment by Godfrey and Lowe (1975) emphasizes this perspective in an experimental variation of the Lerner and Simmons paradigm, and in the process reintroduces us to some critical aspects of the normative structure of our society. These investigators suspected that rejection of a victim would occur only if the victim gave the appearance of someone who was so weak and gullible as to "suffer for the wrong reason." On the other hand, if the victim suffered for "intrinsic" reasons, presumably ones that had meaning and value to her, then the observers, as in real life, would not condemn her.

To test these ideas, they employed a confederate who helped create one of four scenes just prior to the victim's receiving the electric shocks. In all conditions the subjects were seated in a circle, waiting to begin a study on the perception of persons under stress. They then learned that one of them would have to be the person receiving a "series of mildly severe electric shocks," the selection being determined by random designation associated with the number of the "seat" they had selected. Of course, the confederate was always the "randomly chosen" victim.

In one condition (Random), the victim left the room without comment to meet her fate. In a second condition (Unwilling) the victim protested, but appeared to be persuaded by the experimenter of the value of the experiment, and then agreed. A third condition (Good Reasons) was created by having the "victim" accept her fate immediately, announcing as the basis for her decision the same reasons used by the experimenter in the Unwilling condition. In the fourth condition (Volunteer), the experimenter asked for volunteers, and the confederate "victim" volunteered straightaway, giving the same "good reasons" as in the previous conditions.

Although the study would have been cleaner if the investigators had not oriented their subjects to believe they were in an experiment associated with reactions to "accident or disaster victims," the main findings are very compelling (Table 12). In all conditions, the victim was seen in a relatively neutral to positive light, with no evidence of victim "derogation." Further, as might be expected, when the victim felt that her fate was worthwhile and acceptable, if not desirable as in the Good Reasons and Volunteer conditions, the observers rated her as a considerably more admirable and worthy person.

What might we conclude about the implications of these findings for the Just World Theory, and the way we react to victims? There are two related aspects to this question. The first is substantive, and can be dealt with in a rather straightforward manner. The data provide firm confirmation of a series of earlier findings and theoretical hypotheses (Lerner, 1970; 1974; Lerner & Lichtman, 1968; Lerner & Matthews, 1967). From these earlier studies, we had learned that, if people enter a situation where there appears to be limited access to a desired resource—and where everyone is equally entitled to the desired outcome—then a situation of "parallel competition" is perceived by the participants. Under these conditions, most people in our society have come to accept certain "rules" as a fair or just way to decide who gets the more or less desirable outcome. For the person who gets less than the others, or "suffers," those are the "breaks," "it was a fair way to decide"; the result is not considered an injustice, and the person is not a victim.

One set of fair rules involves the reliance on "chance." The psychology of this situation can be rather complex, because of the influence at times of rather primitive attribution processes. However, we found in a number of experiments that, if observers believe that (a) they and the victim have an equal chance of being the one to suffer, and (b) the actual choice of the victim is de-

Table 12
Mean Evaluations Given to Victim
(Bipolar Adjectives)[a]

Experimental condition	Evaluation
Volunteer	12.00
Good reasons	9.67
Random	− 2.67
Unwilling	− 3.29

[a]Adapted from Godfrey & Lowe (1975).

termined by the victim's "act" or random selection by the experimenter, they do not feel their sense of justice threatened, and they do not condemn or derogate the victim, although they may feel sorry for her. Actually the findings go beyond this, and as we described in Lerner (1974), even when the observers' concern with justice is satisfied by this "fair procedure," they do not stop evaluating the victim. Rather, they simply view her in terms of their other values and goals. If she meets their values and facilitates their goal acquisition, then they are apt to like her and evaluate her positively.

A typical example of such findings was described in Lerner, 1970. In that experiment, the subject was led to believe that either she or the other girl would be shocked in a learning task. The experimenter then informed them that the choice of one of them as victim would be a matter of random "chance"; the nonvictim subject would be the control, and receive verbal feedback (or positive reinforcement in half of the conditions—money for each correct answer). In all conditions there were two slips in a bowl, which designated the two possible fates. In one set of conditions (Subject Picks), the subject drew the first slip, which designated that she would be in the desirable condition, and therefore the other girl would receive the electric shocks. In the other condition, the Experimenter drew the slips without looking at them, and again the subject had the desirable condition. Subsequently, the subject evaluated the victim. The results of these ratings can be seen in Table 13. Although this is not the appropriate place to discuss the derogation scores when the subject drew the slip, it is important to note that the fair "lottery" system, where the experimenter drew the determining slip, produced no devaluing of the victim.

What can we conclude, then, from Godfrey and Lowe's findings? To begin with, in all conditions the subjects believed that they could have been the victim. The critical event deciding who was to suffer was the seat that person had elected to sit in—by chance. As a result, one would expect what the experimenters found; there was no evidence of a lowering or negative evaluation of the victim in any of the experimental conditions.

Also, the positive ratings given the victim in the Volunteer and Good

Table 13
Ratings of Other's Attractiveness[a]

	Shock control	Shock–Money	Control/control
Experimenter picks	− 2.75 (N = 12)	+ 1.17 (N = 12)	+ 4.91 (N = 11)
Subject picks	− 4.92 (N = 13)	− 11.77 (N = 13)	

[a]From Lerner (1970).

Reasons conditions indicate that the subjects admired the victim—and possibly felt grateful to her when she took charge of her own fate and decided to be helpful, thus removing the observers from any further jeopardy. And this is exactly what one might have predicted, given the fair procedure for deciding the victim's fate. There was no injustice, no innocent or martyred victim.

Of course, where there is no situation of equal risk or "parallel" competition, then the observer of an innocent or martyred victim is confronted with having to make a judgment of deserving and justice, and that is where the "belief in a just world" becomes so critical. It is not entirely clear, however, when we see ourselves as observers of a victim's fate and when we regard ourselves as participants in a zero-sum competition which eventuates in the victim's suffering. It is important to recognize that these perceptions involve different processes, with differing consequences for the way we react to the victims. In either case, considerations of fairness, justice, deserving are involved, but they take different forms and follow different rules. (See Lerner, 1975, 1977; Lerner, Miller & Holmes, 1976, for a more complete discussion.)

What remains after a discussion of these substantive issues is the question of "Why?". Why, given the data described earlier, would anyone believe that the derogation of victims, when it occurs, is the result of an "objective appraisal" of the victim's attributes, including the implied "weakness" in her character? One hunch is that we all, including Godfrey and Lowe, would like to believe that their findings do indicate that we may admire victims who suffer nicely and maybe enjoy their fate, but they certainly do not threaten our sense of justice. Of course we do not reject truly innocent victims. We are rational information processors, who only condemn those who have truly "weak" characters! Of course, we would like to believe that, but what happened to all the evidence?

We May Reject Some Victims, but We Already Knew about That!

The most intriguing reactions to the Just-World-related findings are those which concede that victim derogation may happen from time to time, but that it happens for reasons that we already know about from familiar social psychological theories. For example, Stokols and Schopler (1973) found that observers considered a young woman who became pregnant as the result of rape by a virtual stranger just as undesirable as one who suffered a similar fate because of careless use of contraceptive devices during her sexual liaisons with her boyfriend. The crucial factor in the evaluation of these two "victims" was the extent of misery and suffering associated with the event and ensuing miscarriage. The more severe her suffering, the lower the evaluation, regardless of the "cause."

Stokols and Schopler attributed this effect to the observer's attempt to achieve "cognitive balance," even though the "careless" victim was seen as clearly causally connected to her fate, whereas the innocent rape victim was rated as not "deserving," not "responsible" for her suffering. Since both the clearly responsible and the not responsible victims were equally "devalued" in the severe condition, the balance interpretation becomes more than a bit strained.

A more recent effort identifies victim derogation as a guilt-reduction process. Cialdini, Kenrick, & Hoerig (1976) proposed that, in the Lerner and Simmons paradigm (Victim situation), the subjects felt guilt; this guilt arose from a sense of complicity in the harm done to the victim in the learning experiment conducted in the "other" room by the "other" experimenter. The observers' rejection of the victim was caused by the "tendency for subjects to justify complicity in the production of harm."

The strategy elected by Cialdini *et al.* to test their hypothesis was a replication of the Lerner-Simmons situation, with the addition of similar conditions with instructions "designed to be unambiguous in communicating to the subjects that the collection of their data was not the reason that the victim was performing in the learning experiment" (p. 721). The actual instructions they received were as follows:

Low Complicity

We have been asking subjects to rate a wide variety of stimulus persons including photographs from magazines, other subjects, experimenters, and so on. Today, we are taking advantage of a research program going on in the education department which we heard about last week. They're evidently running subjects in a learning experiment under varying conditions of stress, and they consented to have a couple of sessions piped in through a closed-circuit TV system which KAET (the campus television station) has set up for us. This experiment is going on right now, and we're not sure what's going to happen in any given condition, but it should get at the type of thing we're interested in. You'll be seeing the subject for a short period of time, and many of these cues are subtle, so it's important to pay close attention. (p. 721)

The following instructions, although differing in some ways from those used in the Lerner-Simmons experiment, were designed to create a sense of "high complicity" (guilt) among the observers.

High Complicity

Today we are taking advantage of a human learning study which Dr. Stewart is conducting to observe someone performing in an emotion-arousing situation. This is going on right now down the hall, and we'll be watching it over closed-circuit TV. Your job will be to observe closely the emotional state of the worker and watch for cues which indicate her state of arousal. The subject will be working on a rather difficult serial learning task. You'll be seeing the subject for a short period of time, and many of these cues are subtle, so it's important to pay close attention. (p. 721)

Half the subjects then saw the victim in a Shock condition, and half in a Non-Shock condition presumably involving no suffering. The results in Table 14 indicate quite clearly that the victim was assigned negative attributes when she received the shocks after the observers had read the "high complicity" instructions. The victim's fate did not affect the subjects' evaluation of her if they had read the low complicity instructions.

How should these results be interpreted? There are various ways in which one might interpret the differing effects the two sets of orienting instructions had on the subjects' perception of the situation. It is not immediately apparent, however, that what is being varied with these two sets of instructions is either a single dimension, or the degree of the subjects' complicity. It seems rather strange that the investigators employed this subtle way of creating a condition of low guilt-producing complicity. And, given this subtlety in the crucial experimental manipulation, it is even more odd that we find no report of evidence, either from the subjects or through pretesting, that the subjects' sense of complicity was affected at all by either set of instructions. Consider, now, the following points.

1. There seems to be no obvious reason to believe that the observers in the Lerner–Simmons experimental paradigm questioned the objective realities of the situation in which they observed the suffering victim. That situation defined them as "innocent" bystanders. It was made clear to each observer that (a) they and their experimenter were involved in a totally separate investigation from the one that "caused" the victim to suffer; (b) the experiment they observed involved the effect of two kinds of reinforcement, strong shocks and strong rewards, and it was a matter of random consideration that they were observing the shock condition that day rather than the reward condition; (c) the experiment was going on in a separate room, and neither they nor their experimenter had any power to alter the victim's fate.

2. It is reasonable to expect that, if the subject-observers were motivated by "ego-defensive" needs to view the situation in a particular way, they would be most willing to accept the "realities" of the situation and their role. Why would they not want to believe that which was true "in fact," that they were "innocent observers"? They were unable to prevent the suffering or alter the victim's fate, but they had nothing to do with the experiment or experimenter who inflicted the suffering on the victim.

Table 14
Difference Score Measure of Derogation[a]

	Complicity	
	High	Low
Shock	-19.93^{b}	-7.23
No shock	0.00	-6.28

[a]From Cialdini et al. (1976).
[b]The more negative the score, the more the victim was devalued relative to "the average college student."

3. There is good reason to believe that experiencing a sense of responsibility for harmdoing engages different processes than being an observer of an injustice. This is an issue worth discussing at some length.

For example, when observers in the Lerner and Simmons experiment (1966) were given the opportunity to vote anonymously concerning the fate of the victim in the second session, they virtually all voted for her to be run in the "positive reinforcement" condition where she would no longer be shocked, and would in fact receive a considerable amount of money. In one such condition, the subjects learned that the victim would be run in the reinforcement condition before they evaluated her. These subjects showed no derogation of the victim (Reward condition). However those in a similar condition who were not told of the outcome of the voting before they made their ratings (Reward Decision condition), showed as much derogation of the victim they voted to help as those who had no such opportunity. The crucial factor in the "observer" subjects' evaluation of the victim was her fate—whether she was to be rewarded or not—and not whether they chose to vote for her compensation.

Compare this finding with a situation in which subjects were indirectly responsible for the victims' being in a shock condition. In that experiment (Mills & Egger, 1972) they drew the slip which determined the victim's fate; half the subjects were instructed midway through to change a dial and reduce the victim's suffering. The other half were given the choice of doing the same, which of course they accepted. As in any familiar "dissonance" situation, only those subjects in the choice condition did not derogate the victim. They had chosen to help her, and obviously did not have to feel guilty. In fact, this derogation effect held even when the subjects were led to believe that something had happened with the machine, so that the victim's suffering actually increased, thus meaning that their *act of help had not been effective.*

In this guilt-inducing situation the victim's fate was virtually irrelevant. All that mattered for the subsequent evaluation of the victim was the subjects' sense of responsibility for harming, and then having chosen to help. When you compare these results with those of the "Reward" and "Reward Decision" conditions, it is obvious that the psychology of harmdoers is quite different from that of the "innocent" witnesses of an injustice.

Regan (1971) employed an entirely different situation, but obtained some rather remarkable findings which support this conclusion. The subjects in her study who either witnessed or felt some sense of responsibility for the ruining of someone's research were inclined to be altruistic in the next situation. She also found that, if an interview in which the subjects were encouraged to confess and be reassured intervened between the injustice and the opportunity to be altruistic, there was an important differential effect on her "witnesses" and her "harmdoers." After the interview, the observers remained relatively altruistic, but the guilty harmdoers were no longer inclined to be of any help. Apparently, as expected, the experience of confession and absolution worked for the "guilty" subjects, but had little effect on the witnesses—who were essentially concerned with justice for the victim, and not absolution for their own souls.

Mills and Egger's harmdoers seem to have been equally preoccupied with their own guilt, and so, after choosing to act on behalf of the victim, they were relatively unconcerned about her actual fate. It was their guilt-reducing choice that mattered to them. The innocent observers in the Lerner and Simmons situation apparently were not at all satisfied by their choice to vote for a better fate for the victim. What mattered to the observers was the awareness that the victim's fate had actually been altered.

Regan (1971), on the basis of her findings, concluded:

> Whether the just-world operates at all when one feels responsible for the harm and whether guilt is ever a factor when one is not at fault are moot points. . . . The two mechanisms are perhaps distinguished by a shift in the focus of attention. After witnessing unjust suffering, the observers' attention is focused on other people, on the sufferer and people like him who deserve better outcomes than they have received. After causing harm oneself, attention may be focused on oneself and the harmdoer may be less concerned with alleviating the suffering of the victim and more concerned with reducing his own unpleasant feelings of guilt. (p. 131)

Given the findings described above, which point to distinctly different processes elicited in a harmdoer versus a witness of an injustice, and the explicit features of the Lerner and Simmons experimental situation, some provocative questions come to mind. The foremost of these is, what would have led Cialdini *et al.* to attempt to show that the observers' victim condemnation in the Lerner–Simmons situation was the result of the desire to reduce guilt feelings engendered by their complicity in the victim's suffering?

Some Concluding Thoughts

One possible answer that emerges from all the experiments we have discussed in this section, is that most of us will not accept the idea that we walk around with a Pollyanna-like Belief in a Just World, and that this childish fantasy is so important to us that we are capable of condemning innocent victims in order to hold onto it. The experiments we just reviewed were all designed to show that this is not the case, that in fact we are actually very sympathetic (empathic?) to innocent victims, and only condemn people who suffer when we have been tricked by the experimenter into ignoring our true empathic feelings. There are also those investigators who are willing to concede that we may seem to condemn some victims, sometimes, but (a) only when they "objectively" deserve it, or (b) only because we have a tendency to organize our cognitions into harmonious relationships with one another (cognitive balance), or (c) when we are made to feel guilty, albeit rather indirectly, for everything that happens in our world, including what happens to the poor victim in someone else's experiment.

Regardless of the problems associated with each of these experiments, they all begin and end on a relatively comfortable note. By comparison, our belief in a Just World Theory reminds us not only of our folly and possible cruelty, but also suggests that the "just world" is a myth we invented. Making the theory explicit forces us to face what we want to forget.

Of course, this is all rather wild conjecturing on my part. But, quite seriously, how do we come to terms with the untimely death of innocent children? How do we come to terms with the way diseases, accidents, natural disasters, wars, intrude themselves into the lives of people we know and care about? How do we live with the fact that we are essentially impotent to affect the important things that happen in our world, the frightening events that are brought home to us incessantly by the media? Are we totally inured to events like Vietnam, Northern Ireland, inflation and recession, our inner cities, the pollution of our environment, and the almost incredible horror stories which emanated recently from the seats of economic and political power? Far in advance of the data and theory, it was my guess that most of us have experienced the thought that "it doesn't make sense." After coming to that realization, we make bargains and compromises that usually give us some confidence that "by and large," "over the long haul," "at least for most people" in our world, things do work out so that, if you are the right kind of person and do the right things, you can pretty much get what you deserve. In any case, I certainly don't want to be convinced all over again that it is not, and will not ever be, something like a just world.

If our explanation of this "Just World" framing of our lives is valid, then there are some interesting trends in our society that we should consider next. According to recently published survey data, Americans have become increasingly distrustful of their government and big business since 1958 (Katz, Gutek, Kahn, & Barton, 1975). One possible implication of this finding is that, when confronted with an injustice, people are less likely to believe that, since the "system" is good, the victim must have deserved to suffer. Possibly then we will see considerably less willingness to identify with authority figures, and condemn their victims. On the other hand, if it is true that most of us cannot tolerate the thought that we live in a random or unjust world, then where will we turn? In this vein it is probably worth remembering the cautions of Fromm (1941), Heilbroner (1974), Arendt (1965), and be concerned about the appearance of a "true believer," authoritarian solution as a way of eliminating a frightening, possibly intolerable, state of affairs.

CHAPTER **7**

Condemning the Victimized

The Meanings of Identification

Before getting back to "justice," let us consider for a moment the ironic injustice of denigrating innocent victims. What could lead people to view victims in a negative light? One possibility might be simply an esthetic reaction. There is something about the victim that violates our esthetic sense. The victim is ugly looking, acts in a gross or clumsy manner. Poor people often look "wrong," their clothes, their grooming. They may talk in ways that appear gross or crude to members of the middle class. They may eat foods, live in dwellings that arouse feelings of revulsion. And they may smell bad. For most people there is something repulsive about the sight of someone who is clearly disabled, or disfigured (Kleck, 1969; Richardson, Hartof, Goodman, & Dornbusch, 1971). And, given our tendency to empathize with those who are in great distress, there is a limit to which even the most saintly among us can tolerate being in the presence of human misery.

We might add to these elements the fear of losing the freedom to act on our own behalf (Brehm, 1972), if we respond to the victim's needs or the guilt induced by our failure to live up to the internalized standards which dictate that we help those who are in need (Berkowitz, 1972). And there is also the desire to associate ourselves, in our minds, with people who are successful and happy (Cooper & Jones, 1969).

89

It should be no surprise when we find ourselves and others avoiding victims, blaming them, viewing them as different and worse, occupants of a separate world. Add to that the "truisms" that we learn in our society before we can think. "As ye sow, so shall ye reap," "If they didn't like living that way, they would do something about it," "Cleanliness is next to godliness," "Accidents happen to people who are careless," "God helps those who help themselves," "The sins of the father are visited upon the children," "There is just something wrong with those people—genes, bad blood."

If one were to look, however, for a place to begin the search for an understanding of how people react to victims, the prime candidate probably would be some aspect of "identification" with others. The most obvious thoughts about this issue, for most of us, would be some variant of the idea that we would not react negatively toward victims if we identified with them. On the contrary, we would feel compassionate, and try to come to their aid. Conceivably, we might be somewhat indifferent with respect to the fate of someone with whom we felt no sense of identification whatsoever. As for condemning victims, such condemnation, if it ever did occur, would certainly reflect a failure to identify with them.

Once having stated this, we are left with the task of discovering what we mean by identification in this context. And a considerable amount of research and thought has focussed on this question.

Expecting to "Walk in Their Shoes"

Chaikin and Darley (1973), for example, created a situation in which subjects expected that they would either be a worker, who was to follow a supervisor's directions and construct designs in order to win some money, or a supervisor, who would give the instructions and pay the worker. They were then exposed to an event prior to entering that situation in which a supervisor accidentally ruined the highly successful efforts of a worker. For half the subjects, this event was portrayed as having minimal consequences for the worker's payment; but the others were led to believe that the accident would cost the worker everything he had earned.

As one might expect, subjects' reactions to this event were affected by whether they anticipated being workers or supervisors. Generally, those who expected to be workers were inclined to blame the supervisors, rather than chance or the equipment, for the accident. Most interesting for our purposes were the reactions of those who expected to be supervisors. Generally, they tended to blame the equipment and circumstances for the accident; but when it was clear that the accident would cost the worker money he had earned, they then, in addition, saw the worker in a significantly more negative light, as a relatively undesirable person. Since all subjects saw the identical scene, it appears that the observers' evaluation of this victim was a function of his fate, and not of anything that he had or had not done.

It is important to remember that it was only in the condition where observers expected that they too would be supervisors in the near future that we find the tendency to derogate the victim. Those observers who believed that they might be vulnerable workers condemned the inflicter of the undeserved harm, and not the victim. These findings make good sense in terms of our understanding of what leads people to feel an "identity" with the victim and his fate. "That could be me." And of course this same process would account for our identification with the inflicter of the harm. We want to maintain the image of this apparent harm-doer as essentially blameless.

In a way we have returned to the central quandary that each of us faces when we become aware of a seemingly flagrant instance of injustice. If we identify with the inflicter, we are likely to condemn the victim, as a way of maintaining the inflicter's integrity. On the other hand, if we have identified with the victim, then obviously we will blame and condemn the person who "caused" the harm.

You and I Are Partners: You Could Not Be Bad!

A relatively subtle illustration of the way the observer's prior identification with the victim precludes his derogating that person was provided in the Stokols and Schopler (1973) experiment discussed earlier. They found that, if people expected to interact with a victim in a way which implied a bond of intimacy and the sharing of ideas, then they were unlikely to derogate that person.

The subjects in their experiment were all young women, who expected to engage in a discussion with another female undergraduate concerning "female liberation and changing sexual mores." In preparation for that discussion, they read a case history of a student who had become pregnant and subsequently miscarried. A few details of the history were varied to create the impression for some subjects that the entire experience was very distressing, with serious consequences for her future, or that it involved extremely little in terms of suffering or public disgrace. In addition to the "severity of consequences," the apparent cause of the pregnancy was also varied. In one set of conditions, the subjects were led to believe the girl had been raped by a "boy she had been dating for less than a week." The other subjects were led to believe the pregnancy resulted from her careless use of contraceptives while engaging in sexual relations with her long-term boyfriend. Needless to say, these various instructions were highly effective in creating the impression of a victim who was either relatively responsible for and deserving of her suffering, or virtually blameless.

Two findings are of particular interest. One is that these young women tended to condemn the victim as a function of the severity of her suffering. When the consequences were severe, she was seen as equally unattractive whether she was also viewed as primarily responsible for her suffering, or a virtually innocent victim of rape. The derogation of the clearly innocent victim is the theoretically important familiar finding. What happened when these women were led to believe that they would meet and talk with this victim? Apparently, they viewed the event in virtually the same way as the subjects who expected to meet with someone else, including the assignment of blame for the pregnancy. The only difference, and it is a highly significant one, was that they showed no signs of derogating the victim. In fact, they seemed to like her rather well, regardless of who was to blame for what fate. There may be many reasons why the anticipated meeting and discussion prevent derogation of the victim, including the fact that it would be dysfunctional to attempt to engage in extended discussion of serious issues with someone whom you do not like. But what seems to be implied is an awareness of an interdependence with the victim that may not be felt, or can be rather easily denied, by observers who are relatively separated from the participants in the injustice.

We may, at least for the time being, recognize that not only have we found additional experimental evidence that observers may derogate innocent victims, but we also have begun to fit together some pieces which are suggestive of a more complete model of the way people react to victims. The outlines of this model portray the individual as electing or being forced to feel a sense of identity with the victim or the apparent inflicter of the victim's fate. Of course, as we will discuss in more detail later, there are at least two other possibilities. The observer can feel a sense of identity with both the inflicter and the victim, or neither. But for now we will concern ourselves with the relatively simple and probably most frequent portrayal of a serious event as involving a good guy and a bad guy—a hero and a villain. Even this simple scenario based on the identification with one and derogation of the other participant contains many complexities.

"Disidentifying" by the Powerless

A very interesting experiment leads us to some important questions related to this issue. Lincoln and Levinger (1972) presented undergraduates with one of two versions of a photograph of a scene involving a black man and a policeman. In the "aggressive" version, they saw the entire photograph of a policeman and his dog attacking a black man. In the "nonaggressive" version, the part of the photograph which revealed the attack was masked out, so that the subjects merely saw the upper body of the black man and the policeman in a relatively neutral context. In addition, they were all provided with a communication which set the context for each of the photographs.

The two communications were similar in length and format, but differed in theme. In the aggressive condition, the aggressive behavior was portrayed as unjustified; the message stressed that the victims were peaceful demonstrators, civil rights workers, and the like. The nonaggression message described the stimulus person in a similar manner but did not mention either aggression or suffering. (pp. 205–206)

The important data from this experiment are the bipolar adjective ratings of the black man (Table 15). When the subjects believed that they were simply participating in a study designed to investigate awareness and memory of complex "stimuli," some of which were "high-arousing," then they evaluated the black man more negatively when he was being attacked by the policeman. On the other hand, if they were told by the experimenters in addition that:

We have agreed with the Commission for the Investigation of Public Behavior to report our subjects' opinions to them. The Commission will make this information available to the people involved in the slides you have seen (p. 206)

then the reverse held. The black man was evaluated more highly when he was portrayed as the victim of the policeman's aggression than in the nonaggression condition.

There were some interesting additional findings, including the ratings of the policeman, who was seen as considerably less desirable in the aggressive than in the nonaggressive condition. However, in the public disclosure condition, the policeman who attacked the black man was evaluated more highly than in the private condition (Public $\bar{X} = 64.18$, Private $\bar{X} = 56.13$; $t = 1.99$, 176 df).

If we fit this last finding with the variations in the evaluation of the victim, then it appears quite plausible to conclude that the observers in the public disclosure conditions were responsive to the general norms of our society. This would explain why they were less inclined to evaluate negatively both the victim *and* the policeman who attacked him. It is also worth noting that these subjects, who were all students, evaluated the black man much more positively than the policeman in *all* the conditions. Even this preference for the black man, however, was reduced somewhat in the public condition. When subjects knew that their responses would be made known to the victim and the perpetrator, they were "reminded" of the social norm that people should not dero-

Table 15
Mean Evaluation of Victim[a]

	Aggression	Nonaggression
Private	91.78	99.42
Public	94.69	90.09

[a]Adapted from Lincoln & Levinger (1972).

gate victims and that generally we are all supposed to react as positively as we can to other people.

There is, of course, at least one other way to interpret these findings, and that is in terms of "identification" as the mediating process. If we consider the public disclosure condition as equivalent to providing the observers with the opportunity to help the victim and punish the policeman, that might explain why we find no derogation in that condition. The rating is consistent with the assumption that subjects were "identified" with the black man, and apparently when they had the opportunity to act effectively they did so by condemning the policeman, and not his victim. If we follow this line of reasoning, then we must ask what happened to their "identification" with the black man when they made their ratings anonymously in the context of a simple psychology experiment. Why did they appear to devalue the black victim? Did they give up their "identification" with the black man simply because he was a victim, and there was no possibility of their altering the state of affairs? Could that happen? What governs whom we identify with, and when and why we may change these identifications?

The Role of One's Fate in the Identification Process

The Norm of Social Responsibility

The findings uncovered in two related experiments (Simmons & Lerner, 1968) may provide some partial answers to these questions. These experiments were designed initially as a response to the literature that was developing in the area of altruistic or prosocial behavior from our perspective: that people have a need to perceive or create "justice" in their world. One very active line of research at that time was developed by Berkowitz and his students around the reasonable hunch that there is a prevalent norm in our society which dictates that people are supposed to help others who are dependent upon them (Berkowitz, 1972, 1973). Presumably, people in our society know and accept this "norm of social responsibility" as a personal value, a more or less "internalized" rule of conduct. The question of what determines when or if people will help someone else in need becomes translated into the related issues of what determines the presence and strength of this norm for the potential benefactor, at a particular given time.

Most of the hypotheses generated by this model were tested in a situation portrayed to subjects as involving tests of supervisory skills. The basic strategy of this situation was to create the impression in each subject that another student's (the supervisor's) payment would be based upon their efforts as "workers" performing a rather simple task. Although the subjects thus had power to affect their supervisor's fate, their efforts would produce no extrinsic gains for themselves. Their pay was either a standard fee, or absent. As a result, any differences in effort—rather directly measured by the number of units produced in comparison with a base period under neutral motivation conditions—could be quite reasonably attributed to the subjects' motivation to help the dependent supervisor.

Of course, as one might have expected, the subjects' efforts were affected by other concerns (Lerner & Reavy, 1975); but, nevertheless, the findings generated in this situation provided good support for the theoretical assumptions of Berkowitz and his colleagues, as well as the value of the experimental paradigm. For example, they were able to show that the subjects' efforts would increase measurably as the degree of the supervisor's dependence on these efforts for his reward increased. Also, this responsiveness to the supervisor's needs would appear even when the subjects were led to believe that they were performing under conditions of virtual anonymity, thus indicating a certain degree of internalization of the norm.

The Effect of Prior Negative or Positive Experience on Willingness to Meet Normative Demands

Their most interesting hypotheses, however, centered on the effect of the workers' immediately prior experience on their performance for the dependent supervisor. Their reasoning went something like this. If people walk around with a social responsiveness norm, whether they follow the dictates of the norm in any given situation or not will depend upon how salient the norm is at that time, and the extent to which they feel willing to follow its invariably costly dictates, costly in the sense that the norm-follower has to give up doing something else, and expend efforts that will yield no extrinsic gains. A series of experiments was conducted employing the supervisor–worker situation, to show that workers who themselves had just previously received help, or had a good experience in the sense of winning a prize, would show an enhanced willingness to help a subsequently dependent supervisor, while workers who had been denied help, or had just experienced the dysphoria of failure at a task, would be less willing to work for their dependent supervisor (see Berkowitz, 1972, 1973). The results of these experiments generated mixed and quite equivocal support for their hypotheses. In some experiments, there was no increment in willingness to help a supervisor simply because someone else had done so, and rarely were the investigators able to find the expected decrement in willingness to help because one had failed or been deprived of help (Berkowitz & Connor, 1966; Goranson & Berkowitz, 1966). Subsequent research in various paradigms with both adults and children has continued to generate quite mixed and theoretically confusing results concerning the effects of prior experiences of "positive" or "negative" affect on prosocial behavior (Cialdini, Darby, & Vincent, 1973; Freedman, Wallington, & Bless, 1967; Isen, 1970; Isen & Levin, 1972). Although it is possible to explain away and integrate some of these inconsistencies, what remains rather surprising is that quite opposite effects and hypotheses are offered out of the same general set of assumptions involving social learning and the effect of reinforcements.

It has taken me some time, but I now understand somewhat better what these people are talking about. It is probably true that, when I am feeling very cranky, upset, bothered, I am less likely to do someone a little favor, or even notice their presence, unless they break through my private ruminations. I may even go through something like an autistically based frustration–aggression sequence, where I find myself venting my anger on the *next* person who interrupts, appears vulnerable, makes a demand on me for anything. And, on the other hand, if something very nice has just happened to me, the "rosy glow" may carry over, so that I am more likely to feel warmly and act magnanimously toward other people—while the glow lasts. These reactions seem very familiar to me, and fit the way others act.

But, if one thinks about it for a moment, most of these effects seem to appear in relatively trivial, brief human encounters—the kind of generosity or stinginess which is usually associated with nothing more serious than gracious, mannerly, courteous behavior—or a bit of nastiness. To be sure, there probably are many norms which prescribe that we act like nice, decent citizens, and treat each other with courtesy, and help one another when we are in need. And it is quite reasonable to subsume these norms under the general rubric of "social responsibility." However, when one leaves the domain of norms prescribing gentlemanly or gentlewomanly conduct as a variant of the earlier rules concerning "noblesse oblige," what becomes clear is that there is a very important qualification—at least in our culture—on this obligation to help others. It may be a wonderful act of nobility, saintliness, to help others regardless or in spite of their worthiness; however, the powerful normative prescription is that we must intervene on behalf of those who "deserve" our help. There is unequivocal evidence from the structure of our major social institutions to document the centrality of this issue of deserving in the allocation of resources. Whether or not people are helped through a social agency or through judicial decree, this help is based upon their demonstrated degree of deservingness. The terrible truth is that we spend grand fortunes on procedures to insure that we, as a society, come to the aid of only those who are truly innocent of any culpability for their state of dependency. And, for whatever it may be worth, there are also sufficient experimental data available which document the general principle that people are moved to come to the aid of innocent victims, and are relatively indifferent to the needs of those whose dependency was caused by the victim's own behavior or character (Berkowitz & Daniels, 1963; Braband & Lerner, 1975; Schopler & Matthews, 1965).

Also, if one takes the evidence at face value, it appears that one very strong source of the willingness to engage in concerted, costly, even dangerous efforts on behalf of others who are in need is the experience of personal victimization, of having been treated unjustly oneself. There are possibly many reasons other than the need to generate additional evidence that one lives in a just world that this is the case, but the observation is a familiar one. Certainly one of the most commonly cited examples is the proportion of Jews who are to be found working actively for the rights and dignity of other minorities.

The Importance of "Deservingness" in the Norm of Social Responsibility

With thoughts such as these in mind, Carolyn Simmons and I designed an experiment to illustrate the importance of the theme of deserving in altruistic behavior (Simmons & Lerner, 1968). We wanted to use the same experimental situation that Berkowitz and his students had employed, in order to show that a particular kind of prior negative experience would elicit strong motivation to help a dependent supervisor, the experience of being treated unjustly in a similar context. And also that the workers in that situation would be influenced by the "deservingness" of their supervisor. We expected that those subjects who had been made sensitive to issues of deserving by their own mistreatment would be most responsive to information concerning the deservingness of the dependent supervisor.

The basic procedure we employed was thus virtually the same one used by Berkowitz (Berkowitz & Connor, 1966; Berkowitz & Daniels, 1963). The subjects were led to believe that there would be two supervisor–work sessions. Depending upon the draw of lots, one could be a supervisor, a worker, or work alone in a control condition. It was arranged so that subjects for the first session were assigned to be either supervisors or controls. As supervisors, they had to write instructions to the worker in the next room, so that he could, on the basis of the written communications, create checkerboards out of sheets of different colored paper. All the participants were informed that, for every square pasted correctly during the work period, the supervisor would be paid five cents. Normally, the workers were able on the average to do enough work to earn the supervisors approximately one dollar. The control subjects simply worked alone during this first session, and were paid 25¢ for their efforts.

All of the subject supervisors were given one of two experiences. Those assigned to the Rewarded condition were led to believe that their worker had done enough work for them to be paid considerably more than average, $1.75. By contrast, we tried to create a quite different experience for those assigned to the Fail–Betrayed condition. After completing their instructions, these supervisors were shown their workers' efforts after the practice session of five minutes, for which, of course, there was no payment. The worker had apparently understood the instructions very well, and had time to read the instructions and correctly cut out and paste eight squares. At the suggestion of the experimenter, the "supervisor" then sent a form note to the worker to continue the good work. After the "work" session of 10 minutes the experimenter returned and showed the supervisor that the worker had pasted only five squares, which entitled him to 25¢. Five squares! Even though the worker had twice as long as the practice session when, besides everything else, he had done eight squares.

Following that, all the subjects were led to believe that, according to the second draw, they would be workers in the next session. They also learned, inadvertently, about the previous fate of their "supervisor." One third of the subjects were led to believe that their supervisor had been a control or independent worker, and had earned 25¢ in the first session. Another third learned that their supervisor had also been a supervisor in the first session, and had earned $1.75 (Rewarded). The remaining subjects were given similar information, except for the prior fate of their supervisor, who had earned 25¢ (Fail–Betrayed).

The main dependent variable was the number of units produced by each of these subjects for their supervisors. This time they made envelopes instead of pasting checker boards, and, rather than a particular amount of pay for each unit, their efforts would enable their supervisor to be eligible for a large bonus, to be paid at the end of the semester. Additional measures assessed some of their perceptions of their two partners and their reactions to the situation.

What then would you expect to find? First, let us look at some of the ratings of the subjects who had been supervisors in the first session (Table 16). It is apparent that the subjects' reactions were in line, for the most part, with the experiences we had created for them. Those in the Fail–Betrayed condition rated their partners as less adequate workers, and were less willing to participate again with the same partner, or have that person as a roommate, than were those subjects who were led to believe that their workers had earned them much more than average pay. Not quite in line with expectations was the fact that both experimental conditions yielded high ratings for enjoyment of the supervisor role.

For the most part, then, we had good empirical reasons to support our impressions that the experimental manipulations had the expected effect. With that in mind, we can now look at the measure of the main dependent variable, the amount of work subjects did for their supervisor in the second situation (Table 17).

The analysis produced a significant interaction between the two independent variables. There were no main effects, and the only cells which are significantly different from one another in number of units produced are those with means of 14 and 19. In effect, we can say that those workers who had been rewarded in the previous situation were the ones who expended the most effort on behalf of their dependent supervisor, who had been payed very little during

Table 16
Summary Table of Mean Responses and Analysis of Variance
of Supervisor Questionnaire[a]
Study I

	M responses		Analysis of variance			
	Partner rewarded	Partner fail-betrayed	Source	df	MS	F
1. "How would you rate your partner as a worker?"	10.58	5.17	Partner's fate Error	1 48	364.227 1.663	219.018[c]
2. "Willingness to participate again with same partner"	10.46	5.81	Partner's fate Error	1 48	268.416 4.691	57.219[c]
3. "How much did you enjoy being a supervisor rather than a worker?"	10.04	10.22	Partner's fate Error	1 48		
4. "Willingness to have partner as a roommate"	7.79	5.82	Partner's fate Error	1 48	48.423 4.363	11.099[b]

[a]From Simmons & Lerner (1968).
[b]$p < .005$.
[c]$p < .001$.

the first session. On the other hand, those subjects who been betrayed initially, or who had worked alone as controls, produced considerably more if their present supervisor had been previously highly rewarded, than if he had earned only 25 cents, presumably due to betrayal by his previous worker.

All of this is strange. To be sure, the behavior of the previously highly rewarded worker can be explained somewhat if one assumes that the effect of the high pay was to create the impression in the subjects that they were being overpaid, inequitably. And thus they were made more sensitive to issues of "equitable" or just treatment (Adams, 1965). But that is as far as we can go with that "theory." And certainly, this pattern of findings is beyond that which anyone could generate plausibly from the assumptions associated with the "norm of social responsibility." Even the latter more sophisticated version which incorporates some of the assumptions of reactance theory (Berkowitz, 1973) would fare little better.

The best hunch we could come up with to explain these findings went something like this. The rewarded subjects may have been exhibiting a no-

Table 17
Number of Envelopes Completed in Work Period[a]
Study I

| | M cell values | | |
| | | Other's fate | |
Subject's fate	Rewarded	Fail-betrayed	Control
Rewarded	15.75	19.88	18.50
Fail-betrayed	19.60	14.25	17.50
Control	19.33	14.88	16.00

[a]From Simmons & Lerner (1968).

blesse oblige or good citizen response, or reflecting an overcompensation-induced guilt. Overall, they were the least surprising and least interesting to us. The fact that both the fail–betrayed and control subjects exhibited the same pattern of great effort for the previously highly paid, and minimal effort for the previously poorly paid, supervisor, seemed important. Is it possible that these subjects, regardless of their own immediately prior experiences, interpreted information about the supervisor's prior earnings and fate as valid and compelling evidence concerning his personal merit as a supervisor? One bit of additional evidence tended to support this hunch. At the end of the second session, the subjects completed a second set of ratings. Only one of those produced significant differences among the conditions. "Would you want your partner from this task as a roommate?" The reactions to this completely hypothetical question were as follows:

Table 18
Worker Question 9: Study I "Would You Want Partner from This Task as a Roommate?"[a]

| | M cell values | | |
| | | Other's fate | |
Subject's fate	Rewarded	Fail-betrayed	Control
Rewarded	7.50	6.75	7.88
Fail-betrayed	8.20	7.63	8.00
Control	8.11	6.33	8.63

[a]From Simmons & Lerner (1968).

The only significant effect was produced by the supervisor's prior fate. The previously low-paid supervisor (Fail–Betrayed) was seen as less desirable than the others. There was no significant interaction with the prior fate of the subject.

This was all highly speculative, but it began to make sense. The subjects attributed responsibility to their supervisors for their prior fate, and then tailored their reactions to fit this attribution. Not only did they not work very hard for a previously poorly paid supervisor, but they found him a significantly less desirable person. It is interesting to speculate as to why they acted that way. Was it a simple matter of the rather dispassionate processing of the best information available, the prior fate of the supervisor? After all, they knew virtually nothing else about him, except for general peer status. Or was it somehow more motivated as an expression of some other agenda that the subjects were working out? After all, why did not the Fail–Betrayed subjects use knowledge of their own experience as a basis from which to view and understand what had happened to their supervisor? It seemed, instead, as if they ignored how they had been treated. But we already know from the quite different patterns exhibited by the previously rewarded subjects that the prior experience was not completely trivial, that it did make a difference. Is it possible that the subjects, in spite of all of our efforts to the contrary, interpreted their own prior fate as "deserved," so that they actually did not see themselves as "betrayed"? Had we underestimated the extent to which people want to believe that everyone gets what they deserve?

To test some of these notions, we did a second experiment, which differed only slightly from the procedure employed in the first. We wanted there to be little opportunity for any subject to believe that this prior fate had been "deserved." To do that, we introduced the device of the experimenter's objective appraisal of the subject's instructions while performing as a supervisor. All subjects were given the next to top rating, but their total pay remained the same as in the first experiment, presumably because of the appropriately poor or superb efforts of their workers. The subjects' subsequent efforts for their supervisors were much more understandable; overall, the subjects did the least amount of work on behalf of the previously highly rewarded supervisor, and most for the one who had earned less than average (see Table 19). Primarily it was those subjects who themselves had been fail–betrayed who exhibited the maximum effort on behalf of a supervisor who similarly had been poorly paid. Needless to say, in this second experiment there was no evidence of dislike of the supervisor who had previously received little pay.

Some Obvious and Not So Obvious Conclusions

What can we infer, then, from these two experiments? Certainly, the subjects' response to their partner's dependency was affected by their own prior fate (see Berkowitz, 1972, 1973), but this reaction was also shaped by the in-

Table 19
Number of Envelopes Made in Work Period[a]
Study II

| | M cell values | | |
| | | Other's fate | |
Subject's fate	Rewarded	Fail-betrayed	Control
Rewarded	14.50	14.75	14.66
Fail-betrayed	13.25	21.25	16.66
Control	9.67	15.43	16.50

[a]From Simmons & Lerner (1968).

formation they had concerning the prior fate of their dependent supervisor. Certainly there were no simple effects attributable to the salience and willingness to respond to the dictates of a "norm of responsibility." The rewarded subjects were not generally more willing to help their supervisor than those who had a neutral or negative experience (Berkowitz & Connor, 1966; Goranson & Berkowitz, 1966). Nor was the amount of help offered simply a function of the degree of need and dependency (Berkowitz & Daniels, 1963). Although there were certainly unexpected surprises, as in the first experiment, the data taken as a whole make reasonably good sense. The subjects seemed to tailor their efforts to fit the relative deserving of the person who was dependent upon them.

Actually, the more one thinks about it, the more obvious becomes a set of data which illustrates that people will tailor their efforts on another person's behalf to fit what that person deserves. Any reasonably competent member of our society knows that this is the case. Not only do people actually behave that way for the most part, but it represents a norm, a rule of conduct, which is virtually a "given" bedrock truism in our culture. Any deviation from that rule would be sufficiently remarkable to demand an additional explanation in terms of some special agenda or private relationship between donor and recipient.

So much for the obvious; what is less well understood, and considerably more intriguing, is the way the subjects in this experiment decided who deserved what. If we set aside the improbable possibility that the subjects were responding primarily in terms of experimenter-induced demands, then the first experiment becomes considerably more interesting than the theoretically successful second one. The surprising reactions of the Fail–Betrayed subjects are particularly provocative. Not only were they more likely to exert greater effort on behalf of a previously highly rewarded supervisor than one who had earned the same lousy pay as they had in the first session, but they also showed somewhat more liking for the previously rewarded supervisor than for the one who had shared their fate.

One plausible explanation for the behavior of the Fail–Betrayed subjects in the first experiment is that they actually blamed themselves, although probably not exclusively, for their fate, that their worker only pasted enough squares to earn them 25¢. Even if they did not accept blame for their own fate, and held their "lazy" worker totally responsible, they certainly did not seem to generalize from this interpretation of what happened to them to an explanation of why their supervisor in the second session had previously earned the same small sum.

Why did they not see the supervisor who had received only 25¢ in the first session as having been betrayed by *his* worker? Because they didn't believe that they had been mistreated by their worker? Because they suspected that they had, but didn't want to believe it? Why was it necessary to drive home the obvious and seemingly most comfortable interpretation of their experiences with the relatively bludgeoning procedure we employed in the second experiment? After all, it was made "clear" to them in the first experiment that their worker was fully capable of performing the requisite acts. The only interpretation at all reasonable for his poor productivity in the work session was that he did not want to exert himself, not even as much as the average worker did. The facts stacked up quite clearly. The subject had done his job well enough, his worker decided to do considerably less than average for him. But if the Fail–Betrayed subjects in the first experiment saw it this way, then why did they exert so much effort on behalf of their own supervisor when he had already been overrewarded, but do so little for, think so little of, someone who had also received less than average?

Mysterious? Maybe not. But there was something "fishy" going on. What comes to mind immediately, at least by simple association, is the resemblance between these effects and what we found in the experiment which employed a "fortuitous" assignment of large pay to one worker, while his partner received nothing (Lerner, 1965). In that experiment, the information about the assignment of payment led the observing subjects to invent or find evidence which "justified" the workers' highly discrepant fates. The lucky one was "seen" as actually having performed better. One obvious difference between the subjects in that experiment and the Fail–Betrayed subjects in this one is that we have some reason to believe that the outcome-induced attributions were being made by subjects about themselves as well as their supervisors. Why would not these subjects elect what appeared to be the most "rational" explanation, especially since it would be self-esteem maintaining or enhancing?

CHAPTER **8**

The Assignment of Blame

What this all points to is the need to examine what we know and do not know about the way people assign causal blame, *if* we want to understand how people react to the fate of others, to those who are apparently in need. Up to this point, we have looked at some evidence concerning the way a person's need to believe he lives in a just world affects the way he assigns causal blame to people for their fate. Presumably, the person wants to believe that others, especially those who are suffering and deprived, merited their fate by virtue of something they did or failed to do, or the kind of person they are.

Also, whatever future dangers may inhere in distortions generated by the "just world" constructions which fit people to their fate, they have the quality of being multiply self-serving, at least on a short-term basis. The observer who sees a victim's fate as entirely deserved need not feel frustrated or experience any conflicts concerning the potentially costly consequences of intervention. There is no implicit threat to the image of one's self as a good citizen for failure to intervene, no sense of impotence at being unable to compensate the victim and punish the inflicter of the injustice, no reason to risk one's safety or desired resources to restore justice. All of that can be avoided, circumvented, by the simple device of finding or inventing reasons why everyone got what they deserved.

What we are forced to consider now is the possibility that people will make these fate-linked attributions even when they are emotionally costly, including self-blame for a "bad" outcome. And what makes it more interesting and puzzling is that these seemingly self-punitive attributions also appear to be "irrational." They are not at all required or forced upon the person by a reasoned analysis of the best available data.

The Effects of Outcome on Attribution of Responsibility

Fortuitous Reward and Self-Blame

A more recent conceptual replication and extension of the fortuitous-reward experiment provides another illustration of this effect. Apsler and Friedman (1975) had subjects construct designs with a "magnetic play kit" as the initial task in a two-part experiment. Subjects were informed that some of them as part of the experimental procedure would be assigned a reward of an "extra hour credit" as a form of reinforcement subsequent to this initial task, while others would receive no reward. These subjects, as well as others who were assigned the role of observing them at the task, rated their performance. The results showed that both the performing subjects and the unaffected observers rated the "rewarded" subjects as having performed better than those who received no reward. Presumably, the subjects, including those who were full participants in the event and were directly affected by the "fortuitous" assignment of rewards, construed the worth of their efforts to match the outcome they were assigned. Why did the subjects who received no reward rate their own performance as somewhat less adequate than those who were assigned the extra credit? There are a number of plausible answers that come to mind, not the least of which is that some or most of them thought the experimenters, although they said nothing explicit to that effect, would do the most reasonable thing, and assign rewards on the basis of performance, rather than chance. That's usually the way things are done in our society. And there is some evidence from an internal analysis of other ratings to support this explanation.

And that is one class of answers that must be taken seriously. People assign causal blame to themselves and other people on the basis of their analysis and processing of the information they have available. In its barest outlines, it is just as simple as that. We all were taught and learned some fairly sophisticated principles of cause and effect, which we apply to the events that happen around us (Heider, 1958; Kelley, 1973). What may appear to be an error or distortion occurs when the machinery generates the "wrong" answer because it was fed insufficient or "misleading" data. The process though is quite "rational," or at least an understandable application of a set of information-processing principles (Brewer, 1977).

A number of the subjects in this experiment on the basis of their prior experience assumed that it was quite natural for experimenters to assign rewards on the basis of performance. Once the subjects were presented the information about the rewards and were asked to rate performance, they made the obvious inference that rewards indicate good performance. This image of the subject as a detached processor of information in the assignment of responsibility is certainly compatible with the relatively trivial nature of the event, five minutes of rather enjoyable effort associated with the assignment of an unanticipated and possibly unneeded "extra credit" for participating in the experiment.

Although one can't be sure without additional information, it is doubtful that the subjects were terribly aroused by anything that happened in the situation. They simply went about their business of trying to make sense out of what was happening, given the information they had at hand. In this case, it was a matter of making one's best guess that people who are assigned a reward subsequent to working at a task were probably better workers than those who were not given the extra credit.

The answers to the general questions which began this discussion are beginning to take shape somewhat along these lines. People "identify" with and try to help victims who, on the basis of the best information available, appear to be worthy of help by virtue of their innocence, lack of culpability for their fate, and high personal worth. Think about it for a moment. In order to keep your job—to put food in your mouth and a car in your garage—you have to perform up to snuff. And it took a great deal of past effort, sweat, and skill to get the job you have today. Knowing all that, if you see someone who is clearly poor, what is your best bet about why that person is hungry and what kind of "person" he or she is? You may want to continue or qualify your analysis to include more sophisticated notions based upon what you "know" of the effects of early experience, the modeling of parents, the effects of social barriers, but essentially you are still simply making your best bet, based upon the causal schemes you have learned to apply to the information you have available (Kelley, 1973).

Detached versus Involved Participation

A surprising number of studies which illustrate that people try to make sense out of what happens to themselves and to others have appeared in the literature in one guise or another. One such illustration that people can be quite sensible, at times, was generated in a study which gave undergraduates vignettes to read about another student (Shaw & Skolnick, 1971). Supposedly, Jim wanted to complete a lab assignment in his required chemistry course, so he could leave early for Christmas vacation. He went into the lab on his own, and while following the instructions he mixed two chemicals, and there was an accident. The experimental conditions were created by varying the outcome of the accident. In one case the accident created an offensive odor, in another a pleasant odor, in a third on explosion, and in a fourth a major discovery. Students then responded to questions designed to assess how responsible they thought Jim was for what happened, how they viewed Jim, the accident, and their relation to him.

The main finding of this experiment was that subjects tended to ascribe more responsibility to Jim for the accident when the event was associated with one of the odors, and they found Jim least responsible, and felt it was most likely a result of chance, when he produced a "major discovery." Clearly, it is not necessary to assume that these findings were generated by very complex processes. The subjects simply reckoned, quite reasonably, that it is rather commonplace to create odors in laboratories when one fools with chemicals, but explosions and major discoveries are not associated casually with undergraduates following lab instructions—something else must have "caused" the event, and typically we consider these rare inexplicable contingencies fluke accidents. These rational judgments seem most likely to occur when the whole matter is so removed from us that we really don't care a great deal about what happened or why.

But what happens if we begin to get involved emotionally with what is going on? It is probable that the Fail–Betrayed workers in Simmons and Lerner (1968) cared somewhat about what was going on at the time. I am less convinced that in the seemingly less involving Apsler and Friedman study (1975) either the winners or losers, participants or observers, cared much about the extra credit. Are there any differences in the way people assign causal blame, in the way they process information, in the way they react to their own or other people's fate, when the consequences are serious enough to be emotionally involving, rather than relatively trivial, events in their lives?

With these questions in mind, we can look at a rather brave experiment which provides a most tantalizing set of findings for those of us who are interested in how and why people assign blame. On the basis of pretesting, Jones and Aronson (1973) established that a sample of undergraduates at the University of Texas would view a woman who was a divorcee as less respectable than either one who was a virgin or married and presumably not a virgin. Using this information, they created a simulated jury situation where subjects responded to a series of issues associated with a young woman (described as either married, unmarried virgin, or divorcee) who had either been raped or saved from the consummation of the rape by the police, who arrived on the scene in the nick of time. The written description of the event was essentially the same for all the subjects, and it went as follows:

> Following a night class at the University, Judy Wyatt walked across campus toward her car, which was parked two blocks off the Drag. (See police description of the victim, below.) The defendant, Charles Engels, was walking across the Mall in the same direction as the victim and began to follow her. (See police description of the defendant, below.)

For the rape condition, the case account concluded:

> Less than a block from the victim's car, the defendant accosted the victim and a struggle resulted in which the defendant stripped and sexually assaulted the victim. A passerby heard the victim's screams and phoned the police who arrived to appre-hend the defendant within a few minutes after he had completed his sexual assault.

For the attempted rape condition, the case account concluded:

> Less than a block from the victim's car, the defendant accosted the victim and a struggle resulted in which the defendant stripped the victim. A passerby heard the victim's screams and phoned the police who arrived to apprehend the defendant just before he was able to begin his intended sexual assault. (p. 416)

The simulated jury context enabled the experimenters to assess the extent to which the subjects wanted to punish the defendant—a 26-year-old garage mechanic—as a function of the severity of his crime, and the respectability of his victim. They found significant effects for both these independent variables. The defendent was sentenced by the subjects to a longer prison term if the rape was consummated rather than only attempted, and given a shorter sentence for the very same criminal act if the victim was a divorcee, rather than a virgin or a married woman. That seems to fit what one would expect if one were to assume that the subjects were processing the information available by generalizing from past experiences and common wisdom. Most of us might be less punitive toward the defendant who raped a divorcee, rather than a virgin or a married woman, because we would be more likely to believe that the less respectable di-vorcee did something to elicit the crime. That makes sense, given the more or less conscious stereotype of the ''divorcee'' that we have picked up from our culture.

It may make sense, but there is good evidence that this was not what hap-pened at all. The subjects' responses to the question of ''How much do you consider the crime to be the victim's fault?'' revealed a significant difference among the conditions, but not in the direction of our ''common sense'' predic-tion. As it happened, the married and virginal victim elicited greater blame for the crime than did the less respectable divorcee! To be sure, we are dealing here with degrees of very small differences on an absolute scale, but these differences were reliable, and must be taken seriously.

Of course, it is obvious that, depending upon how the issues were framed for the subject, one could find just the opposite results, and what everyone knows would be confirmed by the ratings. One experiment, however, which went so far as to vary respectability of the rape victim by portraying her as a Catholic nun, or a topless-bottomless dancer, also had difficulty getting sub-jects to produce the expected commonsense result (Smith, Keating, Hester, & Mitchell, 1976). For example, their subjects assigned greater responsibility to a victim when she had no prior acquaintance with her attacker, than when she had known him before.

If we accept these findings of Jones and Aronson as valid, though obviously limited in as yet unknown ways by both method and sample, the important
issue is, what do they mean? We can make at least two different sets of assumptions that are relevant to our purposes. One is that the subjects cared about the
rape case, and they were trying to come to terms with its implications for their
own goals and values. It was real and engaging for them. And the other is that
the subjects were only trying to fit together the pieces of an event from which
they were rather removed, emotionally—detached processers of information.

To the extent that we believe the former is true than the findings offer an
interesting elaboration of the way the concern with justice colors people's
reactions to events in their world. Both experimental variables were designed
to influence the severity of crime—the degree of injustice involved. Apparently the subjects assigned punishment to the offender in proportion
to the amount of harm he had done, the extent of the injustice. The assault on the divorcee presumably was less despicable, created less undeserved
suffering, than the same fate inflicted on someone of more sterling virtues, and
so the criminal was given a somewhat lighter sentence, to punish him for the
amount of harm he had done. However, punishing the inflicter of an injustice
does not remove the threat engendered by the awareness of such a heinous
crime, especially one to which all women are potentially vulnerable. The threat
of this potential vulnerability must be considerably greater when one learns
that the victim is a quite respectable person, someone who is least likely to "deserve" the terrible fate of a rape assault by virtue of something she has done, or
by the kind of person she is. The implicit question raised by this event is "if it
can happen to someone like her, as innocent and respectable as she is, then who
is safe from such an awful fate?" The subjects then attempt to reduce this
threat by persuading themselves that this particular victim must have done
something to elicit the attack.

It is also conceivable that the subjects confronted with these circumstances
feel no sense of threat; they simply may be more puzzled by the sexual assault
when it involves a virgin or a married woman. The subjects may believe that it
is more unusual for someone who is highly respectable to allow herself to be in
a position of vulnerability to an attack; according to our common wisdom, it is
statistically more of an exception to the general class of expected events than if
the victim were a divorcee. Is it not quite natural, then, to assume that such a
relatively rare event must reveal something unique about this particular respectable victim? Clearly she must have done something untoward, exceptional, to
elicit this unusual fate. That conclusion follows, then, from a reasonable analysis of the evidence available, and what most of us assume about causal
schemas. Kelly (1973) has noted a general tendency for people to employ mul-
tiple causal explanations for relatively extreme rare events. This would be such
an example. The rarity of the rape of a highly respectable person leads the
observer to assume that more than one factor was responsible. Not only the at-

tacker, but also to some extent the victim's behavior, must have played a part.

Certainly, without more direct evidence concerning the mediating processes, both of these explanations remain somewhat removed from the specific findings. It is worth noting, however, that the commonsense, rational information-processing approach to these issues is not at all simple or straightforward The most obvious prediction on the basis of "common sense" would be that, if any victim were assigned some blame for her terrible fate, it would have been the least respectable divorcee. Most of us would have bet on that prediction, and been dead wrong.

The Appearance of "Primitive" Attribution Processes

Apparently the rules which people employ in attributing causation do not follow necessarily what most of us think we do. We are not that logical or sophisticated in the way we process the information to judge cause and effect (Nisbett & Wilson, 1977). Why not? Is it simply a matter of the quirks in the cognitive processes by which the information is attended to and processed (Ross, 1977; Ross & DiTecco, 1975)? People tend to be overly influenced in their judgments by one kind of information rather than another, and under certain circumstances they are more likely to attend to one kind of information to the exclusion of others. These answers are, of course, a more sophisticated elaboration of the "information-processing" model of causal attribution. We will have more to say about these issues later.

For the time being, we will assume that, for the most part, people are reasonably good at assessing cause and effect or certainly as good as they need to be in order to function adequately in the physical and social world. Most adults understand the difference between proximal and distal causes; between contributing, necessary, and sufficient causes; between accidently "causing" an event which was completely unforeseeable, or causing a foreseeable outcome by some act of negligence, or intentionally causing something to happen. Kelley (1973) and others (Heider, 1958; Jones, Kanouse, Kelley, & Nisbett, 1971) have described very well the naive psychology whereby we discover and attribute causation for human events.

We can add to this reasonably sane, objective image the realization that people often seem to color "whom" they blame for "what" in ways which appear to be self-serving. Although the experimental evidence is less compelling than one might expect (Miller & Ross, 1975), most of us are ready to admit that we are as human as the next person, and so we are more willing to accept credit for ourselves and those we care about when something good happens, and much more likely to claim it was an unavoidable accident or the fault of the other "bad" guys, when things go wrong. The mechanisms and processes which might account for this bias may be more complicated or even totally different than we typically suppose (Ross & DiTecco, 1975). But its presence is so well established in our culture that it is an important factor in the functioning of our most important institutions. It is difficult to imagine two more prominent concerns of social man than the desire to maintain or to enhance one's self-esteem and public image.

Our most solid predictions, then, are that in any given situation, *people will assign causal responsibility in ways that are normatively considered sensible and rational* in our society; and *if they deviate* from a normatively sound cause-and-effect analysis, *it is almost certain to be in the service of making them look and feel good.*

With these predictions in mind, let us take a look at some more data to see how well they fit.

Who Is to Blame in a Chain of Causation?

In one experiment, Lerner and Matthews (1967) had two undergraduates appear for each experimental session, presumably to participate in a study of human learning. When they arrived, they learned that the experiment "required" that one of them receive severe electric shocks for each error made in a paired-associate learning task, while the other would be given either neutral feedback or 25 cents for each correct answer, and no shocks whatsoever. They were informed, as well, that, for purposes of experimental control, the role assignment had to be a matter of chance. There was a bowl with two folded slips of paper designating each of the two conditions. The subjects were then taken to their separate rooms to complete some preliminary tasks, and while they were separated the experimenter introduced the experimental variations.

For one third of the subjects (Self Picks First), the experimenter entered the room and announced that, since they had arrived first (or last), they would draw their slip out of the bowl first. Since the two slips in the bowl both designated the desirable condition, these subjects believed that they would be in the desirable condition; they were also allowed to infer that the other subject would therefore be in the shock condition. Another third of the subjects was led to believe that the other subject picked first (Other Picks First), and were offered the one slip remaining in the bowl; to their visible relief, it had "control" written on it, which meant by clear implication that the other person had drawn the shock-designating slip. And, of course, there was a control condition where there was no mention of either of the two subjects receiving shocks.

Three measures were taken from the subjects before they were given a full explanation of the true purpose of the experiment and engaged in a general discussion of their reactions to it. One of these was an assessment of the assignment of "primary responsibility" for their and the other subjects' fates. The second was a measure of their evaluation of the attributes of the other person in the experiment. And the third was an indirect measure of the desire to help the other person, taken by informing the subjects that they would have to vacate their room while waiting for their training session to begin. Just prior to this information, subjects were allowed to overhear the other subject telling the experimenter that she was very frightened, and did not like waiting alone. The subjects were simply offered the choice of going to a library room with magazines and waiting alone, or going to the room where the other subject was waiting.

The results were rather interesting (see Table 20). The majority of subjects assigned primary responsibility to the person who drew the determining slip of paper. In the Fates Independent condition, they assigned primary responsibility to themselves for their own fate, and to the other subjects for theirs. When the others drew the first slip, they assigned primary responsibility to them for both fates. Similarly, when they drew the first slip, they assigned primary responsibility to themselves for their respective fates. The subjects' evaluation of the other person was assessed by the same procedure employed in most of the "victim" experiments (see Lerner & Simmons, 1966). They described the kind of impression the other person created on the highly evaluative bipolar adjective scales (Table 21). Their ratings of the "average" college student were subtracted from the ratings of the other subject. A minus score indicates that the average student was assigned more positive attributes. It appears from the data that the subjects devalued the others' attributes when they picked first, and enhanced their own attributes when the other drew the first slip. The Fates Independent condition seemed to yield results comparable to the condition where there was no shock involved at all. A rather remarkable set of findings is revealed in Table 22. The overwhelming majority of subjects in both the Self Picks First and Other Picks First conditions elected to return to the room which contained the other subject, while for the most part those in the Fates Independent condition expressed no preference.

Table 20
Number of Subjects Attributing Primary Responsibility
to Experimenter (E), Self (S), and Other (O)[a]

		Fates independent	S picks 1st	O picks 1st
	E	3	2	1
Responsible	O	0	0	12
for S's fate	S	12	13	5
	E	5	2	2
Responsible	O	9	6	15
for O's fate	S	1	7	1

[a]From Lerner & Matthews (1967).

Table 21
$\bar{X}$ Ratings of the Other Person
(Bipolar Adjectives)[a]

	Shock/control	Shock/money	Control/control
Fates Independent	-5.25	-3.57	-6.30
	$(N = 8)$	$(N = 7)$	$(N = 10)$
Other picks first	6.55	3.14	
	$(N = 11)$	$(N = 7)$	
Self picks first	-11.22	-19.33	
	$(N = 9)$	$(N = 6)$	

[a]From Lerner & Matthews (1967).

How do the results of this experiment, taken as a whole, fit the general notion that people are usually quite rational and sensible in the way they assign causal responsibility for events? If and when they deviate from a sound analysis of the best evidence available, do they tend to do so in ways that seem to be self-serving, biased in their own favor?

At first glance, at least, the data point to the need for a different or at least a more complex set of theoretical assumptions. For example, the evidence indicates that the subjects tended to "blame" the person who drew the first of the two slips out of the bowl for the fate of both participants. The subjects' ratings of a primary responsibility, as well as the differential reactions on the other two measures, tend to support this inference in a way that makes sense. Until that first slip was drawn, the breaks could have gone either way; it was only after that event that the participants' fates were sealed.

But assigning primary causal responsibility in the sense of actually "blaming" the person who drew the slip is not at all rational in terms of what we

Table 22
Number of Subjects Selecting Alternative Places
to Await Onset of Experiment[a]

	Fates Independent	Other picks first	Self picks first
With other	4	12	11
With books	1	2	1
No preference	10	4	3

[a]From Lerner & Matthews (1967).

think we know about cause and effect; the subjects were told explicitly that the reason for using the draw to determine which of them was to be assigned to a particular condition stemmed from the scientific dictate that the assignment had to be random, total chance. And, of course, there was no objective way the subjects could tell ahead of time the fate dictated by the particular slip they blindly drew out of the bowl.

Certainly, according to any reasonable analysis of events, neither subject was to blame, since the situation was designed to be random. It is true that, when the subjects were asked to assign primary responsibility, they were not given a category of "chance" to select. Conceivably the subjects really felt that none of them was responsible, or that the experimenter was to blame for everything. After all, it was the experimenter who set up the situation, the conditions, reunited the subjects, and instructed them to draw a slip. An obvious cop-out for these subjects would be to point out that they were merely following instructions—the Eichmannesque defense of "I was just a technician" actually applies here.

The Psychology of "Last Reasonable Chance"

A later study I did with Joe deRivera at NYU revealed that, when the subjects drew the first slip, they would report in a subsequent interview that of course they were not actually at fault, it was simply a matter of chance. However, virtually all these subjects expressed misgivings about the way things turned out, and would have much preferred that the other person had drawn the first slip. Why the bad feelings? Certainly it had nothing to do with the possibility that the other subject might retaliate. They remained separate and were anonymous to one another before and after the experiment. These rather bright, sophisticated undergraduates seemed confused and surprisingly inarticulate in their attempts to make sense out of their "feeling," probably because it did not make sense in terms of their analysis of a reasonable basis for that feeling. Their highly ingrained, overlearned rules of cause and effect simply did not fit what they were experiencing: "I know I am not guilty of any wrongdoing, but then why do I feel this way?"

A follow-up experiment (described in Lerner, 1970) showed, in addition, that subjects in this experimental situation are not at all reluctant to assign responsibility to the experimenter. But, true to the pattern in both experiments, and a subsequent replication (Mills & Egger, 1972), they blamed the experimenter only when the experimenter actually drew the slips out of the bowl.

The evidence seems fairly clear-cut. Most of the subjects assign causal responsibility to whomever draws that slip out of the bowl. That is the person who is blamed for the consequences. The consequences of this assignment of blame also appear in the subject's subsequent reactions. The subjects who draw the first-determining slip appear to devalue the personal attributes of the other subject whom they "caused" to suffer. Is this reaction based upon the desire to reduce one's sense of guilt, as observed in other experimental contexts, by coming to view one's victim as personally reprehensible (Glass, 1964; Jones & Davis, 1965; Walster, 1966)? On the other hand, those subjects who believed that the other subject drew the slip which succeeded in rescuing them from the shocks appeared to enhance their "rescuer's" attributes. Was this an indirect expression of relief and gratitude? And, interestingly enough, when their fates were not linked, the subject seemed to react rather neutrally to the other subject's bad luck.

If this interpretation of what happened in that experiment is at all valid, then we have seen an interesting demonstration of primitive, blaming responses appearing in rather intelligent and highly educated young adults. These responses are primitive in the sense that they treat an accidental association of a person's acts and a set of consequences as a sufficient basis for the assignment of blame. Piaget (1948) and others (Heider, 1958; Shaw & Sulzer, 1964) have shown that very young children often exhibit this kind of blaming process, but by middle childhood or early adolescence at the latest most of us consider the person's intentions and ability to shape events in judging who is to blame for what.

Certainly, whatever the "slip drawer" intended to do, he had no control over the outcomes. They were purely accidental, random, chance. No one is to blame for what happened; or the experimenter is to blame for creating and stage-managing the entire set of events; or everyone is equally responsible for going along with the whole business. But, other than the chance assignment of being the last person involved in the sequence of events which eventuated in one person being shocked rather than the other, there was no rational basis on which one could blame the slip drawer for anyone's fate. Certainly, one could not assign "primary responsibility" to that person. What is even more remarkable, possibly, is that the slip drawers appeared to employ this same primitive process, and seemed to blame themselves for what happened.

There appeared, then, to be two stages or processes in the subjects' reactions. The first was the *assignment of causal blame to the first person involved* —even one's self. Then what ensued was a *reaction to the blaming,* including signs of *trying to reduce guilt by condemning the other person* whom one "caused" to suffer.

On the face of it, there was little evidence that the subjects' reactions followed our initial best predictions. Their behavior was, for the most part, not at all consistent with a normatively sound cause-and-effect analysis of the situation, and though we did see evidence of the attempt to maintain self- or public esteem, it appeared as a secondary reaction to the initial blaming. Of course, if we wish, then, to understand how people react to victims and employ principles of deserving and justice, we must take a fairly serious look at this seemingly primitive tendency to blame people. At the least we should get a clearer understanding of the possible bases for its appearance in adults, who do know more appropriate ways of assigning cause and effect.

Other Examples of Primitive Attributions in Experimental Social Psychology

Think for a moment of Piaget's (1948) compelling demonstrations of how older children differ from younger ones in assigning blame. Given the choice between two hypothetical examples of "Jean who accidently tripped and broke many plates while trying to help his mother and Pierre who broke a few cups while trying to steal cookies," the younger children seem to be more influenced by the severity of the outcome, the amount of damage done, in deciding that Jean was more blameworthy than Pierre. The older children do the opposite, and find the well-intentioned though clearly clumsy Jean less culpable than Pierre, who had larceny in his heart when he accidentally broke the cups. The older children understand, of course, that accidents can happen to anyone, and that blameworthiness is a judgment based upon the assumption that what distinguishes good from bad, guilt from innocence, are the choices that people make, the goals they select, and their wisdom in deciding how to act. Blameworthy people are those whose actions are either foolishly careless, or who intend to do harm.

Having once again stated what appears to be obvious, how then do we explain how it is possible to elicit rather incredible amounts of guilt in bright young adults who cause harm accidentally? A number of investigators have used this by now common effect to study various processes. The prototypical event goes something like this. A subject is ushered into a waiting room prior to the onset of the experiment for which he volunteered. There is only one place for the subject to sit, and, as he pulls out the chair or touches the table which is next to the chair, the "accident" occurs. A set of folders or data sheets are spilled all over the floor. The event is interpreted by the experimenter as a minor disaster for a graduate student's thesis. The anecdotal evidence is extremely compelling. These subjects feel terrible. Why?

Do they actually feel guilty and blame themselves for this clearly unintended "accident"? The evidence seems to indicate that they do. If the subject "causes" the accident, then he will react differently than someone who saw another person "cause" the same accident, and differently than someone who witnessed no accident. The most general finding is that both accidental harm-doers and witnesses will act subsequently in ways that appear designed to make themselves feel better (Cialdini et al., 1973), and that usually involves volunteering to help someone in need (Carlsmith & Gross, 1969; Freedman et al., 1967). In some situations, witnesses actually are more helpful than accidental harm-doers (Konecni, 1972). In others they do less (Freedman et al., 1967).

More interesting for our purposes is the finding that this postaccident "altruism" will be eliminated among harm-doers if they are given the opportunity to vent their feelings about the event to a neutral listener, while subjects who witnessed the same accidental harm are relatively uninfluenced by this opportunity to chat. They remain motivated to help someone in need (Regan, 1971).

Why do these university students blame themselves for a clearly "unintended" accident? What could conceivably lead these people to feel "guilty," and have to engage in some act of expiation? Are they exhibiting the same kinds of processes that lead very young children to blame someone as a function of the seriousness of the consequences?

There is additional evidence that the nature of the consequences does matter to adults in their assigning of blame for "accidents." Tesser and Rosen (1972) found that people are noticeably reluctant to inform someone, even a total stranger, of some terrible news, while this same reluctance does not appear with neutral or more desirable events. One possible reason is that they believe that the recipient of the bad news will blame the "bearer of the sad tidings." Chaiken and Darley (1973) were able to show that observers were considerably more likely to assign blame for an accident when the consequences were potentially serious, than if the identical event caused no apparent obvious harm. Although the observers tended to assign blame in ways which reflected their own temporary allegiances, there was a general avoidance of a "chance" or accident explanation by the subjects when the outcome was relatively serious, rather than benign (Medway & Lowe, 1975).

And, to be sure, there is ample evidence, both in and out of the lab, of wish-fulfilling biases influencing the way people assign causation for events. Gamblers, especially in the heat of the action, genuinely believe that the cards or dice are influenced by "supernatural" forces, special powers that they or others possess (Henslin, 1967). Winning and losing is attributed to the influence of these powers, not natural processes. Langer (Langer, 1975; Langer and Roth, 1976) has provided excellent documentation for this "illusion of control" over win-lose situations.

Motivation and Information Processing: Some Anecdotal Examples

It is time to raise again the question of what "causes" this assignment of "causation." Why do adults, who presumably know better, act this way? And again, we return to the familiar answers. One set of answers is that, except in the few obvious cases where people are so invested in an outcome that they engage in what would otherwise be incredible fantasies of control and power, for the most part people are simply making rather unremarkable systematic errors in the processing of available information. Consider, for example, the accidental harmdoing effect, in the light of our early training. It is a safe bet that, if we "cause" an accident, it is because we were not being careful enough. It was certainly avoidable. And consider the objective contingencies. Not everyone causes accidents; certainly not everyone knocks over a table spilling important data sheets. It is highly probable that the table was solid, and that the graduate student had stored his data in a safe place. If that is the case, then "I must have done something, failed to be careful enough, and that is my crime. Of course I did not intend to cause the accident, but I am guilty of simply not being sufficiently careful." The event itself, with its serious consequences, is *prima facie* evidence that I was not sufficiently careful, as careful as I should have been (Ross, 1977).

One may add to this analysis the reasonable conjecture that, in situations involving fairly strong emotions, people are more likely than otherwise to base their reactions on a limited scanning of the available information. Their reactions will be based on the most familiar and striking aspects of the situation (McArthur, 1972). In the case of these "accidents," the contingency of events and the consequences themselves are clearly the most salient features. The more elaborate qualifying construction of events requires relatively lengthy and dispassionate consideration of alternative possibilities and contingencies. Viewed in this light, there is nothing very mysterious, or primitive, about these "illusions" of control and responsibility. In fact, quite to the contrary, they seem to reflect a rather reasonable process of people trying to make sense out of what happens in light of what they have learned about what are probable causes for certain effects.

One can not accept this as the whole story, however; there is too much evidence that peoples' emotions, needs, and motives come into the picture at one point or another, possibly in determining what they attend to or look for (Ross & DiTecco, 1975), or in what they try to tell themselves and others about what happened, and why. Let us take a closer look at this issue. This time we will begin with anecdotal examples.

Assume for the moment that you are at a rather elegant dinner party. Everything is going along fine, until there is a loud crash behind you; everyone at the table is startled, and many jerk reflectively as you do. In your case, however, your movement knocks over a glass of water—or a plate of soup if you prefer—onto the lap of the person sitting next to you. How do you feel at that moment? Setting aside what you say, which of course will contain in various combinations expressions of regret, apology, attempts to make restitution, what will you actually feel? My hunch is that you will feel terrible, and define that feeling for yourself as a whopping load of plain old guilt. You could probably change the scene to include just the two of you, eliminating the public exposure, face-saving elements, and my strong hunch is that you might reduce thereby somewhat the "embarrassment" component, but you would still feel guilty. Of what?

Back to the large party for a moment. My experience with similar events leads me to believe that something of a "reversal" in attributions occurs. Some part of this may be a genteel ritual in our culture, but I believe that there is a genuine component in the self-flagellating guilt of the "spiller," and the excusing declarations of the victim and the uninvolved bystanders. Everyone else is telling you that of course you couldn't help it, it was a natural and unavoidable accident, while you are genuinely regretful, and allow other people to hear you call yourself a clumsy fool. If people are motivated to maintain a positive image of themselves and a good level of public esteem, then we have discovered one rather convoluted technique for accomplishing these ends. If they are involved at all. And there is some reason to suspect that they are not.

Consider the following set of circumstances. I am assigned responsibility at the clinic for a patient who is a "sex offender." During the initial sessions, I spend hours listening to details of the patient's perverted assaults on young girls and boys, while probing for some understanding of the meaning of these acts in terms of the patients' past history—what had been done to *him*. You see, as any reasonable psychologist will tell you, all behavior is "caused" by a combination of antecedent events and the genetic endowment of the individual. I accept this assumption, not simply because it is a useful way to proceed, a valuable heuristic device, but because I genuinely believe it to be true. With sufficient information, I could explain, understand, any and all behavior. As a clinician, I search for and hopefully find information I need to understand the patient, the causes of his behavior. And although I may not find this sex offender particularly admirable, it is virtually inevitable that I will view him as the "innocent victim" of circumstances that were inflicted upon him by his genes and the events that happened to him, especially as a youngster. There will be little if any tendency to condemn him for the evil acts he committed. After all, given the chain of events involved, I realize that *he* was not the "real cause;" he was merely the transmitter of a series of antecedent conditions. I employ a similar perspective as a social analyst when I interpret the violent behavior of a black gang in the ghetto as an expression of a natural (inevitable?) response to the environment in which they were raised and now live.

None of this should seem at all remarkable. But now, juxtapose that scene to what happens later in the day. I blame myself for not getting more work done at the office, especially for the three reviews I have owed editors for some weeks now. At home I am truly disappointed in the way my daughter manages her time, and her full allegiance to the local caricature of upper-middle-class material values. And there is no disguising the fact that I become furious when my teenage son mouths off at his saintly mother—which he does all too frequently.

How could that be? How is it possible to excuse, explain away, externalize the causal blame for my patient's miserably cruel behavior, or for the violence committed by anyone who is poor and lives in a "ghetto," and yet take on enormous amounts of grief because I blame myself and members of my family for the "cruel," "stupid," and "clumsy" things we do? Why don't I apply the same causal analysis to myself and the people with whom I am so closely identified, if I believe that (a) the way people act is determined by their past experience and their biological inheritance, and (b) this perspective neutralizes the condemning or blaming reaction to what people do, and (c) I do not enjoy the "pain" of getting upset with myself or members of my family? Why would I not apply in my own life the principles which I believe are true, and which at the same time would cause me considerably less grief?

It is, of course, the thrust of the anecdote to illustrate that these primitive procedures are employed widely by people, such as orthodox psychologists, who have other more sophisticated ones easily available in their personal repertoire. And the primitive procedures prevail even when they bring with them relatively painful, conflict-ridden consequences.

Conceivably, the reason that people who "know better" continue to blame themselves and others for "accidents," stupid, thoughtless decisions, not doing enough, letting themselves go, not having enough courage, being selfish, cruel—is because these blaming reactions are so ingrained in our own thinking and our cultural assumptions that they are simply the automatic expression of a long-standing habit. They are automatically elicited, habitual reactions, which one cannot turn off simply because one has learned subsequently that they are inadequate or inappropriate.

The fact that these reactions have a habitual component with strong roots in our culture cannot be a sufficient explanation for their ubiquitous presence in people's lives. The evidence, some of which was cited earlier, is that people can and do employ more sophisticated procedures for attributing causation. So the "habit" can be, and often is, given up.

Even more to the point, possibly, the experimental data seem to confirm what each of us can observe in ourselves and others: most of us want, possibly need, explanations for important human events that are something else, something more than the elaboration of a natural process. We certainly do not view ourselves in those terms. We of course assume that we have choices, opportunities to alter the course of events, bring about things we want to happen. If we make good, wise decisions, and are willing and able to put forth the effort, then, by and large, we can realize our intended goals, get what we want, and avoid the pitfalls.

Whether or not, this bedrock belief in our own ability to choose our fate and influence what happens to us is supported by the direct evidence of our everyday experiences, we do manage to locomote reasonably effectively. Could any of us conceive of what life would be like if we felt powerless, helpless? The glimpses we have each had of what it means to want something desperately, or to be frightened of an impending event and feel impotent to make a difference in the course of events, is enough to convey the strong affect associated with the sense of powerlessness. It should be no surprise, then, that there is considerable evidence which links a wide range of "pathological" consequences to chronic or severely induced states of "helplessness" (Lefcourt, 1976; Rotter, 1966; Seligman, 1975; Wortman & Brehm, 1975).

Viewed in this light, the willingness to blame one's self and those whom one loves is seen as a strongly motivated event. I want to, must, believe that people have "effective" control over important things that happen, and I will hang on to this belief, even when it requires that I resort to rather primitive, magical thinking, and even when it is costly in terms of the negative feelings engendered by the personal judgments which arise out of the assignment of blame—shame, guilt with oneself, and a sense of humiliation, anger, disappointment with those whom one loves. Of course, I may subsequently go through additional efforts to maintain a positive image of myself and those I care about. As we shall see in more detail later, it is not the sense of control that is crucial, but rather the confidence that things will turn out all right, that eventually, you, I will get what we deserve.

CHAPTER 9

The Response to Victimization
Extreme Tests of the Belief in a Just World

The Self as "Victim": Some Puzzling Reactions

Certainly one of the most extreme tests of the motivation to see justice in one's world occurs when the person is inflicted with suffering or deprivation.

One set of investigators who worked with rape victims posit the strong need for a sense of future control as the basis for self-blame:

> What appears to be guilt . . . may be the way the woman's mind interprets a positive impulse, a need to be in control of her life. If the woman can believe that some way she caused it, if she can make herself responsible for it, then she's established a sort of control over the rape. It wasn't someone arbitrarily smashing into her life and wreaking havoc. The unpredictability of the latter situation can be too much for some women to face. If it happened entirely without provocation then it could happen again. This is too horrifying to believe, so the victim creates an illusion of safety by declaring herself responsible for the incident. (Medea & Thompson, 1974, pp. 105–106) (quoted from Wortman, 1976)

Although these conjectures obviously need additional examination, they do make sense. But the need to create the illusion of future safety by inventing an equally illusory degree of control for one's terrible fate does not seem to

123

apply easily to other examples. Rubin and Peplau (1973) found that young men, immediately after learning that the random draw of the Draft Lottery placed them in imminent jeopardy of being drafted, showed signs of lowering their own self-esteem. In other words, they seemed to devalue themselves as a function of their miserable but clearly arbitrary fate.

One could offer many hunches as to what was going on in the minds of these unfortunate young men, but Rubin and Peplau offer an interesting possibility. Their bet is that the lowered self-esteem was simply based on a form of generalizing or "spillover" of affect. The victims felt so terrible and angry about their fate, that everything they thought about took on the same sickening coloration, including themselves. They were mad at life and the world, every part of it.

I think I understand this reaction somewhat better since my father's most recent visit. My father grew up in a Galician shtetl, came to America as a young man, and now lives in Miami with so many others who followed the same long and most improbable path from shtetl to condominium. My very bright son is convinced that his grandfather is the "smartest person I have ever met," and so I tend to agree, and listen more attentively to him now than I did when I was my son's age. One thing he said surprised me then, especially given his fine analytic mind.

He was talking about why, even at his vulnerable age and given his orthodox upbringing, he cannot believe in a God the way man has described. He cannot reconcile the Nazi holocaust which destroyed so many people including his parents and relatives with the presence of "God"—Jehovah or otherwise. He related how he became "ashamed" as he learned of the terrible things that were happening to the Jews throughout Europe. The basis of this sense of shame, as he described it, was simply the event itself; that this could happen to Jews made him feel ashamed as a Jew.

Analogous reactions have been reported in experimental contexts. A fascinating experiment by Comer and Laird (1975) involved negative consequences which were relatively unique to that situation—eating a worm! Out of this most improbable set of events they were able to generate rather compelling data concerning the way victims breathe meaning into their fate. Their subjects exhibited three kinds of reactions to the discovery that they were assigned to the condition where they would have to eat a worm. They devalued themselves, presumably becoming more deserving of their suffering; they altered their self-image in a positive way; or they decided the worm-eating would not be so bad after all.

These results make sense if one accepts the fact that the subjects had come to view themselves as deserving their fate—by virtue of the kind of people they were. They wanted what happened to be "meaningful." Whatever else is involved, the sense of appropriateness about "what' happens to "whom" seems to shape their reaction. If one is a shnook, it is all right for one to suffer—eat a worm. If one is brave and noble, then it is appropriate to eat a worm for a worthy cause.

Is it possible that the attempt to see one's world as just is only one way that people create a meaningful world? Bulman and Wortman (1977) studied twenty-nine accident victims who were paralyzed from the waist (paraplegic) or neck (quadriplegic). They wanted to know how these young people were coming to terms with their fate. Taking the respondents' answers at face value, the authors concluded that there was little evidence that people are motivated to avoid blame for their victimization, as the defensive attribution hypothesis would predict. In general, the respondents tended to attribute more blame to themselves than objective circumstances would warrant.

But Bulman and Wortman also found evidence that these victims were motivated to do much more than construct functional answers to the questions of how it happened and who, if anyone, was to blame. All but three of the victims construed their being crippled within a context which provided meaning for the event. Some saw their fate as natural and just. Another explanation, found primarily among those who exhibited a high degree of self-blame, portrayed the crippling accident as a "positive" event. By far the most frequently employed explanation placed the accident within God's plan, or that of another supernatural power. So it was, in fact, no "accident," and no "harm" was done.

The conclusion from these findings, generated in diverse situations, is that people are impelled, possibly by habit and certainly by a strongly felt need, to perceive what happens to themselves and others in their world as manifestations of a "just world." This perception is maintained by interpreting all nontrivial events as not only understandable or controllable, but as evidence that everything ultimately turns out for the best. At times, this requires that the person find or invent reasons why seemingly innocent victims are inflicted with deprivation and suffering. Although we really don't know enough to predict ahead of time what kinds of reasons the person will find, we do know in outline the form these reasons will take, and have a much better idea of the strength of this drive.

The person may, for example, find the victim responsible for his own fate by virtue of his actions, and that attribution may be sufficient to satisfy the demand that the fate be just. When the assigning of behavioral responsibility is not sufficient, then people look for more reasons for why it is a just world after all. It must be true that people deserve what happens to them, deserve in the sense that "good things" happen to good people, and only the "bad" are made to suffer! Since there can be no doubt about this rule of life, then being betrayed by one's partner, or raped, or forced to eat a worm, or assaulted by a policeman, or inflicted with severe electric shocks, or crippled from the waist down—all of these fates are not "injustices," they are deserved by virtue of who you are, what you have done, what Life or God has planned for you.

I need to believe all this so strongly that I am willing, eager to find, if necessary, the justifying theme in the transgressions, failings, weaknesses, evil ways of myself and those I love. Why? Maybe because we need it to survive at all. That may be true, but certainly there are differences in the extent to which each of us must hold on to this kind of "fairy tale" view of life, and there are probably differences in the particular scenario, or "style," we employ to create the justness of our world. More about that later.

The Dangers in Identification with Victims

What Can We Learn from a Horrible Example?

No matter how much I try to take a good hard look at life, it doesn't really work. The unresolvable issue is not a matter of being afraid, or wanting to avoid suffering. Most people can accommodate to pain, given enough time. And there are ways to neutralize the awareness that there is a great deal one cannot control or predict, by building in to our plans a margin of expected "error." We treat the uncontrollable, unanticipatable as a predictable part of life. All that is familiar and relatively easy. But then those things happen that make me aware that I invent fictions and fairy tales to live by, and, what is more, I realize that I want and need them.

On the front page of our local newspaper, there was a description of a crime. An elderly woman was attacked in her apartment. She was robbed and the thief cut out both of her eyes. I know this much only because it was contained in the opening few lines of the first of a series of articles on the crime. I could not, would not, read all the first article, much less any of the subsequent reports of the woman's condition, the police efforts to apprehend the criminal, because I cannot live with that event. I have to pretend that things like that just do not happen. Why? I am not sure. There may be many reasons. Possibly, hopefully, if we examine our reactions to such events—those too horrible to accept as real—we can learn something about ourselves and the myths we need to construct.

One place to begin is to ask ourselves what we could add to or change in the scenario that would make it less devastating. What if the threat to our future security were removed? The criminal was apprehended and discovered to be totally insane, and we were informed by the most credible experts imaginable that the probability of such an event occuring again was virtually zero. But is it possible for any form of verbal assurance to be sufficiently persuasive that it eliminates the fear component? Or, what if we learn instead that the criminal was apprehended, that his past was full of suffering and misery, and/or that he will be given an equal punishment—an eye for an eye. Would that have an effect on your reaction? Frankly, that would do little to reduce the horror of the event for me. In fact, it might increase it. To be sure, if somehow I learned that the criminal was gloating over what he had done, and leading a luxuriant happy life, it might add a sufficient increment so that I would conclude that the whole world had gone mad.

Frankly, there is nothing I can conceive of concerning the criminal's past or future that could ameliorate the powerful impact of the crime to any significant degree. What about the victim, then? Is there anything we could learn about her past or future that would make a difference? The evidence one can find in the history of our culture and the research presented here points to two related possibilities. If this victim had herself committed horrible crimes in the past, I might be able to live with her fate. Especially if additional "fairy tale" elements were added, so that the "criminal" had been the husband or the father of one of her victims, and had been driven insane by the tragedy she had inflicted on him. And thus the evil that was done generated its own punishment. "As ye sow, so shall ye reap." The other possibility is that the victim's suffering is more than compensated for by what will happen to her in the future. She is a martyred saint, who finds her just reward in heaven.

Except for a lingering sense of revulsion at the thought of the "crime" itself, these latter scenarios would probably do the job, and not only enable me to live with the event, but prompt me to use it to teach my children about how justice reigns in our world. And, hopefully, they would pass it on to their children, as we do the stories about Joan of Arc, Job, Jesus, what God did to the Egyptians, and those happy ceremonies when we relive how wonderful it was when the evil King Haman got his in the end. Those possibilities, even in kind, are not available to me in this case. Part of the reason they are not leads to a discussion once again of the meaning of "identification" with the victim, while others open up the issue of differences in belief systems, and how they are related to the need for justice.

It is highly improbable that any of us could resort to derogating the elderly woman, no matter how much we might want to do that for our own comfort or sanity. Why not? By this time, we certainly have produced ample evidence from the laboratory, interviews with accident victims, and common examples in our own lives, that we are willing at times to derogate ourselves and people whom we love. "Derogate" in this context means finding or inventing attributes which do provide a sense of appropriateness to an undesirable event, even though they are reprehensible or demeaning.

If we are willing and able to do this with familiar loved ones, why not the old lady who was a complete stranger to us until this moment? The answer is that "identification" of the sort that matters in the way we react to victims is not something that happens with people. We do not identify with ourselves, our children, but rather with attributes, qualities that represent central values for us. And we react to the presence of those attributes in whomever or whatever they appear. Think for a moment of when we are angry with ourselves and our family: we may not only be willing to see one of us suffer, but at times will actively induce an appropriate "deserved" amount of pain. This occurs subsequent to the judgment that we have been clumsy, lazy, selfish, cruel. Compare those reactions to what we feel when we hear of almost any child hurt by an adult. Or happen to hear of or witness someone abusing a puppy. Can you imagine anything more infuriating then the image of some big brute kicking a puppy? Children, puppies, elderly people, represent the attributes of dependency, vulnerability, innocence. They are to be loved, revered, nurtured. They deserve, are "entitled" to, such treatment. In addition, it is virtually inconceivable that children or elderly people could have been sufficiently cruel or selfish to have merited painful fates.

Of course, "identification" with victims can take other forms. One of the more familiar of these occurs when we see ourselves "in the victim's shoes." That, of course, is what the Aderman, Brehm and Katz (1974) experiment was supposed to be about. And it may be true, as their findings suggest, that vicariously experiencing the victim's suffering, along with implicit instructions to be sympathetic, will eliminate the tendency to derogate the victim. But we also know that the vicarious experience, the empathic reaction, by itself is a precondition for derogation of a victim (Lerner, 1971a; Simons & Piliavin, 1972).

A variation of this form of identification occurs when we recognize that we are vulnerable to the same general circumstances surrounding the victim's suffering. The victim's fate is taken as a warning, and we actively seek out ways to insure that we will be more fortunate. Presumably, having been forewarned we discover how to act differently and avoid the pitfall, or generate evidence that in fact we are sufficiently "different" from the victim that we need not concern ourselves with the possibility that "it" could happen to us. But what if we can't do either of those two things, and it is truly a terrible fate, of which all of us are frightened?

Two Experimental Tests of How We React to "Similar Victims"

Two experiments were designed to generate some evidence about how we react in those circumstances. The idea for the first experiment (Novak & Lerner, 1968) actually came out of a rather routine inteview with one of the psychiatrists on the faculty of the University of Kentucky college of medicine. The interview was intended to examine the way physicians maintained their "detached concern" while dealing with patients, and so one standard line of questions centered around those occasions they could recall when they stopped being doctors, and found themselves reacting to a patient as any layman would. This psychiatrist related one incident that was important to him. He had been interviewing a patient who had just been admitted to the psychiatric ward of the hospital, after having had an acute psychotic episode. The psychiatrist was forced to teminate the interview, as he learned that, not only was his patient a young physician as well, but his personal style, early life history, etc., was remarkably similar to his own, or, at least, so it seemed at the time. The net effect of this similarity-establishing information as it emerged was not simply to establish an "empathic" or "sympathetic" set. More than anything else, it scared the hell out of the clinician. "That could be me." "Why not?"

The idea of going crazy probably would frighten any of us, if we were confronted with someone who was very much like us, reminded of us ourselves in important ways. It seems likely that we might wonder if that could happen to us; once having raised the question in any serious way, how could we answer it so as to restore our confidence that we are safe from a similar fate? Can we tell ourselves that we know how to avoid going crazy? Neither science nor common sense offers us any great assurance. The other path to regaining our security is to convince ourselves that we are really different from that poor soul; but reality constraints make this alternative difficult, if not impossible. While we are struggling with that solution, it is fairly clear that we will be rather upset, frightened, and actually have only one alternative left, to try to blot out the entire matter, run away from it psychologically, and physically if necessary. That is what the talented and sensitive young psychiatrist had to do, even knowing a great deal about the origins of mental illness.

As we thought about translating these ideas into testable hypotheses, it became apparent that our findings could speak to the issue of processes involved in interpersonal attraction generally. It is a virtual truism in social psychology that "liking" or positive affect, and "similarity" of any sort between people, are inextricably linked. And since Heider (1958), Homans (1961), and Newcomb (1961), a behavioral component has been added to the "liking" (affect), perception of similarity. People who like one another, or think they are similar to one another, are more likely to want to be together. The perceptions of difference or dislike lead people to avoid one another, or possibly do harm or compete if they are forced to interact.

It was obvious that the situation we had in mind should generate quite contradictory results. We felt confident that we could replicate the results predicted by reinforcement and balance theories (see Byrne, 1971; Newcomb, 1961, Rokeach, 1971), and that people would rate a similar "stranger" as considerably more desirable and likable than a "stranger" who was very different on the same dimensions. In addition, if given the opportunity to meet and chat with a "stranger," they would show a more marked preference for approaching the similar stranger, than one who was "essentially different."

But then we added, in other conditions, the single bit of information which should elicit a rather different set of reactions. Along with the same degree of similarity or difference, we had the subjects learn inadvertently that the other person had been mentally ill—had gone crazy. The "stranger" in the next room wrote on a personal data sheet, ostensibly for the experimenter's benefit:

> I don't know if this is relevant or not, but last fall I had kind of a nervous breakdown and I had to be hospitalized for a while. I've been seeing a psychiatrist ever since. As you probably noticed, I'm pretty shaky right now. (Novak & Lerner, 1968, p. 149)

We of course expected that this news might lessen somewhat the degree of perceived similarity with the other, and have a correspondent effect on measures of liking or ascribed attractiveness. That would fit with virtually all the available theories. But, in addition, we expected a complete reversal in the subjects' desire to meet and interact with the other person, who was mentally ill. These young people would be more bothered by someone who was so remarkably similar to them and had gone crazy—enough to be hospitalized—than by someone who had suffered the same fate, but was totally different from them in virtually every respect (except age and sex). The latter person might actually elicit some interest based on curiosity, a sense of superiority, or a desire to help the poor thing.

The net effect would be to provide a clear instance of "similarity," leading to avoidance, while "difference" elicited a tendency to approach. As we and others had shown in earlier research (e.g. Lerner & Becker, 1965, Lerner, Dillehay, & Sherer, 1967), these reactions of "similarity," liking, and approach–avoidance are not inextricably linked together in people's minds by a simple mechanism of "reinforcement" or "cognitive balance." People interpret and react to information about similarities and differences with others in terms of the particular meaning they have in that situation for the person's values and goals. That was certainly not an original idea. Both Asch (1952) and Jones and Thibaut (1958) had much earlier made very compelling systematic statements to this effect. But apparently they had been temporarily lost in the interpersonal-attraction literature. In addition, of course, we expected to be able to say something about the motives and goals of these young people in our experiment, and how they affect the reaction to a victim—this time someone suffering from "mental illness."

The experiment was cast in the general framework of a study of impression formation; presumably the subjects exchanged information about one another, and then used their best hunches to guess what the other person was like. Of course, the information they exchanged revealed their background, attitudes, and aspirations. The information subjects received was tailored by a tried-and-true formula to be plausibly very similar to, or very different from, their own. In addition, half the subjects in each of those conditions were given the opportunity to learn inadvertently that the other person was mentally ill. The subjects then described their impressions on various measures, including the highly evaluative bipolar adjectives that had been used profitably in this line of research.

The other main measure—the desire to approach or avoid the other person—was fitted in to the general context of the situation by informing the subjects, subsequent to their ratings of the other, that for the second part of the experiment we were interested in studying the way people go about making an impression on others. Each subject was given a choice of actually interacting with the other for 10 or 15 minutes, or spending the same period of time writing out how he generally went about meeting someone else for the first time. In order to turn this choice into a dimension, the subjects were also asked to check on a nine-point scale the extent to which they cared whether their choice was granted. This yielded a dimension from "want to interact" and "very important that I have my choice" to "very important that I am allowed to stay alone in any room and write out my ideas."

The main findings are summarized in the next three tables, taken from Novak and Lerner, 1968. If we set aside the unanticipated, and, for our purposes here, irrelevant findings associated with the sex of the subject, the results are rather clear. The experimental manipulations had their intended effect on the subjects' perception of general similarity to the other person. The "similar" other was seen as more similar than the "different." And the mentally handicapped other was seen as less similar than the "normal." The same main effects appeared on the subjects' evaluations of the other's attractiveness, Similar more attractive than Dissimilar, the Normal more attractive than Mentally Handicapped. Of most interest, of course, were the Approach–Avoidance reactions.

Table 23
Perceived Similarity: Means and Analysis of Variance for "Similarity" Question[a, b]

	Normal		Disturbed	
	Male	Female	Male	Female
Similar	3.250[c]	1.583	4.833	5.083
Dissimilar	7.083	8.333	7.333	9.333

Analysis of variance			
Source	df	MS	F
Similarity (A)	1	450.667	212.458[f]
Handicap (B)	1	60.167	28.365[f]
Sex (C)	1	5.042	2.377
A × B	1	22.042	10.391[e]
A × C	1	10.667	5.029[d]
B × C	1	32.667	15.400[f]
A × B × C	1	2.040	< 1
Within cells	88	2.121	

[a]From Novak & Lerner (1968).
[b]$N = 12$ per cell.
[c]The lower the mean score, the greater the perceived similarity.
[d]$p = < .05$.
[e]$p = < .01$.
[f]$p = < .001$.

Table 24
Subjects' Ratings of Partner's Attractiveness
(Bipolar Adjective Scale): Means and Analysis of Variance[a, b]

	Normal		Disturbed	
	Male	Female	Male	Female
Similar	129.083[c]	123.333	112.583	105.417
Dissimilar	94.083	85.583	96.083	76.250

Analysis of variance			
Source	df	MS	F
Similarity (A)	1	21,033.760	88.561[f]
Handicap (B)	1	2614.594	11.008[e]
Sex (C)	1	2552.344	10.746[e]
A × B	1	1100.260	4.632[d]
A × C	1	356.510	1.501
B × C	1	243.844	1.027
A × B × C	1	147.510	< 1
Within cells	88	237.505	

[a]From Novak & Lerner, (1968).
[b]$N = 12$ per cell.
[c]The higher the mean score, the more positive the rating of attractiveness.
[d]$p = < .05$.
[e]$p = < .01$.
[f]$p = < .001$.

The expected interaction appeared rather clearly for both the young men and women.

Although the findings were in line with our expectations, we did not leave it at that. In a second experiment (Lerner & Agar, 1972), we employed a different "victim," a 20-year-old former university student, male, an opiate addict who was in the hospital in order to withdraw from his serious addiction. Some time earlier, he had been injured in an automobile accident, and had been given morphine while under treatment. An additional independent variable was the source of the addiction. In one set of conditions (Internal Cause), the subjects read the following case history information:

> It has been discovered that while in the hospital Mr. Howel would complain of greater pain than he was actually suffering in order to receive morphine injections. He now admits that he "liked the feeling it gave him," that it was "like being drunk, only better." (p. 71.)

An external cause was established for some subjects by an alternative description:

> It has been discovered that the physician under whose care Mr. Howel had been, had

indiscriminately administered large doses of morphine to him during his hospital treatment. The physician had also inappropriately administered the drug to the patient after his discharge from the hospital. Although aware of the fact that his patient had become addicted, the physician failed to advise the patient of this condition. (p. 71)

Obviously, there was a strong effect on rated attractiveness of the other induced, by the Similar–Dissimilar manipulation (see Table 26). The dissimilar other was assigned considerably less attractive attributes. What is more interesting, however, is that a clear interaction occurs between the two main variables, Addict–Normal and Similar–Dissimilar (combining the two addictions) (F (1/52 df) = 7.34, p <.01). The combination of dissimilar attributes and morphine addiction created a more appealing or admirable impression than these dissimilar qualities associated with a Normal person, a "nonaddict," and the opposite effect holds for similarity and addiction. Although we could easily generate plausible reasons for this finding, they would not add particularly to our present interest. The approach-avoidance index yielded extremely pertinent and interesting data.

If one combines both addict conditions, there is a clear replication of the earlier finding. The similar addict is avoided, and the same degree of similarity

Table 25
Avoidance Index: Means and Analysis of Variance[a, b]

	Normal		Disturbed	
	Male	Female	Male	Female
Similar	6.750[c]	4.750	9.917	10.000
Dissimilar	10.167	10.167	6.583	7.750

Analysis of variance

Source	df	MS	F
Similarity (A)	1	15.844	1
Handicap (B)	1	8.760	< 1
Sex (C)	1	.844	< 1
A × B	1	311.760	11.991[d]
A × C	1	14.261	< 1
B × C	1	15.844	< 1
A × B × C	1	1.261	< 1
Within cells	88	25.999	

[a]From Novak & Lerner (1968).
[b]N = 12 per cell.
[c]The higher the mean score, the greater the unwillingness to interact with the partner.
[d]p = < .001.

Table 26
Subject's Ratings of Patient's Attractiveness
as Measured by Bipolar Adjective Scale[a]

	Addict		
	Internal	External	Normal
Similar	99.70	97.00	107.55
	(N = 10)	(N = 9)	(N = 9)
Dissimilar	78.82	81.50	64.71
	(N = 11)	(N = 10)	(N = 7)

[a]From Lerner & Agar (1972).

except for the addiction leads to a clear tendency to approach, to want to meet and talk with the other. The "dissimilar" normal person is avoided more than if he were a morphine addict about to be withdrawn.

As Table 27 shows, there was also an unexpected difference between the tendency to approach an addict who was portrayed as having brought about his own addiction out of his craving for the drug (Internal Cause), and the clearly innocent victim of a physician's incompetence (External Cause). We had expected that the latter, "Innocent" victim would be more threatening to the subjects' sense of security—after all, anyone could be an innocent victim—and thus elicit the greatest avoidance when combined with the attributes that gen-

Table 27
Approach–Avoidance Index: Means and Analysis of Variance (Addict)[a, b]

	Addict		
	Internal	External	Normal
Similar	3.50	8.22	13.44
	(N = 10)	(N = 9)	(N = 9)
Dissimilar	9.73	14.20	10.57
	(N = 11)	(N = 10)	(N = 7)

Analysis of variance			
Source	df	MS	F
Cause (C)	1	211.67	13.05[c]
Similarity (S)	1	373.64	23.03[c]
C × S	1	.01	< 1
Within cell	36	16.233	

[a]From Lerner & Agar (1972).
[b]The higher the score the stronger the approach.
[c]$p < .001$.

erated a strong impression of similarity with the victim. Just the opposite oc-
cured. The similar addict was avoided more when he was portrayed as the
"cause" of his addiction than when relatively innocent. Why?

One possibility is that, since he brought about his own miserable fate, he
was seen as personally reprehensible. The evidence does not support that explanation. If anything, the similar-internal addict is seen as a relatively attractive person, considerably more attractive and desirable than, for example, the
dissimilar addict who elicits a much greater willingness to approach.

So it is unlikely that subjects avoid the similar blameworthy addict because
they find him personally unattractive. One other possibility consistent with the
general line of thinking underlying this research is that we were dead wrong
about which addict condition would be most likely to elicit the sense of "identification." Of course, the subjects were able to "identify" somewhat with the
relatively innocent victim (external cause), but they truly saw themselves in the
victim who brought about his own grief because he had given in to the good
feeling generated by the drug. Almost all of us have gone through the experience of drinking or eating too much, to our predictable detriment, solely because we wanted the "good feeling" it gave us. Although the internal addict
who was similar in so many ways had "control" over what happened to him, it
is the kind of control that we all misuse.

No data generated in this experiment speak directly to this explanation.
As it happens, the decision to exclude the seemingly useless, direct assessment
of the extent to which the subjects viewed the other as similar or different was
particularly unfortunate. At the least, we might have had some evidence about
whether our similar internal addict was seen as more or less similar than the
similar addict whose physician caused the addiction.

If we put the data from the two experiments together, they provide storng
confirmation of the theoretical hypotheses, and indirectly for the line of reasoning that generated the entire experimental situation. In a sense, though, as
nicely supportive as they appear, it is important to recognize at some point that
the results provide only indirect evidence for the social psychological processes
which interest us. Although I would not have thought of doing so at the time, I
do regret that we did not have our subjects, or others, tell us fairly directly how
upset they were by the victims we created for them. What thoughts did they
have when they learned that another person their same age, sex, and just about
everything else imaginable, had gone crazy? And what was their reaction to the
possibility that they would actually meet and talk with such a person? Was it
truly threatening to their sense of security? Did they want to reestablish their
comfort by derogating the victim, or by trying to find ways in which they were
truly different? And, failing those efforts, did they remain relatively anxious,
insecure, and eager to forget the whole business as soon as possible?

The findings certainly fit very well what one would expect, were these processes actually going on. Although the data generated in somewhat indirectly

related experiments suggest that more than one set of factors may have accounted for the reaction of *some* of our subjects (Cooper & Jones, 1969; Taylor & Mettee, 1971), the overwhelming conclusion is that victims who remind us of ourselves are more likely to be avoided than those who are obviously "different" from us, especially when there is no possibility that we can intervene on their behalf.

Identification with Victims—Some Concluding Thoughts

What does this all mean, then, in relation to identification—the concern with justice, and the way we react to victims? It is a reasonable conclusion that we will be more bothered by the awareness of the suffering of someone with whom we are identified than someone with whom this identification is weaker or nonexistent. And we have good reason to believe that we "identify" with others in different ways, either because we are attached to them, because they embody important virtues and values, or because we see ourselves as vulnerable to the same causal events. And the evidence seems to add up to the conclusion that, although there are probably important differences associated with each of these forms of identification, there are some particularly important common features in addition to the dimension of greater involvement with the fate of the "identified-with" victim.

What seems to prevail as the dominant concern about the "fate" of those with whom we identify is that they have what they deserve, that they are not victimized by themselves or others. The experimental findings from Simmons and Lerner, Comer and Laird, Bulman and Wortman, confirm that we are willing, at times eager, to find "fault" with those we care about, to blame them for things that happened to them. It is acceptable for them to suffer if it is "deserved." We accept and possibly need this view of life and its travails. If anything, the evidence indicates that the more "identified" we are with someone by any of the possible links, the more important it is for us to find this link between what happens to them and what they deserve. We have also uncovered evidence about what we do when our ties to reality prevent us from finding the needed "justification" for what happened. We try to run away from those victims whose suffering makes no sense by any rules of a just world. And if that is not possible, we may discover that no injustice has occurred after all.

CHAPTER **10**

Who Believes in a Just World
Dimension or Style?

Throughout this book, I have been referring to the way "people" react. The clear implication, of course, is that we all need to and do believe that we live in a just world, where rules of deserving and justice apply. But not all people believe that they live in a just world and probably not everyone cares whether the world is just or not. And there probably are some people who would prefer to believe that the world is a miserable jungle run by cynical forces, and that tragedy, pathos, and emptiness are the central themes of human existence.

As it turns out, there are some interesting aspects to this matter of individual differences in the extent to which people maintain their belief in a just world. Many of these are reflected in the kinds of comments and questions I often get after describing the just-world ideas to an audience that has never been exposed to them before. Along with the customary friendly reactions, someone sooner or later announces that of course she/he does not believe that the world is a "just" place. People are out for what they can get, limited only by the constraints induced by the anticipation of internal or external sanctions. At that point, I typically administer the "empathy test"; I describe the signs of human misery and degradation one can see on any tour of the slums, a psychiatric ward, or nursing home for the elderly. Or, I may describe some of the sequences involved in the subincision rites portrayed in the film that Lazarus, *et al.* (1962) used in their research.

137

Some people "flunk" the test. Their cool or condeming indifference is not a defense; they really don't give a damn. I think they are people whose very early life experiences were such that the normal developmental processes, including attachments to other people, never appeared. My diagnosis may be incorrect, but, in any case, from what I can see through casual observation and in research situations, these people are relatively few in number.

A more interesting variation of this same issue appears in another set of questions. "Are you saying, then, that there are no normal individual differences, that everyone needs to and does believe she/he lives in a just world?" Some important aspects of the Just World ideas are revealed by that sort of question. For example, I find myself confessing, privately if not out loud, that my best hunch is that, within the range of what we mean by normal, all people will develop a "belief in a just world" sufficient to enable them to function adequately in their society. Given a reasonably stable and complex environment, they will "naturally" develop a commitment to deserving as the central theme in their goalseeking activities. And, given the "normal" processes whereby people form attachments to one another, this commitment to deserving will be manifested in a commitment to justice for oneself and others—a just world.

The question remains whether those assumptions are tantamount to asserting that everyone has the same degree or form of belief in a just world. Obviously not. Beyond a requisite amount of belief or trust in the justness of their world, people certainly can and do differ in their view of their world, including the way they find justice in it.

The Rubin and Peplau BJW Scale

A Description of the Scale

One way of looking at this issue is to assume, as did Rubin and Peplau, that the belief in a just world is

> an attitudinal continuum extending between two poles of total acceptance and total rejection of the notion that the world is a just place. (1975, p. 66)

Setting aside for the moment the question of whether this is a valid portrayal of the psychometric or psychological properties of the "Belief in a Just World" the facts have borne out the heuristic value of their approach. The items on the scale have a great deal of "face" validity. I cannot imagine a more straightforward way of asking someone if they believe they live in a just world, then asking them whether they agree with the statement, "Basically, the world is a just place," or "By and large, people get what they deserve" (1975, p. 69). To be sure, some of the other items have more explicit referents, and are a little more subtle, but not much more.

In the most recent form of their "Just World Scale," the person is offered three degrees of agreement or disagreement to select from—very much, somewhat, slightly—which yields a six-point continuum for each item. The scores are summed for all the items, yielding a minimum score of 20, with a maximum of 120 indicating complete affirmation of the justness of one's world. The items are as follows:

- Good deeds often go unnoticed and unrewarded.
- When parents punish their children, it is almost always for good reasons.
- It is rare for an innocent man to be wrongly sent to jail.
- People who get "lucky breaks" have usually earned their good fortune.
- Students almost always deserve the grades they receive in school.
- It is often impossible for a person to receive a fair trial in this country.
- Careful drivers are just as likely to get hurt in traffic accidents as careless ones.
- Men who keep in shape have little chance of suffering a heart attack.
- Crime doesn't pay.
- In professional sports, many fouls and infractions never get called by the referee.
- Although evil men may hold political power for a while, in the general course of history good wins out.
- People who meet with misfortune often have brought it on themselves.
- Basically, the world is a just place.
- I've found that a person rarely deserves the reputation he has.
- The political candidate who sticks up for his principles rarely gets elected.
- By and large, people deserve what they get.
- Parents tend to overlook the things most to be admired in their children.
- In any business or profession, people who do their job well rise to the top.
- Many people suffer through absolutely no fault of their own.
- It is a common occurrence for a guilty person to get off free in Canadian courts.

With an "instrument" that measures a personal construct, psychologists often act as if they have found a "peek-a-scope" that enables them to look directly into, or at least catch a glimpse of, someone's psyche. If you believe that, and have a great deal of courage, then opportunities open up for testing theoretically important hypotheses. After all, up to this point our anecdotes, and especially the experimentally generated data, all depend upon a rather elaborate and often unspecified set of inferential leaps concerning what is going on inside those who observe suffering and deprivation. We can only infer that the differences in average scores across the various conditions are a function of something going on inside the observers, that something being the need to believe in a just world. But now, with an "instrument," we can more directly examine the link between the way people react to events in their environment and their belief in a just world. Remember, we are assuming at this point that people have more or less of this belief, and that those with more are the ones most likely to exhibit the characteristics and reactions we have assumed reflect the person's attempt to maintain this belief.

BJW Scale—Reactions to the Victims of the Draft Lottery

Let us look frst at the empirical validity of the Just World Scale. What meaningful behaviors are correlated with the person's total score on this scale?

It is only right that the most ambitious, and in some ways the most severe, test of the validity of the Rubin and Peplau "BJW" Scale should have been conducted by the authors. Using the draft lottery created during the Vietnam war, they gathered together 58 draft-eligible young men in groups of approximately six each to listen to the broadcast of the 1971 lottery which would determine the likelihood, and in some cases the certainty, that they would be drafted into the armed forces. Fifty of the 58 participants were recruits from the university communities in and around Boston. They came together before the lottery, and filled out a series of questionnaires, including the BJW scale. After learning their respective fates, they completed another series of questionnaires, some of which were repeats.

One of Rubin and Peplau's most remarkable findings was that, regardless of BJW scores, there was a strong association between the person's fate in the lottery and his subsequently measured "self-esteem." It appeared that those who had relatively bad draft rankings were likely to lower their self-esteem, and those who had good ones revealed an enhanced self-concept. Why should that have happened? There may have been something artifactual built into the measure, so that it was inappropriately sensitive to the respondents' shift in mood (Cobb, Brooks, Kasl, & Connelly, 1966). Or is it conceivable that these young men actually went through the primitive response of condemning themselves for their fate, seeing their terrible fate as punishment, retribution, for past sins? It is hard to tell what that single finding means, but it is intriguing.

Their analysis of the relation between the young men's BJW scores and their reactions to one another subsequent to learning their respective fates generated rather remarkable findings. Those BJW whose scores were in the top third of this gorup were affected by the knowledge of the other person's fate in ways that distinguished them from the others. Overall, there was a general tendency to express sympathy and liking for the lottery "losers." However, those in the top third on the belief in a just world displayed the theoretically expected tendency to "reject" these innocent victims. For example, the more probable it was that one of their group members would be drafted, the less liking for and comfort with that person. In fact, they expressed measurably greater "resentment" toward those who were most likely to be victimized by the system (Rubin & Peplau, 1973).

Actually, I find these results rather astounding. Consider, for example, that the measures and ratings employed as dependent variables were rather crude indices of unestablished reliability, let alone validity. Also, their subjects were a fairly homogeneous lot in terms of background, education, and general level of sophistication. The vast majority were members of the subculture found in the Eastern University environment, a very "savvy," bright, politically and socially aware, "liberal" group. These are not the kind of folks that one would expect to endorse the "obvious," almost childlike magical belief in the justness of one's world that is offered by the items on the BJW Scale. Although Rubin and Peplau report no absolute scores, it is most likely that even the third of their sample that achieved the highest BJW scores found it difficult to subscribe fully to most aspects of the belief system assessed by that scale. There is also the fact that these young men had sufficient reason and opportunity to feel closely identified with one another. They had a great deal in common, including a common task and a potentially shared fate. And finally, by the time they learned of their individual fates, they had spent sufficient time together to form some impressions of one another as a background against which the "just world" effect had to appear. All things considered, it is truly remarkable that Rubin and Peplau found any effect at all, much less one that fit their theoretical model.

When I read a study like this, with highly improbable but theoretically exciting findings, I often have two rather different reactions. One, usually the initial reaction, is to be terribly impressed. If, given all the noise in the design, sample, and measures, the results still appear to some significant extent, then it follows that the underlying process being tapped must be very powerful. I am fully convinced. But then, later, I tend to worry. If the odds were so great against the theoretically posited reason for the effects to appear, then a more immediate artifact in the procedure must have created the results. Certainly, with a correlational study, one has to be especially concerned about "third variable" effects.

BJW Scale and Reactions to Injustices in Society

A number of subsequent efforts did more than assuage my doubts about the BJW Scale. For example, more than one investigator has found a clear relationship between people's BJW scores and their responsiveness to issues of justice associated with criminal acts. High BJW "jurists" are both more likely to give stiff sentences to defendants who have been convicted of a crime such as negligent homicide (Gerbasi & Zuckerman, 1975; Izzett, 1974), and also to find the victims more culpable and "deserving" of their fate. This latter effect appeared even with the victim of a clear case of rape (Gerbasi, Zuckerman, & Reis, 1977). Both of these reactions seem to be direct results of the person's greater concern with seeing to it that justice prevails, that no real harm was done, and in any case the harm-doer will certainly be punished sufficiently. There is also the entire set of reactions that are virtually the opposite or mirror image of the tendency to condemn victims: the attempt to restore justice by helping victims.

One could reasonably interpret the meaning of a high score on the Rubin and Peplau (1975) scale in more than one way. Someone who agrees, for example, with the assertion that "All the world is a just place," or disagrees with "Good deeds often go unnoticed or unrewarded," could be reflecting rather directly the belief system that was inculcated by the socializing agents in their environment. This is what their friends, parents, and religious leaders believe, and taught them to believe. And, as a result, they of course tend to interpret what they see happening around them to fit these beliefs.

On the other hand, many of the items on the BJW Scale tap a very naive view of social reality. I can't imagine how anyone could reasonably agree totally with such statements as: "In almost any business or profession, people who do their job well rise to the top," or "Crime doesn't pay," or "People who meet with misfortune have often brought it on themselves," or disagree with the assertion that "Many people suffer through absolutely no fault of their own." The common underlying theme appears to be a strong faith in the presence of an omniscient, omnipotent force, that sees to it that justice and goodness triumphs, and that wickedness is punished, as revealed explicitly in *Item 14:* "Although evil men may hold political power for a while, in the general course of history good wins out."

It seems plausible that the belief in a hand which guides everyone's destiny to ensure that justice prevails requires a motivated effort on the part of a reasonably bright and aware adult in our society. That person either would have to have been raised in an environment which screened out or prevented the processing of a great deal of information, or for some reason have refused to face the facts of life. If the latter is the case, then the condemnation of victims is essentially a "defensive" reaction generated to protect the belief in the all-seeing, all-protecting agent of justice.

Of course, it is difficult to generate definitive evidence concerning the validity of these alternative possibilities, especially when one realizes that, in all probability, some combination of these and many other processes are involved in the complex of reactions tapped by the BJW Scale. It should be possible, however, to approach these issues by examining the way those who manifest more or less of this form of "Belief in a Just World" react when confronted with the opportunity to act on behalf of a "victim"—to prevent or eliminate an instance of injustice.

It follows that, if the BJW measure assesses a motivationally based construction of social reality, then those with a strongly held belief should be more willing to engage in costly efforts to prevent an injustice than those who are more willing to accept the facts of life. Injustices often do occur, and, often enough, the bad guys win out over the good. What I am assuming at this point is that those people who get a high score on the BJW Scale are exhibiting a motivated distortion to meet their own needs, while those with lower scores are more "realistc," and at the other extreme possibly somewhat cynical or anomic. If this is the case, then it is a safe bet that those with high BJW scores will not only be likely to condemn victims, but will also be more altruistic than those with lower scores in the appropriate context. They should be more highly motivated to respond to the legitimate needs of other people.

There is a theoretically interesting qualification to this hypothesis. If high BJW's greater willingness to help is essentially a defensive reaction, then these people should be highly sensitive to the potential for actual restoration or prevention of an injustice. They will help when the circumstances indicate that their efforts will be completely successful, and sufficient to meet the demands of justice. When the complete elimination of the injustice is impossible or improbable to some degree, or when they do not have sufficient assurance that justice will prevail, then they may be less likely to try to help the victim, and more likely to engage in one of the other "defensive" reactions, such as denying the victim's fate, or construing the victim as the kind of person who deserves to suffer or be deprived.

A Test of the "Defensive" Component in BJW

Dale Miller (1977a) translated these ideas into a set of hypotheses amenable to experimental examination. He reasoned that, if a victim were portrayed as a single victim of injustice with relatively finite manageable needs, then those with a strong belief in a just world would be considerably more responsive than those with a weaker belief in a just world. Other things being equal, the latter people would have less motivation to incur the personal costs of helping the victim. If, however, the same victim were construed as one among many of a kind prevalent in society, the extra incentive for the high-BJW people to get involved in helping would be eliminated. In fact, one might conjecture that the high-BJW people would be more likely to avoid helping victims of unrelievable unjust deprivation. Rather than help, they might condemn.

The subjects Dale Miller employed were university students, who participated initially to a fairly pleasant task for experimental credit. At the end of that session, they were given the opportunity to volunteer for further sessions to work on similar tasks. Presumably, the experimenter with whom they had worked had left the situation, and would have no idea of their response to the

Table 28
Mean Number of Sessions Volunteered as a Function of Belief
in a Just World and Presentation of Victim[a]

	Presentation of victim		
Belief in a just world	Isolate	Group	Control
High	8.9	3.1	2.1
Low	3.0	3.9	4.3

[a]From Miller (1977a).

solicitation which appeared as a printed form to be completed by the subject.

The experimental conditions were created by variations in the information contained on this form. In the Control conditions, the subjects were informed that their help would be valuable to the experimenter, and they were asked to indicate the number of sessions they would be willing to do.

In the two experimental conditions they learned that the psychology department had been made aware of the case of a mother who had been deserted by her husband. She had great difficulty taking care of her family, especially since she was trying to go to secretarial school, and could only maintain a part-time job. Life was extremely difficult for her and her young children. It was also explained that there were no funds the department could give directly to this woman, but it would be possible to use the funds allocated for research if the participants would donate the $2.00 for each session they worked to the family. Each subject could volunteer for up to twenty sessions, with the pay going to this desperately needy family.

The only difference between the Isolate and the Group experimental conditions was that in the latter the subjects also learned that there were at least 300 other families in the area with similar needs. The individual need in all cases was emphasized by pointing out that "the welfare of Mrs. R. and her children is of immediate concern," and that they were only going to be asked to help Mrs. R. (Miller, 1977a, p. 117). The main dependent variable was the number of sessions elected by the subjects in each of these conditions.

The subjects had completed the BJW Scale earlier in a different setting, and for purposes of analysis they were divided into those above and below the median of their group. The findings can be seen in the following table. Essentially, there is one discrepant cell. The high-BJW subjects were very responsive to the opportunity to help the single victim. That reaction did not appear when the victim was portrayed as a member of a large group. It is also worth noting that there was no significant correlation between BJW scores and volunteer rates in the Group condition, but there was an $r = .56$ ($p < .06$) between these measures in the Isolate condition.

In a second experiment, Dale Miller varied the nature of the victimization by emphasizing that the solicitation to help was tied to the Christmas season—each year the psychology department raised funds for ten needy families. This he designated the Temporary suffering condition. In the Continuous suffering condition there was no mention made of the time of year. The act of help involved donating (anonymously) some part of the three dollars, or more if they wished, that they were paid for participating in the same sort of task that had been employed in the first experiment. It was clear, in all cases, that there would be no further solicitation of funds linked to their reaction to the appeal. Also, presumably no one could know if they gave anything at all to the victims. Again, for the purposes of analysis the subjects were divided into those who had scored above or below the median of their group on the BJW Scale. The main findings are revealed in the following table.

In this study it appears that the specific Christmas solicitation (Temporary) was more effective than the general request (Continuous), ($p < .025$). There was also an interaction between degree of BJW and kind of solicitation ($F = 3.24$). The high-BJW subjects were much more affected by the nature of the appeal, giving more than the low-BJW in the Temporary condition, and significantly less in the Continuous. The correlations between donations and BJW score is negative in the Continuous condition ($r = -.42$), and positive in the Temporary ($r = +.37$). These two correlations differed significantly from one another ($p < .05$).

Where the act of help is defined as a discrete event legitimized by the society, then the greater the BJW the more responsive the person. When the solicitation is portrayed as the opportunity to get involved in the ongoing suffering and deprivation in our society, then the higher the score on the BJW scale the less likely the person is to act on behalf of the victim. Apparently, then, those who score high on the BJW scale may be more or less willing to help victims than those who appear less "believing." The responsiveness of high-BJW people to the fate of others seems to be tailored to maintain or protect the belief in the pervasiveness of justice in what happens around them. Their reactions fit

Table 29
Mean Donation Rate (in Cents) as a Function of Belief in a Just World and the Duration of the Victims' Suffering[a, b]

Belief in a just world	Duration of the victim's suffering	
	Temporary	Continuous
High	167	62
Low	127[a]	109[a]

[a]From Miller (1977a).
[b]All means except those with a common superscript differ at the 5% level.

very well the motivational, defensively based meaning of a relatively high score on that scale.

The "Functional" Use of BJW-Related Acts: Appeasing the Gods

Some additional evidence for the "functional" basis of the kind of BJW measured by the Rubin and Peplau scale was generated in an ingenious effort by Miron Zuckerman (1975). In the first two of the experiments he reports, the main experimental variable was the "time" of a telephone appeal to volunteer for an altruistic act. The other independent variable was whether the subject's BJW score fell above (High BJW) or below the median for that sample (Low BJW). In the first experiment, subjects were called either five weeks before the midterm or two days before the midterm exam. In the second experiment, the two time periods were either four weeks before the final exam, or at the beginning of the final exam period. In the first experiment, the dependent variable was the number of experimental sessions volunteered. In the second experiment, subjects were asked to volunteer up to five hours to read to a blind student in night school. In the third experiment, the "time" variable was not manipulated. All subjects were called a week before final exams started to participate in a one-hour experiment. The results of the three studies can be seen in the following table.

During the normal course of the year, there was no discernible difference in the way high- or low-BJW students reacted to a request for help. However, just prior to an exam, a critical event in their lives, the high-BJW subjects were clearly more willing to be altruistic, to do a good deed for someone.

What Zuckerman had suspected is that people who held the kinds of beliefs tapped by the BJW Scale would be inclined to comply with a request for "help" at a time in their lives when they were very concerned about what the fates would bring them. It follows that someone who finds it easy to agree with such assertions as "People who get lucky breaks have usually earned their good fortune" is likely to be afraid to do anything to anger the fates, displease the

Table 30
The Effect of a Person's "Belief in a Just World" on Volunteering to Help[a]

	Exp. 1[b]		Exp. 2[b]		Exp. 3[c]
	Mid	Exam	Mid	Exam	Exam
HiBJW	2.83	3.17	2.70	1.35	43.7
LoBJW	3.33	2.17	2.32	.25	25

[a]Adapted from data presented in Zuckerman (1975).
[b]Number of hours volunteered.
[c]% agreeing to participate.

gods. Perhaps some of these students were in the throes of the kind of dialogue that many of us have experienced at times of great expectation or fear: "Just get me out of this one, God, and I will be good for the rest of my life." Before one of the *really* important events, we may engage in our personal set of magical rituals—the clothes we wear, when and how we review the material.

What this chain of reasoning assumes is that, for the high scorer on the BJW Scale, that system of beliefs provides a ready-made sanction for whatever happens to people, including one's self. In addition, it enters into the person's goalseeking in a functional sense. If I truly believe that people almost always get what they deserve, because that is the way the world is constructed, that is the way the "fates" work, then, on those occasions when I have a great investment in a certain outcome, I will take every opportunity to do something "good," I will try to prove to the fates that I am a "deserving" person, someone worthy of their favor.

The Miller and Zuckerman experiments accomplished at least two things. They created the basis for some confidence that the BJW Scale is actually measuring a relatively stable personal attribute involving a kind of belief in the way justice appears in one's world. Second, they shed considerable light on the motivational processes associated with this kind of belief system. Those who are in relatively great agreement with this view of the world will defend the viability of this belief, even when it is relatively costly to themselves in terms of other resources—their time and money. And at the same time, they will design their actions to meet the dictates of the belief system, being "extra" good in order to be "extra" deserving.

BJW as a Correlate of Social Attitudes

Possibly the most important test of the validity of the BJW measure is the extent to which it predicts the way people interpret what they see happening around them. We would expect, for example, that those who score relatively highly on the BJW measure construe virtually everything that happens to fit the general rule that essentially justice prevails, and the evidence indicates that this appears to be the case. For example, in their initial study, Rubin and Peplau (1973) reported survey data which indicate that, among a sample of university students, there was a significant correlation between BJW scores and the belief in an active God, the tendency to justify the plight of blacks and women, and a negative relation to their measures of social activism. Surprisingly, they found no significant correlation with attitudes toward the poor.

Peplau and Tyler in a U.C.L.A. study (1975) found the expected positive relation between BJW scores and the tendency to see political events in a positive sense, to see the status quo as desirable, and to be politically and economically conservative. Their high-BJW respondents were less cynical about politics and politicians; they were, for example, more likely to be opposed to impeachment and finding fault with Nixon's handling of Watergate.

Another Look at Reactions to the "Innocent Victim": BJW in the Lerner and Simmons Paradigm

Given the scale's demonstrated relation to the tendency to justify the status quo, including condemnation or lack of sympathy for victims in society at large, it would be valuable to go back to the situation that generated a great part of the experimental findings, and see if, in fact, "the Belief in a Just World" was an operative factor in determining how the people reacted to that victimization. Fortunately, Miron Zuckerman and his colleagues decided to do just that. (Zuckerman, Gerbasi, Kravitz, & Wheeler, 1975.)

Their design included three experimental conditions of varying "observational sets." In one, they replicated the instructions given to the Lerner and Simmons (1966) observers to be attentive to cues of emotional and physical arousal. In the second condition, they replicated the Aderman *et al.* (1974) "imagine self" instructions. In the third, designed to be a test of Godfrey and Lowe's (1975) interpretation of their findings, the observers were informed that they were actually watching an "obedience experiment" designed to see how long the victim would put up with the experimenter's instructions and continue to suffer. In addition to the three experimental conditions, the subjects were divided, in the analysis, into those whose BJW scores fell above or below the median of the entire group.

The central findings of the study were that (a) there were no differences in the assignment of negative attributes to the victim among the three experimental conditions, (b) there was a clear difference in reactions to the victim and various aspects of the experimental situation between observers with a High versus a Low Belief in a Just World—regardless of the experimentally induced set.

Not only was there a greater tendency to denigrate the victim's character among the high-BJW observers, but in response to other measures the high scores were more likely to describe the learning experiment as important (High = 81.1%, Low = 57.9%, X^2 = 3.71), less likely to see any cruelty involved (42.3% vs. 71.5%, X^2 = 4.84) and they responded more positively to the experiment in their freely written comments (83.3% vs. 63.2%, X^2 = 3.09). It was also interesting that fewer of the observers classified as high-BJW mentioned the possibility that the victim could have stopped the proceedings (11.2% vs. 42.1%, X^2 = 4.88).

Zuckerman *et al.* also constructed a composite score based upon the observer's response to those items assessing his/her view of the situation, and correlated this measure with the observer's reaction to the victim. Interestingly enough, they found a substantial positive relation between these two measures among the high-BJW subjects ($r = .50, p < .01$), whereas there was a negative relation among the low-BJW observers ($r = -.32$). The differences between these two correlations was highly significant.

What does this mean? According to Zuckerman *et al.*, and I tend to agree with them,

> These different patterns of correlations indicate that LBJW's tended to use either derogation or some situational evaluation to maintain their belief in a just world, while HBJW's supported their belief in more than one way. (p. 11)

The typical high-BJW observers not only derogated the victim, but they also saw the entire situation in a more positive light.

So we are again discussing the way people reacted to the young woman being shocked while she tried to remember pairs of nonsense syllables (Lerner & Simmons, 1966). We inferred then that the different degrees of denigration of the victim reflected the observers' motivated attempt to maintain their belief in a "just world": The greater the undeserved suffering, the more negative the view of the victim's personal characteristics, in order to "justify" her fate. Zuckerman and his colleagues have now provided us with considerably more confidence that the tendency to denigrate the "innocent victim" was, in fact, associated with the observers' commitment to the belief that people get what they deserve, as that belief is assessed by the items on the Rubin and Peplau BJW Scale. That is the same belief system associated with condemnation of the victim to be found in the larger society; an acceptance and active support of the political and social status quo, the willingness to help people in need if the outcome of their actions is almost certain to provide evidence that justice prevails, and, when faced with an impending critical event, engaging in symbolic acts, rituals, in order to appease the fates.

Construct Validity of BJW-Related Personal Dimensions:
"I-E," "F," "PEC," and Social Attitudes

The Belief in a Just World measure has proved most fruitful in generating research that established the "construct validity" of the measure, and at the same time provided important, invaluable, support for the hypotheses that the commitment to the belief that they live in a just world can lead people to condemn victims, and invent functional myths about themselves, social causality, and others.

But that is not all. Throughout this discussion of the Belief in a Just World —its origins, functions, effects, we have considered one or another alternative way of encompassing our findings within other more familiar theoretical explanations—cognitive dissonance, balance, generalization of social learning, various attributional and information processing models. The work with the BJW Scale has added an important dimension to this inquiry, by enabling us to examine the empirical ties between this system of belief and other related personal qualities or beliefs systems.

It is often the case, when describing the processes involved in the Just World hypothesis, that a sophisticated listener will point out that we seem to be talking about a "locus of control" dimension (Rotter, 1966); or that we are describing the psychology of the "Authoritarian" syndrome that Adorno *et al.* (1950) identified some time ago; or that we are speaking only about people who grow up in a culture dominated by the values of the Protestant Ethic (Mirels & Garrett, 1971). And, in fact, there is both some conceptual and empirical evidence to support their insights.

Our assertion that people have a need to believe they live in a world where people can get what they deserve, so that they are willing and able to engage in concerted efforts to get what they want, seems to conjure up the image of people who are highly invested in believing they can and do control important events. That seems to be what Rotter (1966) and his followers have described and measured as an "internal" locus of control orientation. The evidence in support of the predictive utility of this dimension is overwhelming. It is linked in theoretically meaningful ways with a wide range of behaviors.

Similarly, the tendency to see the status quo as desirable, including the condemnation of the "weak" and "inferior" folks in society, and the related adoption of a conservative political and social ideology, is what one would expect from those "Authoritarian" characters who score highly on one or another of the "F" (for Fascist) scales. These people are required, presumably by their own dynamics, to identify with the "strong" and the "status quo," and to condemn those who are "weak" and "different" (Adorno *et al.*, 1950).

The emphasis on deserving—usually through effort and self-deprivation—smacks of the Protestant Ethic ideology, which views hard work and suffering as the path to righteousness. Although salvation may not be achieved in this manner, it is through establishing that one's travails are in fact rewarded with earthly goods that one can find the signs that one is among the chosen, the saved. The items that were constructed by Mirels and Garrett (1971) to tap this dimension seem to reveal many common elements with Just World beliefs.

In their summary of the relevant literature, Rubin and Peplau (1975) report a number of studies which show a substantial correlation between their BJW measure and each of these dimensions. It seems reasonable to assume, then, that they do in fact tap something in common; but what? And what are the implications of these correlations for our understanding of the origins and function of the Belief in a Just World?

Although we may be stretching it a bit, the correlation with the Protestant Ethic measures may imply that there is a strong social learning component in the development of BJW. People adopt the belief as a function of their being socialized into the dominant cultural ethic. The association with the Authoritarian syndrome is consistent with the view that adults who manifest the BJW to any great degree are products of a particularly screwed-up family pattern. Their early history consisting of dogmatic, rigid parents prevented them from having the kind of experiences which would enable them to develop more advanced views of social rules, justice, and causality. They are still fixated somewhat at the early primitive stages of cognitive functioning (Adorno *et al.*, 1950; Kohlberg, 1969; Piaget, 1948). And, certainly, the strong association with Rotter's measure of locus of control (1966) implies that we are not measuring a concern with justice, but rather the belief in a certain kind of predictable and manageable environment, in which people can arrange their own fates.

Miron Zuckerman and his associates have conducted a number of studies to clarify the relation between the Belief in a Just World and the "internal-external" locus of control personal dimension (I–E) (Rotter, 1966). They were first able to show, on the basis of their own and others' work, that one could identify a "just world" component tapped by the I–E measure, and that this component, when looked at separately, did not yield the expected relation with other I–E related variables, such as preference for skill or chance or achievement motivation. The fact that this I–E factor did, however, correlate significantly with the Rubin and Peplau BJW measure helps explain the consistent relation other investigators have found between I–E and BJW (Zuckerman & Gerbasi, 1977a; Zuckerman, Gerbasi, & Marion, 1977).

Even more to the point were their and others' findings which showed that both the BJW component in the I–E and the Rubin and Peplau scales were related to political conservatism, interpersonal trust, and the adherence to traditional values, while the previously measured relations between the I–E total scale scores and these variables is eliminated if the BJW component is partialled out. It also appears that the relation between internality and political activity, as well as the reaction to victims, is mediated by the just world component (Zuckerman & Gerbasi, 1977b,c).

We decided to examine these personal dimensions as part of a course in social psychology; we wanted to see how they appear in the way a group of young adults view the society in which they live. Although there are good reasons, as described earlier, to believe that each of these dimensions—BJW, Internal–External locus of control, Authoritarianism, and Protestant Ethic beliefs, should show great similarities to the others in its relation to the perception of social events, nevertheless, there should be some important and interesting differences which can be teased out. For example, the pessimistic and angry Authoritarian view of the world is clearly at odds with the general optimism associated with the belief that one lives in a just world.

In order to reveal how these personal dimensions appeared in subjects' views of what was happening in their world, we provided them with a variety of social issues. We were particularly interested in how these dimensions were related to people's reactions to the disadvantaged and the "different" victims of society.

The subjects in this study (Lerner, 1978) were 106 university students taking a course in introductory social psychology. Each had at least one previous course in psychology, and almost all were beyond their first year of university. The first five questionnaires included measures of the dimensions discussed above. Subjects then responded to two other questionnaires, assessing their opinions about various categories or groups of people. Other items provided subjects with the opportunity to express their degree of satisfaction with contemporary mores, and their opinions concerning the state and future of their country. The items were combined on an a priori basis to yield twelve measures. The measures and examples of the items are:

Poverty and the poor:
> More money should be spent in caring for the poor.

Contemporary mores:
> The attitudes of the younger generation toward sex are more honest than those of previous generations.

Satisfaction and optimism:
> Canada will _____ in the next ten years. (alternatives from "generally improve" to "generally deteriorate")

Blame of United States and foreigners for holding back the advancement of Canada:
> The growth and advancement of Canada has been held back by the dominance of the culture and education by American influence.

Blame of fellow Canadians:
> Same stem as above followed by: The exploitation of Canadians by the Canadian business community.

Blame of radicals:
> Same stem as above followed by: Radicals and Subversive groups.

Attitude toward "Canadian Identity":
> An increased demand for the expression of a Canadian national identity could lead to greater self-respect.

The *Separatistes* in Quebec:
> Would develop a society that was better for everyone in Quebec, not only the French.
> Are using religious prejudices to create distrust of the Protestant English-speaking Canadians.

The Indians and Metis:
> Are denied the opportunities afforded to other, European-Canadians.
> Will stay on welfare and special grants as long as they can.

The Americans who come to Canada:
> Are a threat to the Canadian way of life.
> Contribute greatly to the Canadian scene.

The Jews in Canada:
>   Are a very warm and generous people.
>   Are among the first to sell out Canada to their American relatives.

The Maritime Provinces:
>   Have genuine pride in their way of life.
>   Expect the national government to take care of them and their problems.

Twenty-five measures were computed for each subject out of all the questionnaires. These scores were intercorrelated, using the Pearson Product Moment. The first principal components of this matrix were extracted and rotated to simple structure according to the VARIMAX criterion (Table 31).

Three of the four factors which emerged form this analysis seem to make good social psychological sense. The first factor resembles a general "Xenophobia." Although not all the minority or "alien" groups were represented on this factor, attitudes toward Jews, the poor, Americans, and Indians and Metis did have substantial loadings. The Xenophobia component also seems reflected in the items designed to measure acceptance of social change concerning sexual mores, marriage, drugs, and agents of change—such as radicals. This ethnocentrism takes on a very familiar meaning, with the high loading of the "F" Scale and Protestant Ethnic Scale. It would be no surprise to anyone to find that

Table 31
The Four Factors and the Items with Loadings Greater than .35[a]

Factor I		Factor II	
Item	Loading	Item	Loading
Protestant ethic scale	+ .66	Just world scale	+ .65
"F" scale	+ .63	Americans	+ .57
Blame radicals	+ .58	Satisfaction and optimism	+ .55
Contemporary mores	− .37	"Internal" locus of control	+ .36
Indians and Metis	− .39	Protestant ethic scale	+ .35
Americans	− .49	Indians and Metis	− .50
Poor	− .57		
Jews	− .73		

Factor III		Factor IV	
Item	Loading	Item	Loading
Size of community	+ .76	Social desirability scale	+ .50
Estimated SES	+ .55	Canadian identity	+ .47
Religious commitment (self)	− .56	Religious view of self	− .38
Ethnic ties (self)	− .78	Father's education	− .40
		Ethnic ties (family)	− .76

[a]From Lerner (1978).

those people who score highly on the measure of authoritarianism condemn "out-groups," especially Jews.

By contrast, the second factor seems to represent more of a "Win–Lose" world view. Those who score high on the items with high loading on this scale think the world is a just place where people get what they deserve, generally through their own efforts and sacrifice. The world is just, and life is fine and improving all the time. It is worth noting that the two social categories which load highly on this factor represent both the "archwinners," Americans, and the "archlosers," Indians and Metis, in Canadian society as seen in Ontario. Belief in a Just World is associated with positive loadings, liking, for Americans, and negative loadings, dislike, of losers (Indians and Metis).

Attitudes toward Jews fail to appear on this factor. One reasonable hunch is that they are seen both as winners and losers; socially, they are losers, still restricted from certain neighborhoods and clubs. At the same time, the Jews are often seen as being financially, and, more recently, politically succesful. The "minority" groups which had the weakest loadings on either Factors I and II were the Maritimers and *Separatistes*. Although this was not expected, one might speculate that these categories are less different than the others on important dimensions (Factor I), and probably less clearly defined as either deprived or highly successful (Factor II).

Factor II seems to confirm what most people know. There is a positive association among such factors as the size of community in which one grew up, the degree of identification with an ethnic group, one's sense of commitment to a religion, and the socioeconomic status (estimated) of one's family. To say it all more simply, among the students in this sample, the poor kids were small-town farm boys who felt a relatively strong tie to their ethnic group, and a sense of commitment to their religion. At the other end were the "city slickers," relatively higher social class cosmopolitans, who had little sense of religious identity, or of belonging to an ethnic group.

Given the rather obvious direct quality of so many of the questionnaire items employed in this study, it is interesting that we find a high loading on the Social Desirability Scale (Crowne & Marlowe, 1964) only on the fourth factor. We also find in this factor the first appearance of background variables mixed with social attitudes. Apparently at one of the poles on this factor is a picture of someone who comes from a family with weak ethnic ties, whose father has little formal education, and who does not view himself as a religious person, but rather attempts to present himself in a positive light, including picking up the new public anthem and thereby identifying with "The Canadian Fact."

These results have some important implications for the understanding of how people react to the victims of economic inequality or social discrimination in our society. The evidence from this study indicates that, to the extent to which the Authoritarianism dimension is operative in one's life, one is likely to exhibit a general condemnation of those who are known to be "weak and different,'' or those who would make demands for social change. As a consequence, almost anyone who needs help in our society, or those who would attempt to create effective change designed to meet these needs, would be derogated and resisted by the Authoritarian.

The dimension typified by the Belief in a Just World is for the most part independent of, and orthogonally related to, the Authoritarianism syndrome. Nevertheless, there are some important similarities as well as differences in terms of the specific attributes and attitudes associated with these two dimensions. The strong commitment to a Belief in a Just World is not associated with the general condemnation of the deprived members of society, nor with the resistance to social change typified by Authoritarianism. The deserving component, however, in the Belief in a Just World implies that people can, and should, control their own fate. Obviously, this can lead to a justification of the status quo—those who are highly privileged must have deserved it, and those who are deprived had it coming as a result of their own failures—or, at the worst, it is just a matter of time until they earn their way out of their miserable condition.

As we have seen in a number of our experiments, the irony inherent in the ''justice'' aspect of the belief in a just world is that it often takes the form of *justification.* In this survey of social attitudes, we find the same ironic pattern appearing in the strong association of this dimension with positive attitudes toward Americans, mixed reactions to the Jews, but, again, a negative reaction to the obvious victims of society—the impoverished, discriminated-against Indians and Metis.

The Belief in a Just World: Styles of ''Defense''

The Effect of Experience on BJW: Abandonment or Transformation?

It takes a while to digest the array of findings that have been generated in and around the BJW Measure developed by Rubin and Peplau. The pattern of correlates is impressive and extremely persuasive. There certainly does seem to be an important dimension that is tapped by that scale, and it appears to reflect beliefs about the extent to which one lives in a just world. Although related to other dimensions in meaningful ways, it is psychologically distinct from the Authoritarian syndrome, the acceptance of Protestant Ethic-related beliefs, or an Internal versus External locus of control.

Having stated and accepted all of that, it is time to return to those initial questions concerning how people differ in their view of justice in their environment. Remember that Rubin and Peplau construed the Belief in a Just World as a dimension on which people can vary from what I presume would be the firm belief that the world is an unjust place, through some middling degree of belief that people at least at times get what they deserve, to the equally complete and firm belief that justice prevails at all times. Apparently, people who seem to believe most completely in a totally just environment are most likely to be responsive to the fate of others in the ways that we have examined: condemning or helping victims. Other people, the vast majority, are presumably more objectively reasonable in their reactions.

From their perspective, Rubin and Peplau see the Belief in a Just World as characteristic of the immature, primitive stage of moral development. If maturity accompanies aging, then most mature adults would be "likely to abandon the belief in a just world" (Rubin & Peplau, 1975, p. 75). They summarize their thinking in the following way:

> While most people probably believe in a just world during at least part of their childhood, they come to question this belief as they grow older. This questionning may be fostered by personal experiences of injustice and by the attainment of a principled view of morality that transcends obedience to conventional standards and authorities. (p. 76)

That is certainly an eminently reasonable position. Most adults have seen too much to maintain the naive belief that life mimics the fairy tales where justice always triumphs and the "good" guys win in the end. I was amazed to discover, for example, that every male member of one of my classes had experienced the adolescent trauma of being humiliated by a "bully." The experience left them hurt and angry, with a sense of bitter futility, and eventually the resignation that bullies are one of the ugly facts of life that one has to try to manage and survive from time to time. There are other familiar, "maturing," experiences that come from the recognition that some people get sick, rich, die, are born with superb talents, or ugly features, into poverty or wealth, get old and feeble; all for reasons that have nothing to do with "deserving." But is it true that people gradually give up their belief in a just world as they are "matured" by these experiences? My strong hunch is that the answer to that question is "yes" only if one is speaking about the kind of belief in a just world that is tapped by the Rubin and Peplau scale. For the most part, the items on that scale are too easily contradicted by common experiences to be maintained for long by anyone but the extremely devout or sheltered.

What I suspect, however, is that most of us cannot give up the belief that we live in and attempt to function in an environment in which we can get what we deserve. That belief is so much an intrinsic part of our functioning that, instead of giving it up as a consequene of our experiences with seeming injustices, we modify and shape its form to make it less vulnerable to threats from disqualifying experiences. Initially, the Belief in a Just World is at the foundation of our sense of security, and we erect increasingly elaborate defenses when necessary to protect that belief. Eventually we come to need more than is generally encompassed by the notion of "security." We need to find or create for ourselves meaningful patterns for our experiences. Whatever form the pattern takes, it must be shaped around certain evaluative experiences.

As human beings, we judge events in moral terms. People, acts outcomes, are not only evaluated on some dimension of desirability; they are also viewed in terms of their "appropriateness," and we want it all to fit together in the appropriate way. Of course, as we grow up we are usually able to accept a sufficiently long time perspective, sense of history and future, so that after a period of struggling and grief we are able to encompass any specific set of outcomes, including death. I am suggesting, then, that virtually none of us give up the Belief in a Just World. As the result of contradicting experiences or maturing cognitive processes, we actually develop less vulnerable forms of the belief.

The next question, of course, is how the evidence looks with relation to these conjectures. That is not an easy question to answer, especially since it is not immediately apparent what kind of evidence one would consider pertinent, that would speak to these issues. It should be remembered that, after all, we are looking for evidence of a belief system which is supposed to be framed or constructed in a way which not only meets the needs of the individual, but also encompasses, or at least is made impervious to, the common human experiences.

I have actually put myself in the awkward position of saying that the reason people claim they do not believe in a just world and insist that only a child or a fool would hold to such a belief is *so that* they can maintain another form of the very same belief:

Transformation of BJW: Some Earlier Evidence of Normative Reactions

One good place to begin is by reviewing what we already know. We have ample evidence that it is neither typical or normative for people to abandon the kind of belief in a just world that is measured by the Rubin and Peplau scale. What seems to happen is that people learn to pretend to themselves, as well as to others, that they are rational, objective observers of the human scene, while, in reality, they are responsive to evidence of injustice in ways which indicate that the relatively primitive BJW is still operative. They are still trying to believe in Santa Claus or the Lone Ranger.

For example, the research that developed around the "Innocent Victim" woman-suffering-shocks paradigm showed that, in the initial experiment (Lerner & Simmons, 1966) fully two-thirds of the observers exhibited signs of condemning the victim, while finding the tormenting situation quite legitimate and desirable. I am prepared at this point, after reviewing the evidence available, to push for an interpretation of their reactions as motivated cognitive distortions. The objective reality is that the victim portrayed on that tape appears as a reasonably nice person who is exploited by the experimenter for her own ends. That assertion is not at all brave, since there is ample evidence from subsequent experiments (Lerner, 1971a; Simons & Piliavin, 1972) that disabused observers do not condemn the victim, and see her very much as do observers who believe that she will be compensated appropriately for her suffering. And, further, given the experimental data as well as the Zuckerman *et al.* (1975) effort with the BJW Scale, the observers' condemnation of this victim is obviously a direct response to the degree of injustice implied by her fate.

We have fairly solid evidence that approximately two-thirds of the observers in that situation distorted their image of a victim in order to maintain the belief that an injustice was not committed. And also, they would almost certainly deny to themselves, as well as others, that they would do such a thing. On the contrary, they would insist that they would see her as she is, the nice young woman victimized by that Machiavellian psychologist.

Who were these observers? In the initial experiment, as well as many of the others, they were university students from various disciplines and social backgrounds. Whatever you may believe about the sheltered life of university students, they nevertheless are sophisticated enough to insist that they do not condemn innocent victims, and that they do not believe in fairy tales or that justice always prevails. In that vein, it is worth noting that virtually all of the experimental findings associated with the Rubin and Peplau BJW Measure showed that relatively primitive reactions to suffering and victimization were revealed by a median split of the sample. The 50% who had the higher scores were compared with the lower scoring 50% (see Miller, 1977a; Zuckerman, 1975). In other words, the primitive reactions were prevalent enough in the higher scoring 50% to yield measurable effects.

In sum, it appears that the desire to see justice done in one's environment is sufficient to elicit justice-restoring cognitive distortion among a *substantial portion* of reasonably bright, well-educated young adults. And, further, these observers will deny that they engage in such primitive processes. They are much too sophisticated and realistic to do that.

The Role of Emotional Involvement in the Appearance of Just World Beliefs

We can sharpen somewhat the important theoretical issues that are guiding our inquiry at this point. Actually they should be familiar to us in many ways: reminiscent of many of the earlier efforts to distinguish whether—or at least the extent to which—(a) people function as reasonably rational processors of the information provided by their environment, or (b) their needs and wants shape how they construe their world—what cues they attend to, information they select, and how they organize and process that information.

On the one hand, it seems quite reasonable to assume, as do Rubin and Peplau, that, although very young children may believe they live in a just world where people always get what they deserve, eventually they outgrow that naive view of the real world. They give up this "belief" as their experiences provide evidence that injustices not only do occur, but often persist. Many victims are not compensated, and harm-doers enjoy the fruits of their ill-gotten gains. Also, many of us learn that it is often difficult to disentangle the causal relations of human events to determine who was the victim and who was the harm-doer. And some will question whether it makes sense, in light of the best evidence available, to construe most of the things that happen to people in terms of justice and deserving.

The alternative view is that, for most of us, our portrayal of how we dispassionately process events in our world is a charade, in which we engage most frequently and effectively when we are, in fact, removed form what is happening. We approximate functioning according to this cultural ideal of being "cool, objective, and rational" when what is going on does not affect us very much. Under those circumstances, our reactions do follow somewhat our self–other illusions and the appropriate normative patterns. As the "detached" observers who were informed that the girl was simply acting stated:

> Certainly no one in their right mind could derogate, condemn that nice young woman who is being given electric shocks as part of an experiment. If anything they would question the ethics of the entire proceedings, and probably take steps to see to it that the appropriate authorities are alerted. At least that is what I and the people I know would do.

Most of the time, when things matter to us, either because of the anticipated outcomes or because of what we have just witnessed or experienced ourselves, we begin to look for and find the patterns which meet our needs, especially the need to believe that we live in a just world.

The alternative, quite opposite hypothesis from that assumed by Rubin and Peplau (1975) emerges then: *The more important the circumstances, the more likely that an "experience" of an injustice will be processed, construed in ways which enable the person to maintain the belief in a just world.*

Obviously, both reactions to evidence of injustice do occur. On the other hand, we do act as fairly objective processors of the best information available, and, when confronted with evidence of an injustice, we see it, and adjust our reactions, including the relevant beliefs in the way our world works, to accommodate the information. It also seems, however, that there is a constant monitor of this process which sees to it that the "underpinnings" or is it "overarching construction" of our world view is not threatened by the consequences of this information processing. The content of the monitor's agenda certainly can vary greatly from person to person, but an essential constant can be portrayed as a belief in a Just World—a world in which I can and do get what I deserve.

If these conjectures are correct, then we may expect to find, in our review of the available evidence, that dispassionate, uninvolved observers' reactions will approximate the normative rational information-processing model, whereas emotionally involved observers will be more likely to construe events so that the assumption that people get what they deserve is not contradicted. Certainly the evidence associated with the Lerner and Simmons paradigm fits this pattern very well (Lerner, 1971a; Simons & Piliavin, 1972).

What we also found, however, is evidence that not all involved observers engaged in these justice-fitting distortions of the victim and her fate. In fact, it is plausible to conclude that only those observers who for one reason or another remained at an arrested level in their maturation, holding on to rather naive, almost childlike ways of construing justice in their world, would exhibit signs of justifying the victim's fate in clearly nonrational ways such as derogation. The more "mature" subjects, who were in the lower half of the sample in terms of their agreement with the Rubin and Peplau BJW items, did not seem to need to condemn the victim (Zuckerman *et al.*, 1975).

There are now at least two issues which are important for our search. One is the effect on an observer of witnessing an injustice. Is it true that, as the importance of the event for the observer increases, the more likely that person is to construe the events within a theme of justice and deserving? And the other issue must be one of numbers. Do only a relatively few people reveal this pattern, presumably the ones in an arrested stage of development, or are we able to find signs of this construction among a majority of the observers? Or will we find individual variations in the way people arrange their cognitions—variations with the functional tie of maintaining the belief in a just world?

Victim's Belief in a Just World: A Strong Test of the Importance of the Just World Belief

The closest we come to evidence that can speak to those questions are two studies in which the importance to the observer was clearly established by the fact that the observer was the victim. In one case, the victimization was relatively trivial—discovering that one was slotted to "eat a worm." The second study dealt with profoundly more serious consequences—having been recently crippled in an accident.

In the Comer and Laird (1975) experiment, young men and women who had volunteered to participate in an experiment concerned with the relations among physiological and personality variables and the performance of certain tasks discovered that they were assigned to a condition which required that they eat a worm. Obviously, it was no problem for the experimenters to establish that this was a disgusting, revolting prospect.

How did they react to their fate? Presumably they could have elected to leave the experiment, or refuse to eat the worm. Only three out of 38 chose to opt out in this way. What about the other 35? Comer and Laird present compelling evidence that the vast majority engaged in one or more cognitive changes subsequent to learning their fate. By comparing the reactions of these subjects to others who were assigned the "neutral" task, the experimenters were able to show that the "victims" tended to see themselves as the kind of people who deserved that fate, or began to see themselves in rather "heroic" terms, as brave and courageous. Others decided that worm eating wasn't such a bad thing after all. All of these mechanisms served to remove the sense of being unjustly victimized by their fate.

But how real were these cognitive changes to the victims? How seriously did they take this view of themselves and their fate? The evidence Comer and

Laird generated is extremely persuasive. What better way to see if the subjects really did believe in these justifying cognitions, than by giving them the opportunity to legitimately avoid the terrible fate? And so some of the victims were told there had been a mix-up, and they were actually supposed to have their choice between eating a worm or doing a neutral weight-discrimination task. Twelve out of the 15 subjects in this condition elected to eat the worm after all, or stated that they did not care. Only three chose the "neutral," weight-discrimination task. By comparison, all those in the control group who had not been assigned initially to eat the worm elected the neutral task. I find that persuasive. They elected the terrible fate, because they had engaged in cognitive changes which made that fate appropriate for them, or not so terrible after all.

Comer and Laird presented additional evidence to bolster this interpretation. Some of the victimized experimental subjects were subsequently given the choice, not between worm eating and a neutral task, but between a condition which involved giving themselves painful electric shocks, versus the neutral weight discrimination. If it is true that these victims had actually changed their self-concept to fit their terrible fate, then these justifying cognitions should generalize to other forms of victimization. That is a very brave and powerful test of the hypothesis. Nevertheless, 10 of the 20 victims given that choice elected to administer shocks to themselves. Possibly more to the point was the finding that those victims who, when given their choice, elected to avoid the electric shocks, were those who had adjusted to their initial victimization by deciding that worm eating was not really that bad. Those who had gone through self-concept changes were the ones most likely to act as if they were deserving, or so brave that of course it made sense to choose the painful shocks condition.

Comer and Laird were able to document some of the alternative ways in which people can and do justify terrible fates; they also showed that these justifying changes appeared in most of their subjects—not the immature minority.

An Even Stronger Test: Victim Crippled for Life

By contrast, in almost every respect, there were the accident victims whom Bulman and Wortman (1977) interviewed: young people who had been recently condemned to spend the rest of their lives crippled. I guess it is conceivable that some among these 29 victims had actually sought to harm themselves in this way, but, setting that possibility aside as a serious explanation for the way these people reacted to their fate, we can find some important evidence concerning the forms the Belief in a Just World takes in people's lives.

The central question is how these young people reacted to and came to grips with their fate. As one might expect, all 29 patients had reported asking themselves "Why me?". One of the 29 had not yet come up with an answer. If we take their answers at face value, it appears that there were some victims who, at least at the time of the interview, had accepted a rather straight probability, chance view of what had happened to them. Three of the 28 reported something like this: "Just an accident. Things happen when they happen" (p. 359); or "It just happened to me out of so many people. It could have been the next guy off the board" (p. 358). An additional four gave responses which were similar in form to "Chance" explanation, with possibly a bit more of a "philosophical perspective" to the probabilities inherent in the human condition. One can almost detect the implication of a meaningful pattern in the "probabilities."

> It was bound to happen: things had been going well, so the odds were that something bad could happen. Good things and bad things happen—this was one of those bad things. (p. 359)

The great majority, 21 of the 29, seemed to make sense out of what happened to them in ways which removed the "injustice" of their fate. Only two of them saw their accident as a form of retribution for past wrongdoing. The remainder achieved a perspective that defined their fate as a valuable or desirable consequence. Their having been paralyzed for the rest of their lives was not an undesirable fate. In some cases a "good ending" was fortuitously associated with the accident:

> Since the accident, I've learned an awful lot about myself and other people. You meet different people in a hard-up situation that I never would have met. I was leading a sheltered life, I suppose compared to what it is now. Now I'm just in a situation which I enjoy. (p. 359)

For the majority of respondents, this "good ending" was linked to a religious perspective. Something with Godlike powers guided the events associated with the accident, and, more importantly, would ensure that everything would be made right in this life or later.

> I see the accident as the best thing that could have happened 'cause I was forced to decide my faith, whereas there would have been the possibility that I would have lived and never made a decision—been lost the rest of my life. 'Cause an individual they don't know how lost they are without faith. (p. 359)

or

> It's a learning experience; I see God's trying to put me in situations to help me learn about Him and myself and also how I can help other people. As far as I'm concerned, everybody's whole life is planned by the Creator. So, I guess, given that fact, that I was bound to come into circumstances like this, whether one way or the other. (p. 359)

or

> And it's sort of like the story of Job, you know. He put things in front of you and shows that you can overcome. (p. 358)

If we reflect back on the initial questions, we can see some fairly solid answers emerging from these findings. How do "innocent victims" react to their own fate? From what we have seen, there seem to be at least three kinds of reaction. A minority seem to view what happened to them as "accidents" of circumstance, nothing more or less than that. Another minority reaction construes the victimization as just retribution for past misdeeds. The victim deserves to suffer in this way. The great majority of these people—especially those who suffered the crippling permanent damage to their bodies of the sort that typically precludes living a "normal life"—redefine their fate as one made good by the recognition of a divine plan. These people who have left the just world of "normal" living and entered the world of victims find that it is all for the best, that they are following God's plan; it is certainly a just world then, and, with the presence of the Divine, everything has to be, must be, "just."

The Religious Perspective as a Form of Belief in a Just World

There is some additional evidence that people may adopt a religious perspective to maintain their faith in the ultimate justness of their world. Sorrentino and Hardy (1974) had subjects observe the suffering of an innocent victim in a situation designed to correspond with the learning experiment paradigm from Lerner and Simmons (1966). The entrapped young woman received electric shocks for each virtually unavoidable error she made in a serial learning task. In the Control conditions, the same woman was informed of her errors, and received no punishment of any kind. For purposes of analysis, they divided their subjects (university students) into those who were above or below the median on a measure of the extent to which they reported that religion was "important in their everyday life." Their main dependent variable was a rating of the woman's personality on a series of highly evaluative attributes similar to those employed in the earlier Just World research. They also asked their subjects in the initial phases of the experiment to indicate on a nine-point scale, "To what extent do you believe you live in a just world?".

They found, as had many others before and after them, that there was a moderate and statistically significant correlation between their subjects' belief in the importance of religion in their lives and their belief in a just world—when asked point-blank (r (78) = .38, $p < .01$).

Given this significant positive relation between a measure of BJW and the importance of religion, how would you expect the observers with a high or low comitment to a religious orientation to react to the poor innocent victim? If you make a direct extrapolation and treat the commonly observed correlation of around .38 as if it were in fact representative of a "true" correlation of 1.00, then one should expect to replicate the earlier findings of Zuckerman et al. (1975). The High Religious subjects in this experiment should react as did the

High BJW subjects in Zuckerman's earlier study, and react with the greatest condemnation of the suffering victim and justification of the experimental situation. On the other hand, if it is true that the religious perspective, although related to BJW, is most often a functional alternative with its particular way of finding justice in suffering, then you might expect an entirely different pattern to emerge. In fact, the findings provide support for this latter alternative.

As can be seen in Table 32, adapted from Sorrentino and Hardy (1974), those who were among the lower half of the subjects on the measure of the importance of religion in their everyday life were responsive to the fate of the person they observed. The same person was evaluated as significantly less attractive in the condition where she received electric shocks $\bar{X} = 46.80$) than in the condition where the observers saw her being given neutral feedback ($\bar{X} = 55.50$, $p < .01$). However, the observers who expressed a closer tie to a religious view of life appeared to be virtually unresponsive to the victim's fate. (Control $\bar{X} = 50.50$, Electric Shock $\bar{X} = 50.10$). It did not seem to matter to them, in ways that would appear in their evaluation, whether or not the young woman was being caused to suffer the pain of the electric shocks.

Those findings fit the hypothesis that a religious perspective can encompass an incident of seeming injustice within the larger framework of ultimate justice. Any seemingly undeserved suffering today will of course be rewarded and compensated for later. In effect, there are no innocent victims, no injustices, in the ultimate scheme of things.

It is also worth noting that those with a highly religious view of life had a significantly more negative evaluation of the young woman who was not suffering at all, in the control condition, than did the observers who were less committed to a religious perspective (High Religious $\bar{X} = 50.50$, Low Religious $\bar{X} = 55.50$, $p < .01$). That certainly follows from the religious view of people as at least partially "bad," continually struggling with the evil temptations to their souls.

The Religious Perspective and Society's Victims
Social Class and the Perception of Justice

So far, in our efforts to answer the questions we began with concerning the "functions" and "forms" of the person's belief in a Just World, we have looked at rather special people, or people in special circumstances. It certainly would be no surprise, for even the casual social observer, to discover that "there are no atheists in foxholes." When all other hope fails, then we have no choice but to turn to the supernatural. When faced with the prospect of having to spend the rest of one's life as the paralyzed victim of an "accident," for example, modifying the self-concept in any justifying sense would be tantamount to self-destruction, or a full-blown delusion of grandeur. What appears, then, as a way of eliminating the sense of injustice, as well as hope for the future, is, of

Table 32
X̄ Evaluation of the Learner[a,b]

Observers	Control	Electric shocks
Low religious	55.50a	46.80
High religious	50.50	50.10

[a]Adapted from Sorrentino & Hardy (1974).
[b]An evaluation of learner's attributes on 7-point scales.
The lower the score, the more negative the evaluation.

course, for those of us who grew up in this culture, a supernatural force that will make things right in the end. After all, what other choices are available?

What if we turn away from the special samples and circumstances, and take a look at a cross section of people in the general community? What would we find then? Linda Elkinton and I decided to do just that (Lerner & Elkinton, 1970). We were curious about a number of issues. In the first place, we realized that virtually all the research on reactions to victims, including ours, had been predicated on the researcher's defining who the vehicle was, what constituted a victimization, an injustice. Having realized that, we decided it would be intriguing to see how nonprofessional social scientists in the community viewed justice–injustice in their world.

The approach we settled on was something of a compromise between two main considerations, with the usual limiting conditions of time and money. It was obvious to us that we wanted to do in-depth interviewing. Whatever other data we got from them, we wanted each person to respond freely and completely to general questions of the sort "Do you know any person or kind of person, who gets a raw deal in life, less than they deserve—are treated unjustly?" "Who are they, how did it happen, and what can be done about it?" And, of course, there is the other side to the issue—"any person or kind of person who gets more than they deserve, etc.?" Obviously, these are long and rather intensive interviews. Any attempt to use them with a randomly selected representative sample of a reasonably sized community would be an enormous enterprise. But did we need to do that kind of survey in order to answer our questions? We decided probably not. As an alternative, we did a reasonable number of interviews with people from three distinct social strata, ranging from "very well off" to "barely keeping one's head above water." That would enable us to consider a number of alternative hypotheses.

For example, how does a relatively affluent person view justice in his world? Being in a favored position might lead one to believe in and defend the social order as it exists (Walster & Walster, 1975). In that case, everyone deserves his fate, so there are no victims. On the other hand, the upper classes are usually among the better educated, more aware, and are often found leading reform and welfare organizations—a variant of the "noblesse oblige" tradition. Possibly their education as well as financial and social security enables them to see the inequities in our society quite obviously (Schwartz, 1975).

An alternative perspective would suggest that those least favored in the society would be the ones most likely to see injustice (Deutsch, 1974). Obviously, their own relatively deprived position is seen as undeserved, and those who are better off economically achieved their gains illicitly. An equally good case could be made for the marginally secure middle class as the seat of greatest resentment. Their identification with the Protestant Ethic would lead to condemnation of both the upper and lower classes as getting more than they deserve (Rubin & Peplau, 1973).

Each of these hypotheses, and no doubt many another, is theoretically plausible. To get some data relevant to these issues, we had interviews done with 93 white non-Jewish housewives living in various neighborhoods in the Lexington, Kentucky urban area. Three kinds of neighborhoods were sampled on the basis of their reputation in the community for being relatively homogeneous in terms of social-economic status—Upper Middle, Lower Middle, and Laboring. The selection of homes within each area was random. However, since the interviewing was done during working hours, fulltime working housewives were eliminated.

Perception of Injustice: Extent of injustice. The three samples differed reliably in the extent to which people saw others as getting more or less than they deserved (Table 33). In general, as one might expect from earlier reported findings, the Upper Middle Class respondents were generally more likely to report victims than the other two samples. The understandable exception to this is that, of the eight respondents who mentioned the Lower Middle Class as having less than it deserved, five were themselves from the Lower Middle Class. Similarly, the victims most frequently mentioned by the Laboring respondents were lower income whites (five out of a total 12). There was, then, some tendency for these latter two groups to see people like themselves as underprivileged victims.

There were fewer differences among the three samples in terms of the kinds and numbers of privileged people seen in our society. The Upper Middle group were most likely to report the "rich" and "gangsters" as getting more than they deserved, and respondents in the two upper strata were considerably more likely than Laboring respondents to report *any* groups as overrewarded.

The most striking finding, however, is that people on welfare were by far the most frequently mentioned category of people who got more than they deserved. Approximately one-third of all respondents in each sample spontaneously mentioned either mothers on relief, or people on welfare, as getting more than they deserved. Actually, this category was the incident of injustice *most often reported by the respondents from the Laboring group.* The respondents from both lower strata were more likely to complain about people on welfare than about rich people, landlords, gangsters, Hollywood celebrities, or the lot of the poverty-stricken, elderly, or mentally ill.

Patterns of Injustice. An examination of the respondents' answers to questions concerning both the privileged and victims yielded three general patterns

Table 33
Categories of Reported Injustice[a]

Groups in U.S. who get:

Less than deserve	Upper middle ($N = 31$)	Lower middle ($N = 30$)	Laboring ($N = 32$)
Negroes	11	7	3
Minority groups	22	5	2
Middle class/working man	1	5	2
Lower income whites	12	2	5
Children (of rich or poor)	8	1	-
Old people	2	2	-
Retarded/handicapped	4	-	-
None	3	13	21
Mean Number of Victims reported[b]	2.64	.96	.72
More than deserve			
Rich	9	7	2
Government people/politicians	5	3	-
Gangsters/mafia	5	-	-
People on welfare	9	9	10
Miscellaneous	4	3	-
None	8	11	20
Mean number of privileged reported[c]	1.06	.96	.41

[a]From Lerner & Elkinton (1970).
[b]$F = 23.25, p < .001$.
[c]$F = 6.69, p < .005$.

Table 34
Patterns of Injustice[a]

Frequencies	A Recognize injustice	B Condemn victim	C Complete justice
Upper middle	21	9	1
Lower middle	15	9	6
Laboring	8	10	14
X^2's			
Upper middle vs. lower middle	-	-	4.22[b]
Upper middle vs. laboring	11.48[c]	-	14.25[c]
Lower middle vs. laboring	4.14[b]	-	4.00[b]

[a]From Lerner & Elkinton (1970).
[b]$p < .05$.
[c]$p < .01$.

of responses (see Table 34). Twenty-one respondents saw complete justice in their environment (Type C); no one had more or less than he deserved. Two-thirds of these respondents were from the Laboring group. Only one was from the Upper Middle stratum. A second category (Type B) consisted of those 28 respondents who condemned people on welfare; 17 of those who condemned these victims of poverty also saw some others as victims, but 11 reported this event as the only incident of injustice. The last category of respondents (Type A) were those 44 respondents who recognized injustice in the lot of victims of poverty or illness, and in the ill-gotten gains of criminals or crooked politicians. This category of respondents was most often found among the high Upper Middle sample.

There were differences in social attitudes among those respondents with different patterns of the perception of justice. However, many of these differences varied somewhat as a function of social class. For example, in the Upper Middle group, those who saw injustices (Type A) had a higher mean score on the Internal-External dimension and the Importance of Religion measure than those who condemned victims (Type B). Apparently, those who condemned victims felt more in control of their own fate, and were less concerned with a religious orientation to life.

These differences did not appear among the reactions found in the other two samples. However, in both the Lower Middle and Laboring groups, those respondents who saw complete justice in their environment (Type C) reported having more troubles and obstacles in their life than those who perceived some

Table 35
Social Attitudes of Samples[a]
$(\bar{X}$'s)

	Upper middle ($N = 31$)	Lower middle ($N = 30$)	Laboring ($N = 32$)	F
Condition of U.S. 5 years ago (0–10) (Cantril)	4.63	6.51	6.12	
Expected condition of U.S. 5 years in future (0–10) (Cantril)	6.60	5.27 (Changes)	5.06	8.73^c
Success in attaining life goals (0–10) (Cantril)	8.16	6.70	6.96	4.53^b
Fears and worries about the future (0–10) (Cantril)	7.93	7.10	5.59	8.69^b
Internal-external control (Rotter)	6.54	8.40	8.68	4.79^b

[a]From Lerner & Elkinton (1970).
[b]$p < .02$.
[c]$p < .001$.

injustice (Type A). The respondents who condemned victims (Type B) reported the least troubles and obstacles in their lives. In fact, in the Laboring sample these "victim-condemners" felt more successful in attaining their life goals, and more able to make their lives happy, than the other respondents. This feeling of relative success and power was reversed in the Lower Middle sample: those who condemned victims (Type B) felt least able to improve their lot in life.

There were additional differences among the respondents who exhibited the three types of reactions. Those who saw complete justice (Type C) were more likely to have less than a high-school education, and to identify with "fundamentalist" religion than the other respondents. This finding is confounded, however, with the fact that most Type C respondents are to be found in the Laboring group typified by low education and fundamentalist religious orientation. Unfortunately, there are too few subjects with Type C reactions in the other two social class groupings to partial out the effect of social class.

Among those who perceived some kinds of injustice (Type A and Type B), there were additional differences surrounding their notions of the cause of and remedies for the injustices. In general, Type B respondents (Victim Condemners) were more likely to state that something could be done to eliminate the injustices than were those who saw the underprivileged as victims (Type A). The most consistent differences were found in the reactions to those who were getting more than they deserved. Of course, Type B respondents were much more likely to locate the cause in some personal chicanery, especially on the part of those who were profiting (e.g., the people on welfare.)

Summary and Discussion. It is worth pointing out that less than half of the respondents in this sample (44) recognized the more obvious injustices in our society, and these Types A respondents were most likely to be among the wealthier members, not the supposedly struggling Lower Middle Class or deprived Laboring families. These differences are probably not attributable to some artifact of verbal fluency or response set, since approximately one-third of the respondents in each of the three samples felt free to identify a person on welfare as someone who gets more than he deserves. Apparently, those in the Upper Middle Class are more likely to view the eonomically and socially deprived in our society as victims.

The two other most important findings of this study center around the nature and extent of reaction Type B, the Victim Condemners, found in all three samples, and the degree of complete justice (Type C) reaction found in the Laboring sample. For those who are interested in bettering the lot of the people who find themselves dependent upon public assistance, it is worth noting the characteristics of those who are most likely to condemn these victims. One factor which was significant across all three social classes is that these Victim Condemners were more likely to believe that there is a direct way to solve the problem, and more likely to blame the motives of these victims, the people on welfare, as the cause of their getting more than they deserve. Those who do not condemn these victims, and who actually recognize the injustice of poverty and discrimination, Type A reaction, are more likely to be tentative in their recommendations, and see social determinants underlying the injustice.

Aside from these similarities, the condemnation of people on welfare is likely to be associated with differing characteristics as a function of the social background of the respondent. Those in the Upper Middle Class who condemn victims are people who feel most in control of their own world and fate. Obviously, then, these people are likely to believe that those who are poor caused their own suffering, and want to live that way. In contrast, the frustrated and disappointed Lower Middle Class respondent, and the escaping marginal Laboring person, seem to be the ones in their groups most likely to condemn those who have to be on welfare. The Victim Condemners found in the Lower Middle Class were more likely to be those who felt stymied and unable to improve their position, while among the Laboring Class they were the most optimistic and successful. Conceivably, then, at least three different processes were associated with the tendency to condemn those on welfare.

The most reasonable explanation for the fact that almost half of the Laboring sample saw no one in their world as getting more or less than they deserved is that they have accepted the general norms of our society, and these have been bolstered with a belief in an omnipotent and justice-maintaining God. Therefore, to some people what may appear as inequity on the surface is really the result of sin, or it will be corrected in the future—Heaven or Hell. The evidence that people will seek such explanations when they are deprived and are helpless to alter their state of affairs fits the few findings available from this study. Those who saw complete justice (Type C) were also those who had the most troubles and obstacles in their life, and felt least able to make their life happier; such despondency and helplessness lead to madness, rebellion, *or* a belief that all will be made right eventually (Bettelheim, 1943; Merton, 1957). This fits clearly what we had seen with the victimized people in the earlier research, particularly those who had been paralyzed by an accident.

However, along with these corroborating and elaborating findings, we are left with the indisputably important fact that at least half of the people in our sample were aware that some people in our society get more or less than they deserve. Actually two-thirds of those in the Upper Middle Class sample recognized the injustices that most social analysts would document with objective data.

What, then, about their belief in a just world? They do not condemn the victims in their world, nor do they adopt a religious perspective which can ensure justice in the long run. The obvious conclusion is that these people are realistic enough to recognize and admit that this is a very imperfect world, and there is often a good deal of injustice. In other words, they do not believe in any categorical sense that they live in a just world. They, just as you and I, believe that we live in a world where one can point to great areas of continuing, chronic, festering injustices.

Some Concluding Thoughts

So where does all that leave us? My hunch is that we are in a much sounder position in our social psychological inquiry than as people trying to make our way in life. On the one hand, our commitment to "reality" requires that most of us recognize the injustices in our world. On the other, our psychological needs require us to deny the existence of those injustices. That is an extremely difficult process, which is never fully resolved. It is my hunch that our defenses are not entirely successful in neutralizing all possible cues of injustice, so we remain fairly busy repairing the old or constructing new defenses. That task is considerably more taxing and difficult than having to describe these processes and the relevant evidence we have been able to put together. And that will not be easy.

To be sure, we have reached the most controversial part of this study. If I take my own conjectures at all seriously, then I can construct the following unhappy scenario. As I close in on our defenses, and by so doing render them relatively useless, then I should expect to elicit increasing motivation to resist the evidence and/or find alternative defenses. I know that this entire process sounds like chapter and verse straight from the psychoanalytic couch, but that makes it no less applicable in this context. I not only think it is true, but I will set out to do the best I can to present the evidence and allow the processes to emerge. Later, I will try to answer the question of why I am doing this. There is certainly more at stake here for me than scientific curiosity—or proving that I am a clever fellow.

The Penultimate Defense of the Belief in a Just World: Or the "No-Nonsense-Cut-the-Crap-It's-A-Tough-World-Out-There" Charade

The strategy most of us are forced to adopt sooner or later is almost unassailable by any direct confrontation with reality. At one level, we pretend to ourselves as well as to others that we actually believe in virtually the opposite of a just world, and some of our activities are based on that charade; most of the time, however, we design our lives on the assumption that we do live in a just world. Since we refuse to admit to holding this belief, even to ourselves, then any evidence of an injustice around us should pose no particular threat.

> Although I may not like or want injustices I of course recognize they do exist and I will do what I can within reason and my own enlightened self-interest to arrange to cope with the implications. That is what any even moderately sane decent person would do.

As you have probably recognized, we have come full circle, and are now about to reconsider the system of defenses described in the introductory section. At that point, I tried to establish that the "belief in a just world" was not quite so simpleminded and naive a notion as it might seem at first blush. And that I was sufficiently aware of the questions a reasonably aware reader would raise to have provided some tentative but plausible answers. Now in this last section, as in the main body of the book, I must produce the evidence that will turn the "tentative" and "plausible" answers into the probable and persuasive conclusions.

Rather than try to recreate the hypotheses and arguments offered then, I will recapitulate some of the basic issues described in considerably more detail earlier, and then see what the evidence looks like.

The analysis went something like this. By the time they reach adulthood, most people recognize and have had to learn to manage certain basic facts of life. One is that there are certain people who are condemned to live in an Unjust World by any standards we accept. In the world of victims, people are deprived and suffer undeservedly. It is virtually impossible for anyone to rescue them from that fate, by virtue of the nature of their condition or the social psychological consequences associated with the act of helping, coming to their aid.

The suffering and deprivation of the stigmatized, the ugly, the blacks, the chronically ill or physically damaged, victims of crime, those born into ghettoes of poverty, is so severe and widespread, their inflicted handicaps in life so debilitating, that it is clear that they are different from "us." They live in a totally different environment–world, with different contingencies and life possibilities. You and I live in a world where, whatever else is wrong, whatever accidental or Machiavellian forces may be loose in it, it is still a world, at least by comparison, where we and those we care about can pretty well get what we deserve, where we can earn, deserve the things we want, and avoid those that frighten us.

Along with these powerful impressions, we all come to recognize that there are some dangers to this crucially important status quo. The dangers come from at least two related sources. One is that, psychologically, we remain continually vulnerable to cues, to experiences which indicate that we do care about and feel a sense of responsibility, even identity, with these victims. The awareness, for example, of a sick, starving child and helpless, defeated parents, among a myriad other cues, is sufficient to elicit strong impulses to help. We care deeply for them and their suffering.

Second, we recognize that this powerful impulse contains within it the further implicit demand to continue helping until—when? When can we stop giving, helping? Psychologically we remain open to helping until we have nothing more to give, not only to this victim, but to the untold others whom we know are equally if not more deserving of our help. If we yield to this powerful urge, which one can never fully control or make go away, then that is tantamount to our voluntarily entering the world of victims, and bringing with us those who are dependent upon us. Some people do that, and devote their lives to living in and among the world of victims, in order to do what they can, in that position, to relieve underserved suffering.

Most of us choose, instead, to control the urge to help so that it does not interfere with our own ability to live in the just world, and, at the same time, we wish to maintain the image of ourselves as reasonably normal, decent people. So we often employ the device of comparing ourselves with those around us. I am no different than other people like me who we all know are good and decent folks. I give my full share to help the needy in my community.

Along with this relatively objective assessment of our relation to others, and psychologically valid reference to the reactions of others in order to define social reality, we have characteristically adopted a series of supporting "myths." The most widespread and institutionalized of these is that we are all essentially selfish or at least self-interested. We are all in the business of avoiding pain and maximizing our pleasures. Everything we all do is grounded in the more-or-less enlightened pursuit of our own self-interests. We are always, invariably, attempting to make the best deal for ourselves. In any encounter, we engage in those acts which we believe at the time are the most profitable for us, will reap the most gain for the least cost.

As a result, if at any time we feel impelled to respond to the urge to come to the aid of a suffering victim, we can allude to these facts of life, this view of the way we and others are built, to find the strength to turn our backs and walk away. To give in to any such unilateral acts of help would of course be potentially extremely dangerous since that act would create the kind of evidence that would invalidate the person's basic defense, "I am no better or worse than my neighbors. I do my part, give my fair share." The unilateral act defines the person as "different," and one of "them." How, then, can the person continue to defend against the dangerous but implacable unrequitable impulse to care and help?

The myth that we are all governed by a profit-oriented homunculus is intimately linked with many of the basic institutions in our society, and not the least of which are those associated with the acquisition and allocation of resources, and the maintenance of social integration and control. All of our legal institutions—civil and criminal—assume the same model of man, the same "myth," as the economic institutions. Although we will not go into the social psychological consequences of the institutionalization of this assumption, one obvious implication is that, if it is not a valid model of human motivation, it has served a centrally functional role in our basic institutions, oriented as they are to production, acquisition, and control.

Let's take a look now at some of the evidence relevant to the various elements involved in this analysis. First, we must look at the mythical image of human motivation, because of its central role in our defenses.

The Contemporary Model of Man: What Is It, and How Pervasive in Our Lives?

I am least inclined to try documenting the assertion that most of us pretend to live by this myth. Frankly, I think you can do that best for yourselves. Ask yourself whether or not you think it is true. The "it," the model of man, is most recently described by Hatfield (1980), in the quotes from her distillation of the best wisdom available in the social sciences designed to generate a "General Theory of Social Interaction" (see also Walster, Berscheid, & Walster, 1973, 1976). She begins the description of the model, which presumably is based upon the role of "equity" or justice in social relations, with the following set of assumptions:

> The proposition that individuals prefer pleasure to pain is hardly startling. Theorists in a wide variety of disciplines take it for granted that people are selfish: . . . Equity theory, too, rests on the assumption that people are "wired up" to seek pleasure and avoid pain.
>   Thus our first proposition states:
>   *Proposition I:* Individuals will try to maximize their outcomes (where outcomes equal rewards minus punishments). (1980, p. 2).

Later, she rephrases this proposition as

> Corollary I.I So long as individuals perceive that they can maximize their outcomes by behaving equitably they will do so. Should they perceive that they can maximize their outcomes by behaving inequitably they will do so. (p. 3)

Not only do we have this assertion concerning the central and ubiquitous position of this assumption in contemporary social science, but I can add the bit of intelligence that I know of no theory of altruistic or "prosocial" behavior in contemporary social psychology which does not make a similar assumption. People help others only if and when it is seen as the least painful, most profitable way to behave.

The pervasiveness of this myth in our own lives can be illustrated most readily, I think, by your asking yourself a series of questions concerning your closest most intimate relations.

> Why did I decide to marry _____?
> Why do I spend time with, hang around with _____?
> Why do I take care of my kids _____?

My bet is that in these and virtually all other instances you will come up with an instrumental reason which quickly reduces in your thinking and language habits to "because I get the most out of it in comparison with other available alternatives. It allows me to avoid some painful consequences, my conscience, what other people would do to me or for me."

If this is true, then you should be impressed. Especially when you recognize that that means that we believe that virtually everything we do, at least purposefully, is governed by our own selfish interests.

Is This Model of Man "Mythical"?

There is probably no direct way of providing clearly disconforming evidence. By this time in our lives, we so naturally, almost reflexively, take any such counterevidence involving selfish acts on the behalf of others and assume that the benefactor had other agendas which were guiding his behavior. The apparently selfless act was really a self-interested attempt to reduce guilt, gain social esteem, incur the future indebetedness of the person helped, etc.

There is, however, ample indirect evidence to suggest that we reconsider the viability of this assumption. First, our faith in the assumption is supported by only a limited and biased sampling of the available evidence.

For example, at the macrolevel of analysis, one can find considerable evidence, if taken at face value, that we self-interested creatures devote an enormous amount of our resources to the direct welfare of others. Boulding (1974) has systematized these activities in the study of "Grants Economics." The "grants matrix" is equivalent to the "quantity of one-way transfers: who gives what to whom." In illustrating the magnitude of these transfers, he states:

> According to James Morgan, in the United States one-way transfers within the family in 1968 ran to about $313 billion, close to a third of the GNP. Government transfers, both federal, state and local, were about $71 billion. (p. 17)

Also, the public dialogues around important social movements and extreme acts of sacrifice are not couched in terms of either direct or indirect self-interest. Virtually every demagogue or leader—Hitler, Roosevelt, Martin Luther King—has placed the theme of Justice at the core of his appeal. No other goal or value has the ability to sanction, legitimize, all acts, including the intentional sacrificing of human life and liberty.

To be sure, one can derive the appearance of this commitment to justice in our institutions from a functional analysis of the "social contract" as the rational social invention of selfish people (Campbell, 1975). Nevertheless, it is most important for our purposes here to recognize that this is a rather complex, derived interpretation of the evidence. Taken at face value, it is clear that people value justice more than profit, and at times more than their own lives.

If we change our perspective, and look at the psychology of the individual, what can we find? There are at least two sets of findings that are worth mentioning. On the one hand, there is considerable evidence that people evaluate their outcomes, their profits, in terms of whether they are deserved or not. The absolute level, objective status, of one's fate is of indirect relevance to the person's level of satisfaction. What matters is that people believe that their fate is at least equal to what they deserve. (See Crosby, 1976, for a summary of some of the relevant literature.)

Although its theoretical interpretation is still up for grabs, there is ample evidence that people typically design their activities to get what they deserve, and they will be distressed if they subsequently acquire "more" than they deserve. In fact, a number of careful experiments have shown that workers will engage in considerable "costly" efforts to prevent themselves from getting more than they deserve according to the situationally appropriate rules of entitlement. (See Walster, Walster, & Berscheid, 1978 for a summary of some of this literature.) These findings require substantial theoretical acrobatics in order to fit them in to a set of assumptions based upon the profit-oriented homunculus, whereas the simplest most direct interpretation is that people are motivated by the commitment to deserving and justice.

Second, our confidence in the assumption is supported by relatively non-rational processing of new information to fit this assumption. Without going into considerable detail, I would like to alert the reader to an ironic twist in the history of the "bystander intervention" research. The dramatic incident which admittedly inspired that entire line of research was the Kitty Genovese murder. According to the records, 38 of her neighbors admitted watching at least some part of the prolonged attacks and murder that took place in the streets below their windows. No one called for 35 minutes, while she was repeatedly stabbed and pursued.

The ingenious research that followed examined the effect of various conditions on the likelihood that a bystander would do anything to intervene on behalf of an epileptic having a grand mal seizure, someone fainting and falling down in a subway, falling from a ladder in the next room, a robbery, etc. The research was designed to illustrate that people would be inclined to not intervene if they were able to "diffuse the responsibility" and blame others. The results of the considerable research showed that, where the personal risks and emotional costs for intervening were high, or the definition of the situation was ambiguous, or they were with strangers who might make them feel embarrasssed for acting foolish, then people would be unlikely to intervene. In this way, they were able to show that *even in emergencies, the likelihood of acting on behalf of the victim was determined by the bystanders' cost–benefit analysis.*

I find the slippage between the problem and the theoretically grounded findings intriguing. According to this research, most, if not all, of the observers in the Kitty Genovese murder should have done the obvious thing: made an anonymous call to the police. Most of the observers were with family members or at least friends with whom they could achieve *clear consensus and support,* and an anonymous call would have *cost them nothing* in "risks," and *gained them relief from any self-doubts or guilt.* So why did they not call? I can guess at the reason, on the basis of justice theory, but I am amazed that none of the bystander-intervention investigators has bothered to speak to this issue, or even noticed the discrepancy. They had assumed that, obviously, bystanders operate with the same cost-accounting homunculus as everyone else.

In What Ways Does the "Myth" Create a Functional "Defense"?

I think the best way to approach this issue is to describe two closely related situations which elicited radically different reactions from our subjects. The subjects, by the way, were women undergraduates, a fact that will become more important later.

You may recall the situation created in Lerner and Matthews (1967) experiment. Two subjects appeared for each session. Once they arrived, they learned that one of them would have to be the experimental subject, and receive electric shocks during the paired-associate learning task, while the other would be her control, and be given neutral feedback. It was left up to the blind drawing of slips to determine which of them would be the experimental and which the control subject. When subjects believed that they had, by chance, drawn the control slip, leaving the shocks slip for the other person, they showed considerable evidence of feeling guilty—as if they were harm-doers, who had caused someone to suffer undeserved harm. Besides assigning "primary responsibility" for their own and the other subject's fate to themselves, they tended to derogate their victim, presumably as a way of relieving their own guilt.

In a subsequent experiment, Rosemary Lichtman and I (Lerner & Lichtman, 1968) modified the situation just slightly. The only difference was that one of the pair of subjects was allowed to choose which of the two conditions she preferred (electric shocks or neutral feedback). Presumably, someone had to choose, and a table of random numbers decided that she had won the opportunity. In this situation, we found that 20 out of 22 young women chose the "neutral" condition. And they assigned themselves primary responsibility, not only for their own fortune, but also for the fact that the other person would be assigned to the shock condition. What about their feelings of guilt? As it turned out, these subjects, who quite intentionally chose an alternative which they knew would, at the same that it rescued them, cause someone else to suffer, showed virtually no evidence of guilt. Not only did they not derogate their "victim," they revealed upon subsequent interviewing the firm belief that "anyone would have chosen control for themselves. She would have done the same thing if she had been given the choice" (Lerner & Lichtman, 1968, p. 231).

What might explain these two sets of findings? Let us take a few moments, and consider some conjectures about an important set of norms in our society which rest upon the assumption that everyone essentially is out to get what they can for themselves. Therefore, it is legitimate, if not desirable, for everyone to look out for their own interests. When there is a scarce resource, only enough for one, or there can be only one winner or survivor, then I have a perfect right to pursue that goal, even if it means that others who also have a legitimate claim will lose out.

We can see in these two situations the conditions under which these norms can justify literally causing another's harm. Both experimental situations described above fall under the justice of parallel competition—involving norms of justified self-interest. There is a desired outcome which is indivisible; there is equal relevant investment and claim to the desired outcome, and there are fair rules for determining the winner and loser. Why, then, in the condition where the determining outcome is the "chance" drawing of the slip, should we find signs of guilt, while in the conditions where the subject's intended choice gives her the desired outcome, and thereby causes the nonchoosing subject to suffer, do we find no sign of guilt or self-condemnation? This seems to fly in the face of naive psychology and associated findings (Heider, 1958). Certainly we excuse accidentally caused harm considerably more readily than intended harm! Our legal structure reflects this judgment.

The answer to this apparent anomaly is located in the psychology of justified self-interest. The main hypothesis can be stated quite simply—*norms* (public rules about what people can and cannot, should not do) can only justify "intentions." They can justify outcomes only if the intention was justifiable, and the intention caused the act which led to the intended outcomes. Sounds like complex fantasy, but it isn't. Let us simplify it by looking at some data.

Remember, women were employed in the justified self-interest studies described above. When we attempted to replicate the effect with men, we found that the choice of shock or nonshock for one's self was about evenly divided, and whichever condition they chose for themselves, we found significant condemnation of the other person (Table 36). Why did this occur? Our hunch was that, even in this situation of parallel competition, it was not appropriate for *men* to use the desire to avoid pain to justify intentionally causing another person to suffer. *The male-appropriate norms could not legitimize the intended outcomes.*

To test this, we altered the situation slightly, by giving the "fortunate" male subject the choice between a shock condition and one where he could earn a considerable amount of money (positive reinforcement). Here we replicated the effect found with females, when the choice was between shock or control. The men overwhelmingly chose the positive reinforcement, with no signs of condemnation or guilt. ($\bar{X} = +1.83$) Apparently, the intention to earn money legitimized the intended act–outcome sequence. P was led to believe O won the right to choose and had chosen the desirable condition, thus causing P to suffer the shocks. When P was led to believe that O's choices were between shock and a neutral control condition, he denigrated O. ($\bar{X} = -12.70$) This condemnation did not appear, however, in those male subjects who were

Table 36

Ratings of the Other Person's Attractiveness: Bipolar Adjectives[a]

	Fates available		
	Shock/Control	Shock/Money	Control/Control
S Chooses	−10.58	+1.83	+3.38
O Chooses	−12.70	−3.60	

[a]Adapted from Lerner (1971b).

caused to suffer by someone who chose a money condition rather than the shock ($\bar{X} = -3.60$) The other's act was justifiable—no condemnation, even though P was to suffer.

There is evidence concerning the importance of the other links in this intention–act–outcome hypothesis. Let us say the choosing subject's intentions are good, justifiable, and these good intentions determine his acts. What if, however, the acts do not determine the outcomes? A study by Darlington and Macker (1966) bears directly on this point. In that study, each of two subjects' outcomes depended upon the performance of the other. Knowing this, each worked responsibly for the other. In one condition, however, subjects were led to believe that the other had achieved the desired outcome for them, but that they had failed, and so the other would not be rewarded. They had tried and intended to do well, but thought they had failed. Subsequently, these subjects showed significant signs of attempting to reduce feelings of guilt, in this case by volunteering to give blood.

The situations designed by Freedman *et al.* (1967) and Carlsmith and Gross (1969) to elicit guilt depend upon the effect of an unintended, even well-intended act. For example, a subject quite naturally leans on a table, spilling valuable material all over, or is accidentally distracted by a noise, leading to disastrous results for the experimenter. In the drawing-a-slip situation (Lerner & Matthews, 1967), it is apparent that the choosing subject's intentions did not cause the outcomes. It was her act which did. Subjects did attribute causal responsibility to themselves for this act, but there were no norms—at least none powerful enough—to justify the outcomes.

It should be possible to provide a more careful demonstration of this justification process by modifying slightly the "choice" conditions. Although this is pure conjecture, the bet here is that if, at any point, this chain were *interrupted*—intention causing act causing outcomes—we should find evidence of guilt. For example, a male subject has won the choice between a shock condition and a money condition. We already know that he will most likely choose the desirable condition. However, in this new condition he does not meet the other person, and only after this choice, which is supposedly irrevocable, does he learn that the other is a cripple, a woman, a "nonequivalent" other. His intentions were justifiable, they determined his act (choice), but the intentions did not determine the outcome—his getting money at the expense of someone in greater need, with greater investment, etc. My hunch is that he would experience considerable guilt.

To extend this adventure into fantasy, recall the situation where you are sitting at a formal dinner party, next to a gentleman who is dressed quite elegantly, as is everyone at the table. A loud noise "causes" you to jerk reflexively, thereby causing your elbow to flip a bowl of soup onto the man sitting next to you. How do you feel? Probably a mixture of regret, guilt, embarrassment. Change the situation slightly—the same scene, except this time out of the corner of your eye you notice that the waiter carrying a bowl of soup on a tray has tripped, and the soup is flying toward you. Being lightning-quick, you shove yourself away from the table, realizing that if you do this your neighbor will get the soup on him. Of course, you act according to norms of justified self-interest—and the neighbor gets the soup. Do you feel more or less guilt in this latter case than in the former? In which case were your intentions—intended acts—critical in determining your neighbor's fate? As a final twist, what would your feelings be in the second situation if the flying bowl accidently careened and cut a child nearby? Some justifiable intention, same act, but now an unintended outcome.

I must confess that I knew all along that these hypotheses about the social psychology of justification were only obliquely related, at best, to the issues at hand. But I could not resist the temptation to present them to you here. My excuse for this indulgence is that I believe the experimental findings and anecdotes illustrate and highlight quite nicely a number of relevant points. The most important one, of course, is that *people can justify causing others to suffer if they can locate the "cause" of their acts within a set of norms which assumes that all people have a right, a need, to look out for themselves regardless of the cost to othrs (who presumably are doing the same thing)*. The scene is one of self-centered individuals in competition for a scarce resource. In other words, I can ignore the considerations of what I do to you, or fail to do for you, as I pursue my own interests, as long as I can locate the basis of my action within this normative context.

Obviously, these norms are very powerful social psychological devices, since, as we have seen, if any aspect of the situation interferes with my having access to these justifying norms, then I will have to face the emotional consequences of being a harm-doer. Having inflicted an undeserved fate on another person, I will feel guilty, ashamed, and attempt to repair the consequences of my act, to restore justice, or justify what I did. In a society where there are many victims who might potentially make me feel guilty for what I have done inadvertently to cause their harm, or unintentionally failed to do to prevent their suffering further, norms of "justified self-interest" can be most functional in enabling me to turn my back on their claims, and feel justified in doing so.

It Is a Charade—We Only Pretend to Ourselves and Others that We Believe in the "Myth"

This, of course, is the crux of the issue. There is a commonly accepted strategy among experimental social psychologists for demonstrating that one has discovered an alternative, presumably more encompassing explanation for a published finding. First, you must show that you are able to recreate the finding in question with your procedures—such as condemning an innocent victim, and then you can illustrate how the effect is altered or eliminated when you vary the "true" causal event—the independent variable that is derived from your alternative theoretical perspective. That, of course, was the strategy employed in some of the studies reported earlier that were designed to portray the condemnation of victims as based, not on the observer's defense of the belief in a just world, but on the elicitation of the observer's guilt, indirect complicity (Cialdini *et al.*, 1976), or the interference with the observer's natural empathic reaction (Aderman, *et al.*, 1974).

Although, as we have seen, this method is not at all foolproof, it is an eminently reasonable way to proceed. So, in presenting the evidence that follows, we will first create the events we want to understand more fully. Once having done that, then we will try to probe further, hopefully more deeply.

CHAPTER **11**

Deserving versus Justice

A Demonstration

Some years back, I was invited to attend a conference on altruism and helping behavior, sponsored by the National Science Foundation (NSF). In trying to decide what to present to this illustrious group that would portray most dramatically and succinctly what I thought I had discovered about "how" and "why" people cared for one another, I chose a demonstration that I had been developing with various audiences during the previous year.

The demonstration begins with my announcing that I am not only interested in the theoretical issues associated with reactions to victims, but I am also actively involved in helping families who come through our medical center. I then describe what is contained in the pile of manilla folders that I have placed on the table in front of me. Each folder contains the complete record of a family whose sole breadwinner has been stricken by illness for a considerable period of time. They have long since exhausted all means of public support, and are living in the most miserable of conditions. The children in each family are suffering from severe malnutrition. There is not enough clothing, shoes, etc. for the older children to be able to attend school on a regular basis. Simply staying warm during the chilling Kentucky winters is problematic for them. By the time I have finished presenting this material, it is clear that each of the families is living under the most primitive conditions. They are barely surviving. It is of course intentional that the presence of suffering of young children is made salient. Whatever means one can find to blame adults for their own misery, they are inapplicable to young, unquestionably "innocent" children.

The punch line is the request for funds. The audience is told that each family needs between $50 and $100 a month in order to enable them to eliminate the worst of their suffering. With that amount per month, they would be able to meet the basic needs of food, shelter, and clothing, and the kids could survive, and possibly attend school. I make it clear that there are enough folders (families) for everyone in the room to have their own, and I intend to pass them out to each person in the room to examine; however, since I do not want to subject the families to any additional public exposure, I want a tentative agreement from those in the audience that if, in fact, the families are as I have described, they each would be willing to provide the necessary funds for one family for as long as they are needed. I then ask either for a show of hands, or allow them to send me a folded sheet of paper indicating their willingness to participate. As it turns out, neither of these makes any difference to the rate of volunteering.

The discussion that ensues invariably reveals the following: Yes, I have been effective in eliciting a considerable amount of concern, sympathy, compassion for the families. Yes, there was no question that they were seen as truly innocent victims—especially the children; and the availability of enough folders for everyone handled the question of "diffusing responsibility." But No! There is virtually no willingness to accept one of the folders—with the implication of then providing them with $50 to $100 a month. *And,* there is, for all intents and purposes, no guilt about the whole matter. Some regrets, a willingness to talk more about the entire event, but a remarkable absence of guilt associated with the refusal to accept the folders and the implied responsibility.

Why no guilt? These people were given the opportunity to act on the basis of their feelings of concern and compassion. The amount of money required from them each month was selected because it did not exceed what they, given their incomes and style of life, would typically spend on entertainment. It was a very safe bet that they each spent at least the equivalent of a hundred dollars a month on dinners out, movies, martinis or wine with dinner, summer vacation. Certainly there would be no threat at all to their economic security or that of their children were they to divert that portion of their income to rescue the misserable family from the most primitive form of deprivation and suffering. Is it possible for these decent, concerned people to choose their own liquor and entertainment over the chance to eliminate the terrible suffering of an innocent child? And then, after having made that choice, not be consumed with guilt?

The most obvious interpretation of all this is that, when you pit a person's concern for the suffering of an innocent child against his own desire to enjoy himself, justice goes out the window. Even among the highly selected samples of concerned social scientists at the NSF conferences no one really gives a damn, or really cares about justice for other people.

Of course, one could quarrel with various aspects of the demonstration. The audiences were really suspicious of my presentation, even though they would not admit to such thoughts later. Or, the way I presented the cases elicited enormous, overwhelming amounts of "reactance" in the audience, to the point of being guilt-relieving . Or there must have been something "fishy" going on, because I and many other people actually do send a certain amount of money to an "adopted child" in rural Sicily; or "I and most people" would have contributed if we could have done it anonymously; or "I and many others" would have taken a family if we had a chance to establish a close personal relationship, etc.

I find these reactions transparently inadequate. The easiest, and, as I have discovered, excessively cruel way to handle most of them is to fall back in role and insist that I am in fact able to meet their conditions—the reactance is certainly gone after our little chat. I can arrange anonymity or intimacy. I can show them that I did not invent these families at all—there is nothing "fishy" here, *I am totally serious about all of this!* And then I ask them, implicitly, of course, to "put up." But that is cruel, mainly because it perpetuates their own charade. It has the effect of demonstrating to them and those in the audience that people are not only selfish, but also hypocritical in their "do-gooder" protestations. And that is not true.

Mainly, what I do next is attempt to elicit their candid reactions to a number of alternatives, including some hypothetical scenarios. The one of most interest here involves the request of a political candidate for their support and campaign contributions. The candidate's distinguishing platform is the revision of the system of taxation. If instituted, the usable income of the members of the audience would be reduced to the point where it would be rare for them to be able to afford luxuries such as martinis, restaurants, entertainment, summer vacations. The funds thus acquired through the equitable scheme of progressive taxation would eliminate the conditions of poverty in our society. Virtually everyone in the audience announces their willingness, eagerness, to support such a candidate, even though the net effect on their own usable personal income would be the same as that involved in their helping the suffering family.

So what does that prove? Probably not very much. It is not surprising that people would like to appear to be socially responsible, especially if the gesture is only "make-believe," and costs them nothing. Even if I could convince you that the people were completely sincere, it is still quite plausible that they were trying to recover from the immediate consequences of a bit of residual guilt or anticipated public sanctions for their seemingly callous reactions to the plight of the needy family. But what if it were a genuine and to many of them a familiar response that I merely happened to elicit in ironic juxtaposition to the immediately preceding refusal to help? Certainly many of these people have backed up their liberal socialist ideologies with considerable personal and financial support in the past. Those were genuine unhypothetical attempts to accomplish the same ends with essentially the same personal costs. And, although there has been some wavering back and forth, the system of taxation that has been voluntarily adopted by the general population and support often by large segments of the middle and upper classes in many European countries is virtually identical in consequences and costs to what I described to my audience. The economically privileged electorate in Sweden, when faced with the real choice, did approximately what the members of my audience had stated that they would do, and I believe them.

But that is not the point, either. Besides having to do more than decide whether I or you should believe their altruistic reactions, it is more important, crucial, to understand what the various reactions mean. This is what I think was happening with the audience.

The presentation of the suffering family created a familiar set of threatening "traps" for the audience. The strong impulse, elicited by the emotional reactions to the unjust suffering, was to offer whatever help was necessary. But, as described earlier, giving in to that impulse would make them less able to resist further efforts to help that family, or any other equally deserving victim. Having learned the bitter lesson of their impotence to make all the injustices go away, they must rely on the strong defenses of "doing only my fair share, what everyone else in my position is doing" to resist the impulse which would move them from their own just world into the world of victims. Any unilateral act of help for a deserving victim is very dangerous, because of their vulnerability to being trapped by their own caring in combination with the overwhelming demands from the victims who deserve help. By acting, we demonstrate to ourselves that we belong to "them," or, more aptly, there is no *real* difference between me and those who are condemned to a life of deprivation. They belong to me. There are not "two worlds" with two "kinds" of people—victims and nonvictims. That is too frightening, threatening a prospect for the emotionally vulnerable nonvictim to face voluntarily.

In addition, the validity of that implication is established by the requirement that the person give up a meaningful part of the style of living—what he/she earned and worked for—in order to comply with this urge to help. For most of us, these seeming luxuries—the martini before dinner, the vacation, the dinners out—represent anticipated end points of a long process of trying to "earn" and "deserve" what we want, would enjoy—a way of life. Giving them up would be tantamount to demonstrating that we did not deserve them after all. But that would not be fair. I worked for, deserve, all of this—for myself and my family. It is not right that I be required now to give that up, *even* for the suffering family. What happened to the justice in *my* world? Must I forget that in order to help "them" survive a little better in their unjust world?

The choice is between continuing to maintain one's separation from the world of victims and continuing to live in a "just world"—by not engaging in the unilateral act of help for the family—or choosing to help the family, with the attendant serious risks that one is agreeing to give up the claim to living in the just world in order to join the family and the hordes of others in the unjust world. That is not really much of a choice for even the most vulnerable and tender among us. Most of us would rather not wrestle with these issues. They are best resolved and handled by admitting to one's self and others that it is a "tough world," where each person has to take care of himself and his own.

From this analysis, it is easy to understand the willingness to support the equitable taxation proposal to eliminate the poverty in one's society. Here, the choice is between desired, even deserved, "luxuries," and the possibility of increasing the justness of one's world. And when the threat to one's own deserving is further reduced by the fact that everyone else will have to give up a proportional part of their luxuries, then there is a minimal threat involved in the act of support. The opportunity to reduce the injustice in one's world with virtually no threat to one's own deserving, now and in the future, should have a strong appeal for most people. The particular desired resources in question should be relatively inconsequential by comparison with the urge to help in these circumstances of no threat to one's own deserving, now and in the future.

Deserving versus/and Justice

Dale T. Miller took as his doctoral thesis project the task of generating an experiment that would speak to these hypotheses. He wanted to recreate the elements of the dilemma as they might appear in the normal course of a person's life. To do this, he had undergraduate men work at an experimental task. They were paid for their participation, as they would be with any job. The dependent variable he used in this research was the student's willingness to continue to work at a similar task. What he varied was the circumstances surrounding the rate of pay they were offered for their future work sessions. That seems straightfoward enough.

But how to introduce the victim? And what kind of victim? He stayed close to the kind of victimization used in the demonstration. When they finished their work and went to the office to receive their pay, the students in the "victim" conditions were given a sheet of paper which described a family that was in desperate circumstances. The mother and two children had been abandoned, and she was working at night while going to secretarial school during the day, so that she could take care of them herself. During this time, however, they were poverty-stricken, and the children needed shoes, clothes, and medicine. The psychology department had been alterted to the mother's circumstances by a social agency, but unfortunately there were no funds available except those earmarked by granting agencies for research. The members of a department then had thought of a plan whereby subjects who were paid for participating in the research would have a certain amount of their pay "donated" to the family. In addition, the students learned what the various amounts of money would buy for the children, and also given a maximum number of sessions they could elect to work.

There were four related conditions in this experiment. In one, there was no mention of the family in the written solicitation for further work sessions. The students were offered what had been established as a fair rate of pay for that kind of job, $2.00, and that was all there was to it. In a second condition, they were offered the same pay, but with the additional information about the family, and that one of the two dollars for each session worked would go to help them. In a third condition, there was no mention of the family and they were offered, this time, $3.00 for each session. In the fourth condition, the total amount was the same as the previous condition, $3.00, but this time one of the three dollars would go to the family.

What were these four conditions supposed to reveal? Of course these four conditions were rather brave efforts to capture the psychological processes described in the conflict over deserving for one's self and justice for others. If it were true that these students thought $2.00 was what they deserved for that kind of work, then being presented with the opportunity to help a truly needy family would constitute a threat to one's own deserving. Giving one of the two dollars would be seen as unfair by the workers. As a result, they should be less willing to work if they had to share their $2.00 pay with the family. But what about the $3.00 conditions? If two dollars was seen as fair pay, it is conceivable that the extra dollar for themselves would be seen as a nice bonus—no great overpayment, certainly. How would the incentive to get a $3.00 paycheck each hour compare with the chance to get a fair pay of $2.00, while in addition one dollar went to aid the family? If the theory is correct, and the experimental procedures are successful, then this last condition should reveal the greatest incentive to work—I get the chance to help a needy victim, and there is no threat to my own deserving.

Could it be that simple? The opportunity to help someone in genuine need will be avoided if it is a threat to one's own deserving. The very same opportunity will be welcomed if that threat is removed. The main findings, in terms of number of hours of work the students elected in each of the experimental conditions, can be seen in the following table adapted from Miller, 1977b.

These findings are so nicely in line with the theoretical hypotheses it is good to know that they were replicated in all essential respects in a subsequent experimental test (Miller, 1977b). What we can see in Table 37 is the expected interaction between amount of pay and pay allocation ($p < .01$). The incentive value of being able to keep the additional dollar per hour for one's self was negligible ($\bar{X} = 7.25$ vs. $\bar{X} = 7.58$), whereas the opportunity to help the family

Table 37
Mean Number of One-Hour Sessions Elected[a]

	Pay allocation to family	
Total pay	$0.00	$1.00
$2.00	7.25	3.67
$3.00	7.58	11.91

[a]Adapted from Miller (1977b).

with that dollar was a significant incentive ($\bar{X} = 7.58$ vs. $\bar{X} = 11.91$). And note the remarkable difference in the willingness to work when the money for the family would lead to the worker's having less than he deserved, in comparison to the same amount of money being taken from a pay which would leave him a fair rate of pay ($\bar{X} = 3.67$ vs. 11.91).

It is clear that in this prototypical situation these workers were much more highly motivated by the desire to get what they deserved, and *then* to help those in need, than by the simple desire to maximize their outcomes. If people were governed in their actions solely by the attempt to maximize their own profits, then the condition where they could keep the large pay for themselves should have provided the strongest and most effective appeal. That was not at all the case.

What we find here are data which clearly disconfirm the "myth" that we are all out to get the most we can for ourselves, regardless of what it might cost others. On the contrary, these people's behavior indicated that they cared about deserving for themselves, first, and then justice for others. That is radically different from the image contained in the "myth."

Additional data in Dale Miller's thesis add an extremely important dimension to these findings. He did a separate study in a classroom containing students who provided the population from which the workers in the experiment were selected. These students were equivalent in every essential respect to those who were given the chance to work for the needy family. In this study, he handed out to each student a full description of one of the conditions contained in the experiment, including, when appropriate, the material which described the family. Their task was to read the material, and then indicate on the questionnaire how many hours they thought "someone like themselves" would sign up for. Of course these subjects remained anonymous, and there was every incentive for them to try to be as accurate as possible.

What were the results? If we look at Table 38, adapted from Miller's thesis, we can see the "myth" in full operation. Their best guess-prediction was that they and others like them would be motivated by how much they could keep

Table 38
Mean Number of One-Hour Sessions Predicted[a]

Total pay	Pay allocation to family	
	$0.00	$ 1.00
$2.00	7.25	3.67
$3.00	7.58	11.91

[a]Adapted from Miller (1975).

for themselves. In fact, these people believed earning two dollars for one's self would be *less* attractive if that rate of pay reflected having to give up one of three dollars to the family, than if it were simply their total pay—with no mention of family at all. ($\bar{X} = 8.30$ vs. $\bar{X} = 11.33$). That is just the opposite from the way people reacted in the actual situation.

Consider the irony in all of this. There is no doubt that we all care about feeling secure, and we also want very much to think well of others, and have them think that we are good, decent, even admirable at times. In spite of all this, or actually in part because we have these needs for security and esteem, we construct a set of myths about how ultimately selfish we all are. We pretend very hard to believe in them—because we think we must, in order to protect ourselves. But, in fact, whenever the occasion arises, we act in ways which contradict the myth. We act in ways which reveal that we care about deserving and justice—about living in a just world. Nevertheless, we continue with the "charade," because we think we have no choice.

The "Charade" as a Social Device

John Holmes, Dale Miller and I (1971) did research which highlighted the elaborate social mechanisms people have invented to maintain the charade. In this case, we focused on a common if not tacit conspiracy between "victims" and benefactors from the Just World. The rules of this transaction are easily portrayed. The victims or their representatives must couch their approach to the nonvictim in a way that enables the nonvictim to pretend that he is not being a benefactor. An ideal context is a commercial transaction in which the benefactor is allowed to construe his act, to himself or others when needed, as a normal straightforward purchase, an economic exchange. When employing this "Exchange Fiction," the victim–supplicant must provide enough information so that the potential benefactor recognizes the degree and validity of the victim's genuine needs; at the same time, the message must be underplayed to the point where both parties pretend to ignore it while they go about the normal routine of an economic exchange. And it can be very effective—as any-one knows who has bought light bulbs or address labels from war veterans, sheltered workshops for the retarded, the blind.

In order to take a close look at the processes we thought we had identified in this social mechanism, we decided to sell decorator candles to people in the community. In the first experiment, we varied the nature of the "appeal" associated with either the economic transaction or the request for a donation. The Low Need appeal went as follows:

> Hello, I'm from the Kitchener-Waterloo Recreational Society. We are interested in helping our midget softball team buy equipment for their members who are 7 to 10 years old. They are being sponsored for some of the necessary equipment but we'd like them to be fully fitted out and feel they should have the best available equipment.

The Moderate Need appeal was:

> Hello, I'm from the Kitchener-Waterloo Perceptually Handicapped Society. We're starting a training programme for handicapped children about 7 to 10 years old who have problems in performing many normal activities. We hope that with this programme we will be able to help them deal with their problems. There are over 200 children in the programme and we need a lot of support to make it effective.

The High Need appeal was:

> Hello, I'm from the Kitchener-Waterloo Society for Emotionally Disturbed Children. We're starting a training and remedial programme for handicapped and emotionally disturbed children from 7 to 10 years old who have severe problems in coping with most normal activities. We hope that with this programme we can avert the tragedy that will result if these children are left to cope alone with their problems. There are over 200 children who could remain damaged for life if they don't get help, so we need a lot of support to make the programme effective.

This last appeal in particular might seem strong enough to evoke the benefactor's defenses, but in fact it is very brief, and then the major issue becomes the purchase of the candles. The interaction then turns into a straightforward sales pitch. It is explained in some detail how useful these candles are as gifts for friends and relatives. And, as any wise purchaser would want to know, the candles are "of excellent quality and are long-lasting."

The three comparable control conditions omitted any mention of candles, and terminated with the request for a donation of 75¢ or more. That figure was settled on because it was the price of the least expensive candle shown in the Exchange conditions. The proportion of people complying with either form of request and the amount of money contributed either by direct donation or via the mechanism of the purchase can be seen in the following table.

In this first experiment, we found that the opportunity to purchase a candle was not particularly attractive to people (Table 39). If anything, with the Moderate appeal, a greater proportion of people were more likely to respond to the direct request for a donation. However, as the intensity of the appeal increased, to the point where initially the respondent was made aware of serious

Table 39
The Average Amount of Donations and the Proportion of Persons Contributing in Study I[a, b]

Condition	Level of deserving			Marginal Means
	Low	Moderate	High	
Donation	14.47	34.06	40.50	28.78
	0.16	0.44	0.44	0.33
Exchange	38.46	33.33	131.25	66.89
	0.23	0.17	0.69	0.35
Marginal means	24.22	33.75	79.39	
	0.19	0.32	0.54	

[a]Adapted from Holmes, Lerner, & Miller (1976).
[b]The first number in each cell is the amount of contribution in cents. The second number is the proportion of people who make a donation.

undeserved suffering that could be prevented, the difference between the Exchange context and the direct request for help appeared most dramatically. The Strong appeal seemed to have relatively little effect on the potential donor. The amount given was, on the average, not appreciably different from that elicited by the Moderate appeal, or the opportunity to help the kids get nice baseball equipment. When couched in the framework of the purchase of candles, however, people were extremely responsive to the needs of the emotionally and perceptually handicapped children. They contributed, indirectly, more than three times the amount offered in all the other conditions.

The second experiment varied the terms of the exchange. One kind of decorator candle was offered for $3.00 each, which was about the fair retail price. In one condition (Fair Price) the potential purchaser was informed of that, and told that the $1.00 profit would go to the "cause." In the Altruist's Price condition, they were told that the normal cost was $2.00, and the additional $1.00 was added on for the cause. In a third condition (Bargain condition), the candle was portrayed as normally going for $4.00 in the local stores. All of these pitches were equally plausible. There were two "causes" combined wih each of these appeals. A *Low Need*, which was identical to that used in Study 1 (baseball equipment) and a *High Need*, which was a hybrid of the Moderate and High conditions from that initial study. In a sense, it is probably a misnomer to construe the request for funds to equip a baseball team as a "need"; but this way it sounds more like a dimension.

And there was direct solicitation of donations associated with each of the appeals. In one case, the request was for a dollar or more, and in the other for three dollars.

The major findings can be seen in Table 40.

Requesting a direct donation was rather ineffective, regardless of the needs of the beneficiary. The average amount donated was around 30¢. Combining the purchase of the candle with the opportunity to help the kids with their sports equipment was no more productive. That too yielded an average of about 30¢. There was, however, an enormous leap in the amount collected when the serious appeal of genuine need was combined with any of the offers to buy a $3.00 decorator candle. And as the value of the exchange for the purchaser increased, so did the average amount contributed. After all, who could resist a true bargain; haven't we all been waiting for the chance to buy a $3.00 decorator candle, especially if it was marked down from $4.00? Would you believe that more than 60% of us have been waiting to make the purchase of two or more of these candles? Frankly, no! I think it was all a well-constructed and familiar charade. A social mechanism based upon exchange fiction: People pretending to care about candles and bargains so that they can care for other people. We have come full circle, just as we should.

A Last Thought

If it is true that a central concern in people's lives is maintaining the belief that they live in a Just World, and that a variety of acts which we appropriately label as cruel or indifferent stem directly from their attempt to protect this belief, it is also true that this commitment remains a powerful untapped source for generating constructive social change. We have seen persuasive evidence that people are strongly motivated by the desire to eliminate the suffering of innocent victims, and that the main barrier in the way of this motivation's appearing in social action is people's fear of losing their place in a just world. The desire to maximize one's own outcomes is a relatively trivial motive in people's

Table 40
The Average Donations and Proportion of Persons Contributing in Study II[a]

| Condition[b] | Solicitation procedure | | | |
	Donation	Altruist's price	Fair price	Bargain price
Low need	31.25/0.25[c]	27.27	27.27	30.00
	25.00/0.08	0.09	0.09	0.10
High need	41.97/0.40	120.00	150.00	184.62
	50.00/0.17	0.40	0.50	0.62

[a]Adapted from Holmes, Lerner & Miller (1976).
[b]The first number in each condition is the amount of the contribution in cents. The bottom number is the proportion of people making a contribution.
[c]These findings are for the one-dollar donation condition. The findings listed below are for the three-dollar condition.

lives, that gains its importance only as it enters into the person's concerns with deserving and justice.

If I have been able to demonstrate the validity or at least plausibility of all this, what then? Much remains to be done. As scientists and people who care about one another we need to understand more about the social psychological processes which generate this commitment to deserving and justice. Why do people care about justice? This concern is ultimately tied to the need to solve the riddle of what decides the particular form that justice takes in a given situation. At times, people feel that justice is served when people's needs are most effectively met; at other times, people's deserving is seen as relative to their effort, their contributions to a task, their station in life, what they can win in a fair competition (Lerner, 1975). And both of these sets of problems are inextricably bound up with the way people decide who is in their "world," and what place they have in that world (Lerner, 1977).

And, of course, these are good, exciting problems, which signify in bold terms how far we have come already. We needed to know a great deal before we knew what questions to ask, and even before we knew how important the questions were to us.

References

Adams, J. S. Inequity in social exchange. In L. Berkowitz (Ed.), *Advances in experimental social psychology*. New York: Academic, 1965.

Aderman, D., Brehm, S. S., & Katz, L. B. Empathic observation of an innocent victim: The just world revisited. *Journal of Personality and Social Psychology,* 1974, *29,* 342–347.

Adorno, T. W., Frenkel-Brunswick, E., Levinson, D. J., & Sanford, R. N. *The authoritarian personality.* New York: Harper, 1950.

Allport, G. W. *The nature of prejudice.* Cambridge, Mass.: Addison Wesley, 1954.

Apsler, R., & Friedman, H. Chance outcomes and the just world: A comparison of observers and recipients. *Journal of Personality and Social Psychology,* 1975, *31,* 884–894.

Arendt, H. *Eichmann in Jerusalem: A report on the banality of evil.* New York: Viking, 1965.

Aronson, E. The theory of cognitive dissonance: A current perspective. In L. Berkowitz (Ed.), *Advances in experimental social psychology,* (Vol. 4). New York: Academic, 1969.

Aronson, E. *The social animal.* San Francisco: W. H. Freeman, (2nd ed.). 1976.

Asch, S. F. *Social psychology.* Englewood Cliffs, N. J.: Prentice-Hall, 1952.

Bandura, A., & Rosenthal, T. L. Vicarious classical conditioning as a function of arousal level. *Journal of Personality and Social Psychology,* 1966, *3,* 54–62.

Bar-Tal, D. *Prosocial behavior: Theory and research.* Washington, D. C.: Hemisphere Publishing Co., 1976.

Berkowitz, L. Social norms, feelings, and other factors affecting helping and altruism. In L. Berkowitz (Ed.), *Advances in experimental social psychology* (Vol. 6). New York: Academic, 1972.

Berkowitz, L. Reactance and the unwillingness to help others. *Psychological Bulletin,* 1973, *79,* 310–317.

Berkowitz, L., & Connor, W. H. Success, failure and social responsibility. *Journal of Personality and Social Psychology,* 1966, *4,* 664–669.

Berkowitz, L., & Daniels, R. Responsibility and dependency. *Journal of Abnormal and Social Psychology,* 1963, *66,* 429–436.

Bettelheim. B. Individual and mass behavior in extreme situations. *Journal of Abnormal and Social Psychology,* 1943, *38,* 417–452.

Boulding, K. Social justice as a holy grail: The endless quest. In M. J. Lerner & M. T. Ross (Eds.), *The quest for justice: Myth, reality, ideal.* Toronto: Holt, Rinehart & Winston of Canada, 1974.

Braband, J E., & Lerner, M. J. A little time and effort: Who deserves what from whom? *Personality and Social Psychology Bulletin,* 1975, *1,* 177–181.

Brehm, J. W. *Responses to loss of freedom: A theory of psychological reactance.* Morristown, N. J.: General Learning Press, 1972.

Brewer, M. B. An information processing approach to attribution of responsibility. *Journal of Experimental Social Psychology,* 1977, *13,* 58–69.

Bulman, R. J., & Wortman, C. B. Attributions of blame and coping in the "real world": Severe accident victims react to their lot. *Journal of Personality and Social Psychology*, 1977, *35*, 351–363.

Byrne, D. *The attraction paradigm*. New York: Academic, 1971.

Cahn, E. *The sense of injustice*. New York: New York University, 1949.

Campbell, D. On the conflicts between biological and social evolution and between psychology and moral tradition. *American Psychologist*, 1975, *30*, 1103–1127.

Carlsmith, J. M., & Gross, A. E. Some effects of guilt on compliance. *Journal of Personality and Social Psychology*, 1969, *11*, 232–239.

Chaiken, A. L., & Darley, J. M. Victim or perpetrator? Defensive attribution of responsibility and the need for order and justice. *Journal of Personality and Social Psychology*, 1973, *25*, 268–275.

Chein, I., Gerard, D. L., Lee, R. S., & Rosenfeld, E. *The road to H: Narcotics, delinquency, and social policy*. New York: Basic Books, 1964.

Christie, R., & Geis, F. L. (Eds.). *Studies in Machivellianism*. New York: Academic, 1970.

Cialdini, R. B., Darby, B., & Vincent, J. Transgression and altruism: A case for hedonism. *Journal of Experimental Social Psychology*, 1973, *9*, 502–516.

Cialdini, R. B., Kenrick, D. T., & Hoerig, J. H. Victim derogation in the Lerner paradigm: Just world or just justification? *Journal of Personality and Social Psychology*, 1976, *33*, 719–724.

Cobb, S. Brooks, G. W., Kasl, S. V., & Connelly, W. E. Health of people changing jobs—A description of a longitudinal study. *American* Journal of Public Health, 1966, *56*(a), 1476.

Comer, R., & Laird, J. D. Choosing to suffer as a consequence of expecting to suffer: Why do people do it? *Journal of Personality and Social Psychology*, 1975, *32*, 92–101.

Cooper, J., & Jones, E. E. Opinion divergence as a strategy to avoid being miscast. *Journal of Personality and Social Psychology*, 1969, *13*, 23–30.

Crosby, F. A model of egoistical relative deprivation. *Psychological Review*, 1976, *83*, 85–113.

Crowne, D. P., & Marlowe, D. *The approval motive: Studies in evaluative dependence*. New York: Wiley, 1964.

Darlington, R. B., & Macker, C. E. Displacement of guilt-produced altruistic behavior. *Journal of Personality and Social Psychology*, 1966, *4*, 442–443.

Deutsch, M. Awakening the sense of injustice. In M. J. Lerner & M. Ross (Eds.), *The quest for justice: Myth, reality, ideal*. Toronto: Holt, Rinehart & Winston, 1974.

Efron, E. "You are finks." *TV Guide,* April 17, 1971, 16–18.

Erikson, E. H. *Childhood and society*. New York: Norton, 1950.

Etzioni, A. *The active society: A theory of societal and political processes*. New York: Free Press, 1968.

Festinger, L. *A theory of cognitive dissonance*. Evanston, Ill.: Row, Peterson, 1957.

Freedman, J. L., Wallington, S. A., & Bless, E. Compliance without pressure: The effects of guilt. *Journal of Personality and Social Psychology*, 1967, *7*, 117–124.

Fromm, E. *Escape from freedom*. New York: Holt, Rinehart & Winston, 1941.

Gerbasi, K. C., & Zuckerman, M. *Experimental investigation of jury biasing factors*. Paper presented at the meeting of the Eastern Psychological Association, New York, April, 1975.

Gerbasi, K. C., Zuckerman, M., & Reis, H. T. Justice needs a new blindfold: A review of mock jury research. *Psychological Bulletin*, 1977, *84*, 323–345.

Glass, D. C. Changes in liking as a means of reducing cognitive discrepancies between self-esteem and aggression. *Journal of Personality*, 1964, *32*, 540–549.

Godfrey, B. W., & Lowe, C. A. Devaluation of innocent victims: An attribution analysis within the just world paradigm. *Journal of Personality and Social Psychology*, 1975, *31*, 944–951.

Goffman, E. *Stigma: Notes on the management of spoiled identity*. Englewood Cliffs, N. J.: Prentice-Hall, 1963.

Goranson, R. L., & Berkowitz, L. Reciprocity and reactions to prior help. *Journal of Personality and Social Psychology*, 1966, *3*, 227–232.

Harding, J., Proshansky, N., Kutner, B., & Chein, I. Prejudice and ethnic relations. In G. Lindzey & E. Aronson, (Eds.), *Handbook of social psychology* (Vol. 5). Reading, Mass.: Addison-Wesley, 1969.

Hatfield, E. Equity: Theory and research: A review. In E. Hatfield (Ed.). *Love, sex, and the marketplace*. New York: Academic, 1980.

Heider, F. *The psychology of interpersonal relations*. New York: Wiley, 1958.

Heilbroner, R. L. *An inquiry into the human prospect*. New York: Norton, 1974.

Henslin, J. M. Craps and magic. *American Journal of Sociology*, 1967, *73*, 316–330.

Hess, R. D. & Torney, J. V. *The development of political attitudes in children*. Chicago: Aldine, 1967.

Holmes, J. G., Lerner, M. J. & Miller, D. T. Symbolic threat in helping situations: The "exchange fiction." Unpublished manuscript, University of Waterloo (Ontario), 1971.

Homans, G. C. *Social behavior: Its elementary forms*. New York: Harcourt, Brace, 1961.

Horowitz, I. A. Effects of choice and locus of dependence on helping behavior. *Journal of Personality and Social Psychology*, 1968, *8*, 373–376.

Isen, A. M. Success, failure, attention, and reaction to others: The warm glow of success. *Journal of Personality and Social Psychology*, 1970, *15*, 294–301.

Isen, A. M., & Levin, P. E. The effect of feeling good on helping: Cookies and kindness. *Journal of Personality and Social Psychology*, 1972, *21*, 384–388.

Izzett, R. Personal communication, 1974. Cited in Rubin, Z., & Peplau, A. Who believes in a just world? *Journal of Social Issues*, 1975, *31*, 65–90.

Jecker, J., & Landy, D. Liking a person as a function of doing him a favor. *Human Relations*, 1969, *22*, 371–378.

Jessor, R., Graves, T. D., Hanson, R. C., & Jessor, S. L. *Society, personality and deviant behavior: A study of a tri-ethnic community*. New York: Holt, Rinehart & Winston, 1968.

Jones, C., & Aronson, E. Attribution of fault to a rape victim as a function of respectability of the victim. *Journal of Personality and Social Psychology*, 1973, *26*, 415–419.

Jones, E. E., & Davis, K. E. From acts to dispositions. In L. Berkowitz (Ed.), *Advances in Experimental Social Psychology* (Vol. 2). New York: Academic, 1965.

Jones, E. E., & Thibaut, J. W. Interaction goals as bases of inference in interpersonal perception. In R. Tagiuri & L. Petrullo (Eds.), *Person perception and interpersonal behavior*. Stanford: Stanford University Press, 1958.

Jones, E. E., Kanouse, D. E., Kelley, H. H., Nisbett, R. E., Valins, S., & Weiner, B. *Attribution: Perceiving the causes of behavior*. Morristown, N. J.: General Learning Press, 1971.

Kaplan, J. A legal look at prosocial behavior: What can happen for failing to help or trying to help someone. *Journal of Social Issues*, 1972, *28*(3), 219–226.

Katz, D., Gutek, B. A., Kahn, R. L., Barton, E. *Bureaucratic encounters: A pilot study in the evaluation of government services*. Ann Arbor: Institute for Social Research, 1975.

Kelley, H. H. The process of causal attribution. *American Psychologist*, 1973, *28*, 107–128.

Kelman, H. C. Violence without moral restraint: Reflections on the dehumanization of victims and victimizers. *Journal of Social Issues*, 1973, *29*, 25–61.

Kesey, K. *One flew over the cuckoo's nest*. New York: Viking, 1962.

Kleck, R. Physical stigma and task oriented interaction. *Human Relations*, 1969, *22*, 53–60.

Kohlberg, L. *Stages in the development of moral thought and action*. New York: Holt, Rinehart & Winston, 1969.

Konecni, V. Some effects of guilt on compliance: A field replication. *Journal of Personality and Social Psychology*, 1972, *23*, 30–32.

Krebs, D. L. Altruism—An examination of the concept and a review of the literature. *Psychological Bulletin*, 1970, *73*, 258–302.

Langer, E. J. The illusion of control. *Journal of Personality and Social Psychology*, 1975, *32*, 311–328.

Langer, E. J., & Roth, J. Heads I win, tails it's chance: The illusion of control as a function of the sequence of outcomes in a purely chance task. *Journal of Personality and Social Psychology*, 1976, *33*, 951–955.

Lazarus, R. S., Speisman, J. C., Mordkoff, A. M., & Davison, L. A. A laboratory study of psychological stress produced by a motion picture film. *Psychological Monographs*, 1962, *76* (34, Whole No. 553).

Lazarus, R. S., Opton, E. M., Nomikos, M. S., & Rankin, N. O. The principle of short-circuiting of threat: Further evidence. *Journal of Personality*, 1965, *33*, 622–635.

Lefcourt, H. *Locus of control.* Hillsdale, N. J.: Erlbaum, 1976.

Lerner, M. J. Evaluation of performance as a function of performer's reward and attractiveness. *Journal of Personality and Social Psychology*, 1965, *1*, 355–360.

Lerner, M. J. The desire for justice and reactions to victims. In J. Macaulay & L. Berkowitz (Eds.), *Altruism and helping behavior.* New York: Academic, 1970.

Lerner, M. J. Justice, guilt, and veridical perception. *Journal of Personality and Social Psychology*, 1971, *20*, 127–135.(a)

Lerner, M. J. Justified self-interst and the responsibility for suffering: A replication and extension. *Journal of Human Relations*, 1971, *19*, 550–559.(b)

Lerner, M. J. The social psychology of justice and reactions to victims. Canada Council Grant No. S–70–1251, September, 1973.

Lerner, M. J. Social psychology of justice and interpersonal attraction. In T. Huston (Ed.), *Foundations of interpersonal attraction.* New York: Academic, 1974.

Lerner, M. J. The justice motive in social behavior: Introduction. *Journal of Social Issues*, 1975, *31*(3), 1–19.

Lerner, M. J. The Justice Motive in social behavior: Some hypotheses as to its origins and forms. *Journal of Personality*, 1977, *45*, 1–52.

Lerner, M. J. "Belief in a Just World" versus the "Authoritarianism" syndrome . . . but nobody liked the Indians. *Ethnicity*, 1978, *5*, 229–237.

Lerner, M. J., & Agar, E. The consequences of perceived similarity: Attraction and rejection, approach and avoidance. *Journal of Experimental Research in Personality*, 1972, *6*, 69–75.

Lerner, M. J., & Becker, S. W. Interpersonal choice as a function of ascribed similarity and definition of the situation. In I. D. Steiner (Ed.), *Current studies in social psychology.* New York: Holt, Rinehart & Winston, 1965.

Lerner, M. J., & Elkinton, L. Perception of injustice: An initial look. Unpublished manuscript, University of Kentucky, 1970.

Lerner, M. J., & Lichtman, R. R. Effects of perceived norms on attitudes and altruistic behavior toward a dependent other. *Journal of Personality and Social Psychology*, 1968, *9*, 226–232.

Lerner, M. J., & Matthews, P. Reactions to suffering of others under conditions of indirect responsibility. *Journal of Personality and Social Psychology*, 1967, *5*, 319–325.

Lerner, M. J., & Reavy, P. Locus of control, perceived responsibility for prior fate, and helping behavior. *Journal of Research in Personality*, 1975, *9*, 1–20.

Lerner, M. J., & Simmons, C. H. The observer's reaction to the "innocent victim": Compassion or rejection? *Journal of Personality and Social Psychology*, 1966, *4*, 203–210.

Lerner, M. J., Dillehay, R. C., & Sherer, W. C. Similarity and attraction in social contexts. *Journal of Personality and Social Psychology*, 1967, *5*, 481–486.

Lerner, M. J., Miller, D. T., & Holmes, J. G. Deserving and the emergence of forms of justice. In L. Berkowitz (Ed.), *Advances in Experimental Social Psychology* (Vol. 9). New York, Academic, 1976.

Lincoln, A., & Levinger, G. Observers' evaluations of the victim and the attacker in an aggressive incident. *Journal of Personality and Social Psychology*, 1972, *22*, 202–210.

MacDonald, A. P., Jr. More on the Protestant Ethic. *Journal of Consulting and Clinical Psychology*, 1972, *39*, 116–122.

Maslach, C. Burned-out. *Human Behavior*, 1976, *5*, 16–22.

McArthur, L. The how and what of why. Some determinants and consequences of causal attribution. *Journal of Personality and Social Psychology*, 1972, *22*, 171–193.

Medea, A., & Thompson, K. *Against rape*. New York: Farrar, Straus, & Giroux, 1974.

Medway, F. J., & Lowe, C. A. Effects of outcome valence and severity on attribution of responsibility. *Psychological Reports*, 1975, *36*, 239–245.

Merton, R. K. *Social theory and social structure* (Rev. ed.). New York: Free press, 1957.

Miller, D. T. *Personal deserving versus justice for others: An exploration of the Justice Motive*. Doctoral dissertation, University of Waterloo, 1975.

Miller, D. T. Altruism and threat to a belief in a just world. *Journal of Experimental Social Psychology*, 1977, *13*, 113–126. (a)

Miller, D. T. Personal deserving versus justice for others: An exploration of the Justice Motive. *Journal of Experimental Social Psychology*, 1977 *13*, 1–13. (b)

Miller, D. T., & Ross, M. Self-serving biases in the attribution of causality: Fact or fiction? *Psychological Bulletin*, 1975, *82*, 213–225.

Mills, J., & Egger, R. Effect on derogation of a victim of choosing to reduce his distress. *Journal of Personality and Social Psychology*, 1972, *23*, 405–408.

Mirels, H. L., & Garrett, J. B. The Protestant Ethic as a personality variable. *Journal of Consulting and Clinical Psychology*, 1971, *36*, 40–44.

Nader, L. *Powerlessness in Zapotec and U. S. societies*. Paper presented at the meeting of the American Association for the Advancement of Science, San Francisco, February, 1974.

Newcomb, T. M. *The acquaintance process*. New York: Holt, Rinehart & Winston, 1961.

Nisbett, R. E., & Wilson, T. D. Telling more than we can know: Verbal reports on mental processes. *Psychological Review*, 1977, *84*, 231–259.

Novak, D. W., & Lerner, M. J. Rejection as a consequence of perceived similarity. *Journal of Personality and Social Psychology*, 1968, *9*, 147–152.

Peplau, L. A., & Tyler, T. *Belief in a just world and political attitudes*. Paper presented at the meeting of the Western Psychological Association, Sacramento, Calif., April, 1975.

Piaget, J. *The moral judgment of the child*. New York: Free Press, 1948.

Piliavin, I. M., Hardyck, J. A., & Vadum, A. *Reactions to a victim in a just or non-just world*. Paper presented at the meeting of the Society of Experimental Social Psychology, Bethesda, Md., August, 1967.

Rawlings, E. I. Reactive guilt and anticipatory guilt in altruistic behavior. In J. Macaulay & L. Berkowitz (Eds.), *Altruism and helping behavior*. New York: Academic, 1970.

Regan, J. Guilt, perceived injustice, and altruistic behavior. *Journal of Personality and Social Psychology*, 1971, *18*, 124–132.

Richardson, S. A., Hartof, A. H., Goodman, N., & Dornbusch, S. M. Cultural uniformities in reaction to physical disabilities. *American Sociological Review*, 1971, *26*, 241–247.

Rokeach, M., *The open and closed mind*. New York: Basic Books, 1960.

Rokeach, M. Long-range experimental modification of values, attitudes, and behavior. *American Psychologist*, 1971, *22*, 453–459.

Rosenhan, D. L. On being sane in insane places. *Science*, 1973, *179*, 250–258.

Rosenthal, R. *Experimenter effects in behavioral research*. New York: Appleton-Century-Crofts, 1966.

Ross, L. The intuitive psychologist and his shortcomings: Distortions in the attribution process. In L. Berkowitz (Ed.), *Advances in Experimental Social Psychology* (Vol. 10). New York: Academic, 1977.

Ross, M., & DiTecco, D. An attributional analysis of moral judgments. *Journal of Social Issues*, 1975, *31*, 91–109.

Rotter, J. B. Generalized expectancies for internal versus external control of reinforcement. *Psychological Monographs*, 1966, *80*, (1, Whole no. 609).

Rubin, Z., & Peplau, L. A. Belief in a just world and reaction to another's lot: A study of participants in the national draft lottery. *Journal of Social Issues*, 1973, *29*, 73–93.

Rubin, Z. & Peplau, L. A. Who believes in a just world? *Journal of Social Issues*, 1975, *31*, 65–90.

Ryan, W. *Blaming the victim*. New York: Pantheon, 1971.

Schopler, J., & Matthews, M. W. The influence of the perceived causal locus of partner's dependence on the use of interpersonal power. *Journal of Personality and Social Psychology*, 1965, *2*, 609–612.

Schwartz, S. The justice of need and the activation of humanitarian norms. *Journal of Social Issues*, 1975, *31*(3), 111–136.

Seligman, M. E. P. *Helplessness: On depression, development, and death.* San Francisco: Freeman, 1975.

Shaw, J. I., & Skolnick, P. Attribution of responsibility for a happy accident. *Journal of Personality and Social Psychology*, 1971, *18*, 380–383.

Shaw, M. E, & Sulzer, J. L. An empirical test of Heider's levels in attribution of responsibility. *Journal of Abnormal and Social Psychology*, 1964, *69*, 39–46.

Simmons, C. H., & Lerner, M. J. Altruism as a search for justice. *Journal of Personality and Social Psychology*, 1968, *9*, 216–225.

Simons, C. *The effect of deception manipulations within an experiment on reactions to victims of misfortune.* Unpublished Honors thesis, University of Pennsylvania, 1968.

Simons, C., & Piliavin, J. A. The effect of deception on reactions to a victim. *Journal of Personality and Social Psychology*, 1972, *21*, 56–60.

Smith, R. E., Keating, J. P., Hester, R. K., & Mitchell, H. E. Role and justice considerations in the attribution of responsibility to a rape victim. *Journal of Research in Personality*, 1976, *10*, 346–357.

Sorrentino, R. M., & Boutilier, R. G. Evaluation of a victim as a function of fate similarity / dissimilarity. *Journal of Experimental Social Psychology*, 1974, *10*, 83–92.

Sorrentino, R. M., & Hardy, J. Religiousness and derogation of an innocent victim. *Journal of Personality*, 1974, *42*, 372–382.

Stokols, D., & Schopler, J. Reactions to victims under conditions of situational detachment: The effects of responsibility, severity, and expected future interaction. *Journal of Personality and Social Psychology*, 1973, *25*, 199–209.

Stotland, E. Exploratory investigations of empathy. In L. Berkowitz (Ed.), *Advances in Experimental Social Psychology.* New York: Academic, 1969.

Sutherland, E. *Principles of criminology.* Philadelphia: Lippincott, 1966.

Tajfel, H. Experiments in intergroup discrimination. *Scientific American*, 1970, *223*, 96–102.

Tannenbaum, P. H., & Gaer, E. P. Mood changes as a function of stress of protagonist and degree of identification in a film viewing situation. *Journal of Personality and Social Psychology*, 1965, *2*, 612–616.

Taylor, S. E., & Mettee, D. R. When similarity breeds contempt. *Journal of Personality and Social Psychology*, 1971, *20*, 75–81.

Tesser, A., & Rosen, S. Similarity of objective fate as a determinant of the reluctance to transmit unpleasant information: The MUM effect. *Journal of Personality and Social Psychology*, 1972, *23*, 46–53.

Walster, E. Assignment of responsibility for an accident. *Journal of Personality and Social Psychology*, 1966, *3*, 73–79.

Walster, E., & Piliavin, J. A. Equity and the innocent bystander. *Journal of Social Issues*, 1972, *28*, 165–189.

Walster, E., & Walster, G. W. Equity and social justice: An essay. *Journal of Social Issues*, 1975, *31*, 21–44.

Walster, E., Berscheid, E., & Walster, G. W. New directions in equity research. *Journal of Personality and Social Psychology*, 1973, *25*, 151–176.

Walster, E., Berscheid, E., & Walster, G. W. New directions in equity research. In L. Berkowitz & E. Walster (Eds.), *Advances in experimental social psychology* (Vol. 9). New York: Academic, 1976.

Walster, E., Walster, G. W., & Berscheid, E. *Equity: Theory and research.* Boston: Allyn & Bacon, 1978.

Warner, W. L. *Yankee city.* New Haven: Yale University Press, 1963.

Wortman, C. B. Causal attributions and personal control. In J. H. Harvey, W. J. Ickes, & R. F. Kidd (Eds.), *New directions in attribution research*. Hillsdale, N. J.: Erlbaum, 1976.

Wortman, C. B., & Brehm, J. W. Responses to uncontrollable outcomes: An integration of reactance theory and the learned helplessness model. In L. Berkowitz (Ed.), *Advances in experimental social psychology* (Vol. 8). New York: Academic, 1975.

Zuckerman, M. Belief in a just world and altruistic behavior. *Journal of Personality and Social Psychology*, 1975, *31*, 972–976.

Zuckerman, M., & Gerbasi, K. C. Dimensions of the I–E Scale and their relationship to other personality measures. *Educational and Psychological Measurement*, 1977, *37*, 159–175. (a)

Zuckerman, M., & Gerbasi, K. C. Belief in internal control or belief in a just world: The use and misuse of the I–E Scale in prediction of attitudes and behavior. *Journal of Personality*, 1977, *45*, 356–378. (b)

Zuckerman, M., & Gerbasi, K. C. Belief in a just world and trust. *Journal of Research in Personality*, 1977, *11*, 306–317. (c)

Zuckerman, M., Gerbasi, K. C., Kravitz, R. I., & Wheeler, L. The belief in a just world and reactions to innocent victims. *JSAS Catalog of Selected Documents in Psychology*, 1975, *5*, 326.

Zuckerman, M., Gerbasi, K. C., & Marion, S. Correlates of the just world factor of Rotter's I–E Scale. *Educational and Psychological Measurement*, 1977, *37*, 375–381.

Index

Accident victim, 81, 161, 196
Accident victims, 125, 127, 161
Aggression, 93, 196
  personal, 15
  self-ascribed, 76
Aggressive behavior, 93
Altruism, 183, 195, 196, 197, 199, 200. *See also* Altruistic behavior; Helping behavior; Prosocial behavior
  postaccident, 118
Altruistic act, 146
Altruistic behavior, 94, 97, 174, 198, 199, 201. *See also* Altruism; Helping behavior; Prosocial behavior
  guilt-produced, 196
Altruistic motives, 44, 58, 60, 68
Altruistic reactions, 186
Altruistic victim, 68, 69. *See also* Martyr victim; Innocent victim
Appalachian victims, 5
Approach–avoidance, 130. *See also* Avoidance
Approach–avoidance index, 133, 134
Approach–avoidance reactions, 131
Appropriateness
  experience of, ix
  judgment of, 10
  sense of, ix, 10, 124, 127, 156
Arousal, 15, 44, 59, 65, 75–77, 84
  inhibition of, 78
  vicarious, 78
Attraction, 198
  measures of, 34
  index of, 79
Attraction paradigm, 196

Attractiveness. *See also* Attraction
  bipolar scales, 47
  evaluations of, 131
  measure(s) of, 46, 130
  performer's, 198
  personal, 35
  rated, 133
  ratings of, 60, 82, 132, 134, 178
Attractiveness ratings, 79
Attribution, 101, 125, 197. *See also* Attributions
  defensive, 125
Attribution analysis, 196
Attribution process
  distortions in, 199
Attribution processes, 81, 111
Attribution research, 200
Attributional analysis, 199
Attributional models, 150
Attributions. *See also* Attribution; Responsibility
  fate-linked, 105
  outcome-induced, 103
  primitive, 117
  "reversal" in, 120
  self-punitive, 106
Authoritarian personality, 195
Authoritarian personality research, 5
Authoritarian syndrome, 150, 151, 155
Avoidance, 3, 134, 198. *See also* Approach–avoidance
  and dissimilarity, 134
  and perceptions of difference, 129
  and similarity, 130, 133–135
Avoidance index, 133

Balance, 14, 37, 38, 149. *See also* Balance
    theory; Cognitive balance
  system of, 38
Balance interpretation, 84
Balance theory, 37, 129. *See also* Cognitive
    balance
Belief in a just world, ix, 7, 9, 11, 12, 14–17,
    19, 21, 24, 25, 27, 30, 36, 37, 44, 48,
    73, 74, 83, 87, 88, 137, 138, 140,
    142, 143, 148–150, 155–157, 159–
    161, 163, 165, 170, 171. *See also* Be-
    lief in a Just World Scale; Just World
    hypothesis; Justice; Need to believe in
    a just world
  defense of, 171, 181
  threats to, 26
  underpinnings of, 22
Belief in a Just World Scale (BJW), 138ff. *See
    also* I–E Scale; Locus of control
  and authoritarian syndrome, 151
  and internal-external locus of control, 151
Bipolar adjective ratings, 93
Bipolar adjective scales, 113
Bipolar adjectives, 46, 49, 60, 79, 81, 114,
    130, 132, 134, 178
Bipolar scales, 47, 66
Blame, 28, 40, 103, 108, 109, 111, 117, 125
  assignment of, 92, 105, 115, 116, 118, 122
  attributions of, 196
  causal, 105, 106, 108, 120
Bystander intervention research, 176. *See also*
    Altruism; Helping behavior; Prosocial
    behavior

Caste, 24
Caste system, 24
Castes, 24, 26
Causal analysis, 121
Causal attributions, 198, 200. *See also* Attri-
    bution; Attributions
  model of, 111
  process of, 197
Causal explanations, 110
Causal responsibility, 112, 114, 179. *See also*
    Responsibility
Causal schemas, 107, 110
Causality. *See also* Causal attributions
  attribution of, 199
Causation
  assignment of, 118
Chance, 18, 22, 31, 61, 81, 82, 106, 108,
    112, 115, 116, 177, 197

Chance explanation, 118, 162
Classical conditioning
  vicarious, 195
Cognition, 38, 48
Cognitions, 6, 10, 12, 30, 37, 38, 48, 52,
    160, 161
  dissonant, 10, 37
  negative, 14
  organization of, 14
Cognitive balance, 83, 87, 130. *See also* Bal-
    ance; Balance theory
  theory of, 37
Cognitive changes, 160, 161
Cognitive constructions, 6
Cognitive discrepancies, 196
Cognitive dissonance, 36, 50, 149. *See also*
    Dissonance theory
  theory of, 10, 36, 195, 196
Cognitive dissonance prediction, 48
Cognitive distortions, 157, 158
Cognitive elements, 14
Cognitive functioning, 151
Cognitive imbalance, 37
Cognitive orientations, 22
Cognitive processes, 111, 157
Cognitive templates, 12
Collective behavior, 53
Common fate
  perception of, 57, 58
Competition, 180, 194
  direct or indirect, 61
  parallel, 61, 81, 83, 177, 178
  zero-sum, 83
Compliance, 196, 197
Control, 9, 10, 118, 122, 135, 170
  degree of, 123
  illusion of, 118, 119, 197
  internal-external, 168
  locus of, 198
  personal, 200
  sense of, 28, 122, 123

Defenses, 2, 6, 22, 138, 156, 171, 173, 181,
    186, 191. *See also* Psychological de-
    fenses
  functional, 176
  irrational, 29
  styles of, 155
Defensive reactions, 142, 143
Dehumanization, 197
Denial, 3, 28, 29, 52. *See also* Defenses;
    Psychological defenses

Dependence
   locus of, 197, 199
Dependency, 96, 101, 102, 195
Deserving, 18, 83, 150, 156, 158, 183, 187,
      188, 190, 194, 198
   bases for, 11
   commitment to, 19, 138, 176, 194
   issues of, 19, 96, 97
   judgment of, 11, 16, 83
   personal, 199
   principles of, 116
   relative, 102
   rules of, 137
   sense of, ix
   theme of, 15, 97, 160
   threat to, 187, 188
Deservingness, 96, 97
Deviant behaviors, 37, 197
Deviant statuses, 16
Disaster victims, 81
Discrimination
   intergroup, 200
   injustice of, 170
Dissimilarity. See also Approach–avoidance
   and avoidance, 134
Dissonance, 36, 38, 48, 49. See also Cognitive dissonance
Dissonance prediction, 48, 49
Dissonance situation, 86
Dissonance theory, 37
Dissonance theory explanation, 48, 49
Dissonance theory predictions, 48, 49
Dogmatism scales, 5

Ego–defensive needs, 85
Emotional arousal. See also Arousal
   cues of, 41, 65, 74, 148
   check list, 45
Emotional behavior, 10
Emotional cues
   study of, 59
Emotional cues study, 44
Emotional disturbance, 10
Emotional reactions, 6
Emotional state, 42, 75, 84
Empathic arousal, 74, 76, 77. See also
      Arousal; Empathy
Empathic distress, 74
Empathic feelings, 86
Empathic involvement, 51
Empathic observation, 195
Empathic orientations, 77

Empathic pain, 6
Empathic reaction, 128, 181
Empathic responses, 76
Empathic set, 129
Empathy, 56, 77, 78, 200. See also Sympathy
Empathy-arousing situation, 76
Empathy-inhibiting condition, 75, 76
Empathy-inhibiting instructions, 74
Empathy test, 137
Entitlement
   bases for, 11
   forms of, 12
   rules, 11, 175
Entitlements, 17
   disqualification of, 16
   reduction of, 16
   status, 16
Equality
   rules of, 17
Equity, 174, 200
   psychological, 29
Equity research, 200
Equity theory, 174, 200
Ethnic relations, 197
Ethnocentrism, 153
Exchange fiction, 190, 193, 197

F-scale, 5, 149, 150, 153
Fault. See also Blame
   attribution of, 197
Fate control, 80
Female liberation, 91
Focus of attention, 87
Frustration aggression explanation, 56
Frustration aggression sequence, 96
Fundamentalist women, 64

Good citizen myth, 27–29. See also Myth;
      Myths
Grants Economics, 175
Guilt, 29, 63, 68, 84, 87, 89, 100, 116–120,
      122, 123, 175–177, 179, 180, 181,
      184, 185, 196, 198, 199
   anticipatory, 199
   feelings of, 63, 68, 179
   observers', 70
   reactive, 199
   sense of, 116
   signs of, 14, 178

Helping, 172, 195, 197
Helping behavior, 183, 197–199. See also

Helping behavior *(cont.)*
    Altruism; Altruistic behavior; Proso-
      cial behavior
Helping professions, 51, 66, 67
Helplessness, 170, 200
  states of, 122
Human behavior. *See also* Social behavior
  regularities in, 10
Human learning, 42, 43, 45, 59. *See also*
    Social learning
  study of, 112
Human motivation
  model of, 173
  mythical image of, 173

Identification, 15, 76, 90–92, 94, 136. *See
    also* Identity
  with attributes, 127
  degree of, 200
  with ethnic groups, 154
  meanings of, 89
  with Protestant Ethic, 166
  sense of, 90, 135
  with "underdog," 61
  with victim(s), 57, 61, 64, 77, 91, 126–
    128, 136
Identification process, 94
Identity
  Canadian, 152, 153
  religious, 154
  sense of, 77, 78
  spoiled, 196
  with victim(s), 14, 25, 91, 92, 172
I–E Scale, 149, 151, 201. *See also* Control;
  Locus of control
Immanent justice, 15, 18, 22, 26
Impression formation, 65, 130
Information-processing, 118, 159
Information-processing approach, 111, 195
Information-processing models, 111, 150,
  159
Information-processing principles, 106
Injustice, 19, 20, 22, 27, 50, 52, 55, 56, 61,
    81, 86, 88, 92, 105, 143, 158, 160,
    162, 164–166, 168–170
  complicity in, 68
  cues of, 171
  degree of, 43, 47, 56, 71, 110, 157
  evidence of, 19, 157, 159, 171
  experience of, 156, 159
  extent of, 110, 166
  incident of, 168

Injustice *(cont.)*
  instance of, 91, 142
  magnitude of, 55
  perception of, 166, 198
  response to, 55
  scene of, 50
  sense of, 10, 15, 165
  victim of, 143
Injustices, 19, 22, 73, 125, 136, 158, 168–
    171, 186
  experiences of, 18
  reactions to, 27
Innocent victim, 39, 40, 44, 50, 56, 83, 120,
    134, 135, 149, 163, 180, 195, 198,
    200. *See also* Innocent victims; Vic-
    tim; Victims
  condemning of, 56
  derogation of, 92
  observers of, 53, 77
  reactions to, 64, 148
  rejection of, 74
  suffering of, 43
Innocent victim paradigm, 157
Innocent victim study, 58
Innocent victims, 4, 5, 7, 30, 39, 55, 56, 74,
    80, 83, 87, 89, 92, 96, 125, 140, 158,
    163, 164, 184, 193, 201. *See also* In-
    nocent victim; Victim; Victims
  deprivation of, 73
  derogation of, 39
  suffering of, 73
Internal control. *See also* Control; I–E Scale
  belief in, 201
Interpersonal attraction, 198. *See also* Ap-
    proach–avoidance; Similarity
Interpersonal perception, 197
Interperonal relations, 197

Just World hypothesis, x, 7, 11, 38, 44, 48,
    55, 81, 150
Just World paradigm, 196
Justice, 10, 13, 15, 17–19, 39, 40, 50, 55, 87,
    105, 127, 138, 142, 147, 155, 158,
    159, 164, 165, 168–170, 175, 180,
    185–188, 190, 194
  belief in, 28, 145
  cognitive orientations, 22
  commitment to, 19, 41, 138, 175, 176, 194
  concern with, 82, 110, 151, 194
  evidence for, 38
  issues of, 17, 141
  need to perceive, 94

Justice *(cont.)*
  perception of, 168
  principles of, 116
  role of, 174
  rules of, 137
  sense of, 10, 40, 61, 82, 89
  social, 39
  theme of, 160, 175
  views of, 151, 155
Justification
  social psychology of, 180
Justified self-interest, 198
  norm of, 61
  norms of, 177, 180
  psychology of, 178
Justified self-interest studies, 178

Learned helplessness model, 201
Locus of control, 150, 151. *See also* Control;
    I-E Scale
  and BJW scale, 151
  Internal-external, 150, 151, 153, 155, 168
Locus of control measure, 151

Machiavellian orientation, 9
Machiavellianism, 196
Martyr, 44, 48, 56-58, 61, 69. *See also* Inno-
    cent victim; Victim; Victims
  condemnation of, 57
  evaluation of, 69
  rejection of, 69
Martyr victim, 44, 47, 57
Martyred victim, 55, 68, 83
Martyrs, 44, 56
Moral development, 156
Myth, 26, 88, 173, 174, 176, 180, 189, 190
Myths, 26, 126, 149, 173, 190

Need to believe in a just world, 19, 139-140
Negative reinforcement, 42-45, 47, 57, 59,
    65
Negative reinforcement conditions, 58, 59
Norm, 94, 102
  generic, 16
  internalization of, 95
  social, 93
  social responsiveness, 95
Norm of social responsibility, 94, 96, 97, 99.
    See also Responsibility
Norms, 15, 16, 61, 93, 96, 170, 177-180
  denial of, 29
  humanitarian, 28, 29, 200

Norms *(cont.)*
  male-appropriate, 178
  perceived, 198
  personal, 28
  preexisting, 28
  suitability of, 28

Opinionation scales, 5

Parallel competition, 81, 83. *See also* Compe-
    tition
  justice of, 177
  situation of, 178
Perceived similarity, 198, 199. *See also*
    Avoidance; Similarity
  to victim, 46
Positive reinforcement, 42, 44, 47, 82, 86,
    178
Positive reinforcement condition, 48, 86
Power, 15, 19, 85, 94
  fantasies of, 118
  feeling of, 169
  interpersonal, 199
  observers', 50
  supernatural, 125
Powerlessness, 199
  sense of, 121
Prejudice, 197
  nature of, 195
Prejudices
  religious, 152
Profit motive, 28
Prosocial behavior, 94, 96, 174, 195, 197. *See
    also* Altruistic behavior; Helping be-
    havior
Protestant Ethic, 13, 150, 198, 199
  identification with, 166
Protestant Ethic beliefs, 151, 155
Protestant Ethic Scale, 153
Psychological defenses, 20. *See also* Defenses
  denial-withdrawal, 20
  reinterpretation
    of the cause, 21
    of the character of the victim, 21
    of the event, 40
    of the outcome, 20
Psychological reactance. *See also* Reactance
  theory of, 195
Punishment, 11, 15, 16, 21, 64, 140,
    163
Punishments, 15, 26, 174
  equitable, 18

Rape, 83, 108, 123, 199
  attempted, 109
  victim of, 92, 142
Rape assault, 110
Rape case, 110
Rape condition, 109
Rape victim, 84, 109, 123, 197, 200
Rational Man Myth, 27, 29
Reactance, 185, 195. *See also* Psychological
    reactance
Reactance theory, 99, 200–201. *See also* Psy-
    chological reactance; Reactance
Reciprocity, 196
Reinforcements, 10, 42, 85, 96, 106, 130
Reinforcement condition, 86
Reinforcement theory, 129
Rejection, 41, 60, 61, 69, 73, 198
  of counterevidence, 4
  of model, 61
Relative deprivation
  egoistical, 196
Religion, 163
  commitment to, 154
  fundamentalist, 21, 169
  importance of, 164
  measure of, 168
  Western, 13
Religious belief, 21
Religious commitment, 153
Religious orientation, 168
  commitment to, 163
  fundamentalist, 169
Religious perspective, 162–165, 170
Religious view, 164
Religiousness, 200
Responsibility, 101, 108, 109, 115, 120, 195,
    200. *See also* Attribution; Attribu-
    tions
  assignment of, 200
  attribution of, 106, 195, 199, 200
  causal, 115, 179
  defensive attribution of, 196
  illusions of, 119
  indirect, 198
  norm of, 102
  perceived, 198
  perception of, 28
  primary, 112–116, 177
  sense of, 28, 86, 172
  for suffering, 198
Reward, 40, 64
  fortuitous, 31, 106

Reward *(cont.)*
  performer's, 198
Rewards, 26, 29, 85, 106, 107, 174
  equitable, 18

Self-blame, 106, 123, 125
Self-concept, 140, 165
Self-concept changes, 161
Self-destruction, 165
Self-esteem, 103, 112, 116, 124, 140, 196
Self-image, 73, 124
Self-interest, 173. *See also* Justified self-
    interest
  direct or indirect, 175
  enlightened, 171
  justified, 177, 178
  norms of, 180
Self-respect, 152
Sexual assault, 109, 110. *See also* Rape
Shame
  sense of, 124
Similarity. *See also* Approach–avoidance;
    Perceived similarity
  and avoidance, 130, 133–135
  degree of, 129, 130
  and interpersonal attraction, 129
  perceived, 131
  perception of, 129, 131
  with victim, 49
Social behavior, 10, 29, 197, 198. *See also*
    Human behavior
Social change, 39, 153, 154, 193
  resistance to, 155
Social class, 165, 168, 169. *See also* Socio-
    economic class
Social contract, 175
Social desirability, 46
Social Desirability Scale, 153, 154
Social interaction
  general theory of, 174
Social learning, 96. *See also* Human learning
  and BJW Scale, 150
  generalization of, 149
Social norms, 195. *See also* Norms
Social responsibility, 195. *See also* Responsi-
    bility
Socialization
  processes of, 15
Socioeconomic class
  laboring, lower middle, upper middle,
    166–170
  lower, 166

Socioeconomic class *(cont.)*
  lower-upper, 25
  middle, 24, 89, 166, 167
  upper, 165, 166
  upper-lower, 25
Status, 16
  peer, 101
  social, 24
Statuses, 16, 21, 24
  identifiable, 24
  minority, 16
  special, 16
Stereotype, 109
Stereotypes, 5, 39
  negative, 16
Subculture, 24, 141
Subcultures, 21
Sympathetic reaction, 15
Sympathetic set, 129
Sympathy, 61, 77, 78, 140, 148, 184

Ultimate justice, 22
  assumptions of, 26
  belief in, 22
  framework of, 164
  source of, 22

Victim, 6, 20, 27–29, 40, 41, 43–53, 55–58,
    61, 63–65, 67–71, 74, 76, 79–85, 87–
    89, 91–94, 105, 109–111, 116, 127,
    128, 132, 135, 136, 143–145, 148,
    149, 157, 160, 163, 165, 173, 177,
    187, 188
  behavior of, 71
  character of, 21
  characteristics of, 28
  choice of, 81
  compassion for, 50
  condemnation of, 50, 56, 71, 78, 149, 157,
    164
  denigration, derogation
    devaluing of, 41, 77, 82, 86, 92, 128,
    149
  enhancement of, 57
  evaluation of, 48–50, 57, 77, 82, 86, 91, 93
  fate of, 50, 86
  image of, 50, 158
  impression of, 45
  indebtedness to, 68
  perceptions of, 64
  personality of, 65
  ratings of, 47, 48, 66, 69, 76, 77, 78

Victim *(cont.)*
  reactions to, 49, 50, 69, 70, 130, 148
  rejection of, 64, 67, 68, 76–78, 80, 84
  response to, 76
  suffering of, 44
  view of, 75
Victim condemnation, 87
Victim derogation, 40, 81, 83, 84
Victim rejection experiments, 76
Victims, 26, 30, 39, 40, 56, 61, 71, 74, 78,
    80, 83, 88, 90, 93, 94, 107, 116, 124,
    125, 127, 135, 136, 142, 143, 145,
    149, 154, 155, 160, 161, 165, 166,
    168–170, 186, 190
  compassion for, 74
  condemnation of, 142, 181
  degradation of, 39
  deprivation of, 25
  derogation
    devaluing of, 71, 83
  evaluation of, 83
  lack of sympathy for, 148
  motives of, 169
  reactions to, 55, 56, 74, 140, 151, 152,
    155, 165, 183
  rejection of, 4
  relationship to, 19
  suffering of, 25
  world of, 25, 26, 163, 172, 186, 187

Xenophobia, 153